# MY HEART IS THIS

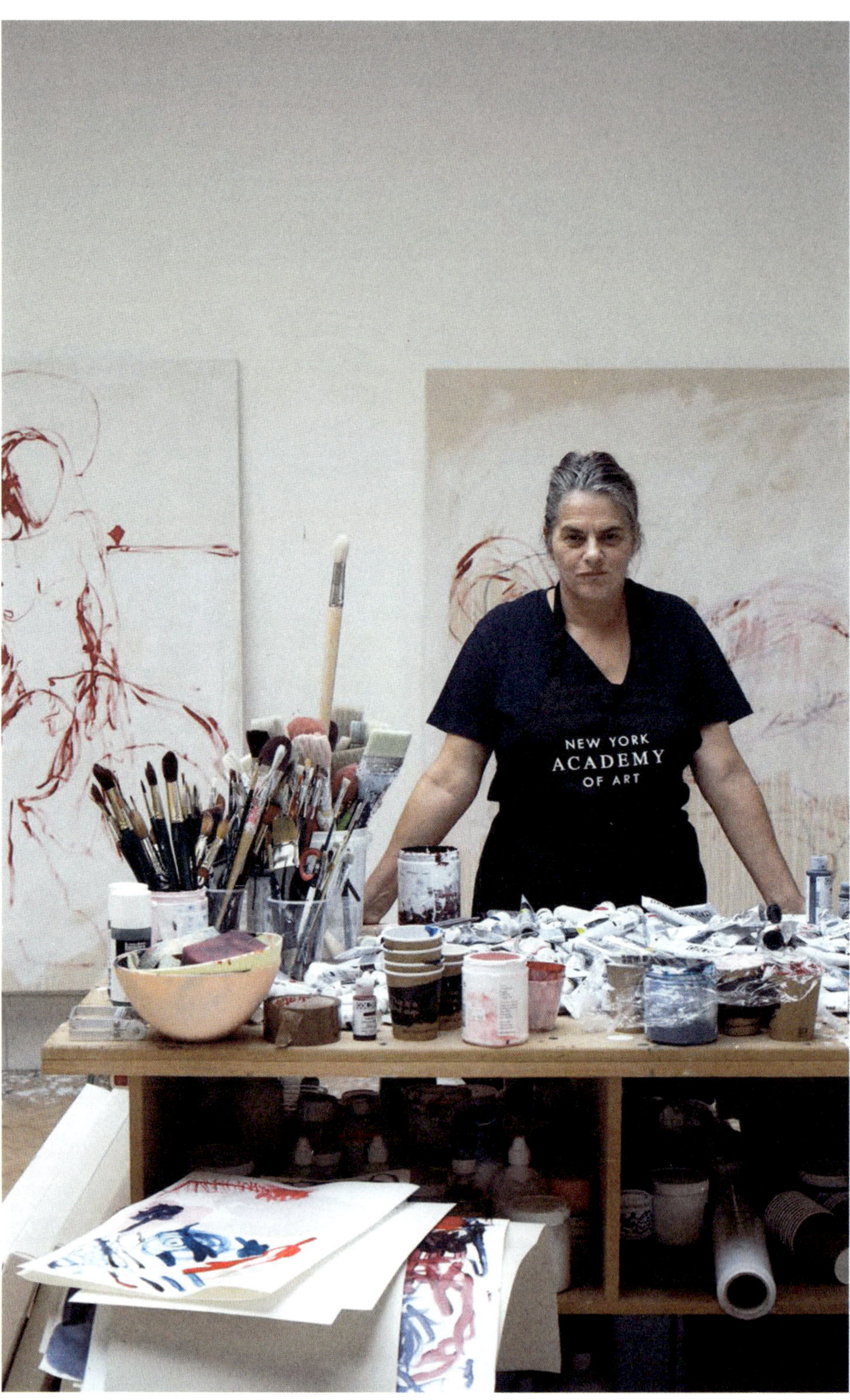

# MY HEART IS THIS

## *Tracey Emin on Painting*

*Martin Gayford*

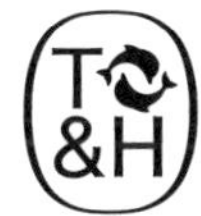

On page 2:
Tracey Emin in her London studio, 2024

First published in the United Kingdom in 2026 by
Thames & Hudson Ltd, 6–24 Britannia Street, London WC1X 9JD

First published in the United States of America in 2026 by
Thames & Hudson Inc., 500 Fifth Avenue, New York, New York 10110

*My Heart Is This: Tracey Emin on Painting*
© 2026 Thames & Hudson Ltd, London

Texts by Martin Gayford © 2026 Martin Gayford
Texts by Tracey Emin © 2026 Tracey Emin
Works by Tracey Emin © 2026 Tracey Emin

Edited and designed by Andrew Brown



EU Authorized Representative: Interart S.A.R.L.
19 rue Charles Auray, 93500 Pantin, Paris, France
productsafety@thameshudson.co.uk
interart.fr

A CIP catalogue record for this book is
available from the British Library

Library of Congress Control Number 2025947490

ISBN 978-0-500-03101-8

02

Printed and bound in Italy by Printer Trento SpA

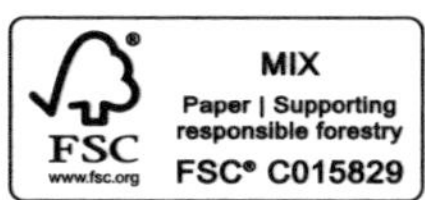


Be the first to know about our new releases,
exclusive content and author events by visiting
**thamesandhudson.com**
**thamesandhudsonusa.com**
**thamesandhudson.com.au**

# CONTENTS

# I

## *A little cork tree*

Outside Tracey Emin's studio in the south of France there used to grow a little cork oak tree. The artist loved it, but then it withered and seemed to have died. 'I broke the stem, saying that I didn't know trees could die', she remembers. 'I thought maybe it had been struck by lightning, or perhaps it had got a disease.'

After a while, she noticed that various parasitical plants were growing out of its stump, suggesting that deep within it life might still remain. She thought, 'Even if the tree was dead, these other living things were coming out of it, so somehow what is inside the tree must be alive.' Then, after five years, the tree itself began to grow again. And that, she concluded, is what had happened to her: 'I was struck by lightning!' Now she is regenerated.

In June 2020, Emin was diagnosed with squamous cell bladder cancer and underwent radical surgery involving the removal of her uterus, ovaries, lymph nodes, urethra, part of her colon, urinary tract, and her entire bladder. She thought she might have six months to live, but four years later, when I came to visit her in her two spacious, light-filled studios in Margate, the signs of new growth fill the place, hanging and leaning against the walls. A bumper harvest of extraordinary paintings, they are fraught, tender, powerful, harrowing, beautiful.

**TE** The other day I was thinking about why I paint. It's like nature. Why does nature grow? Art, painting, these things that come out of us, for me they are our own nature.

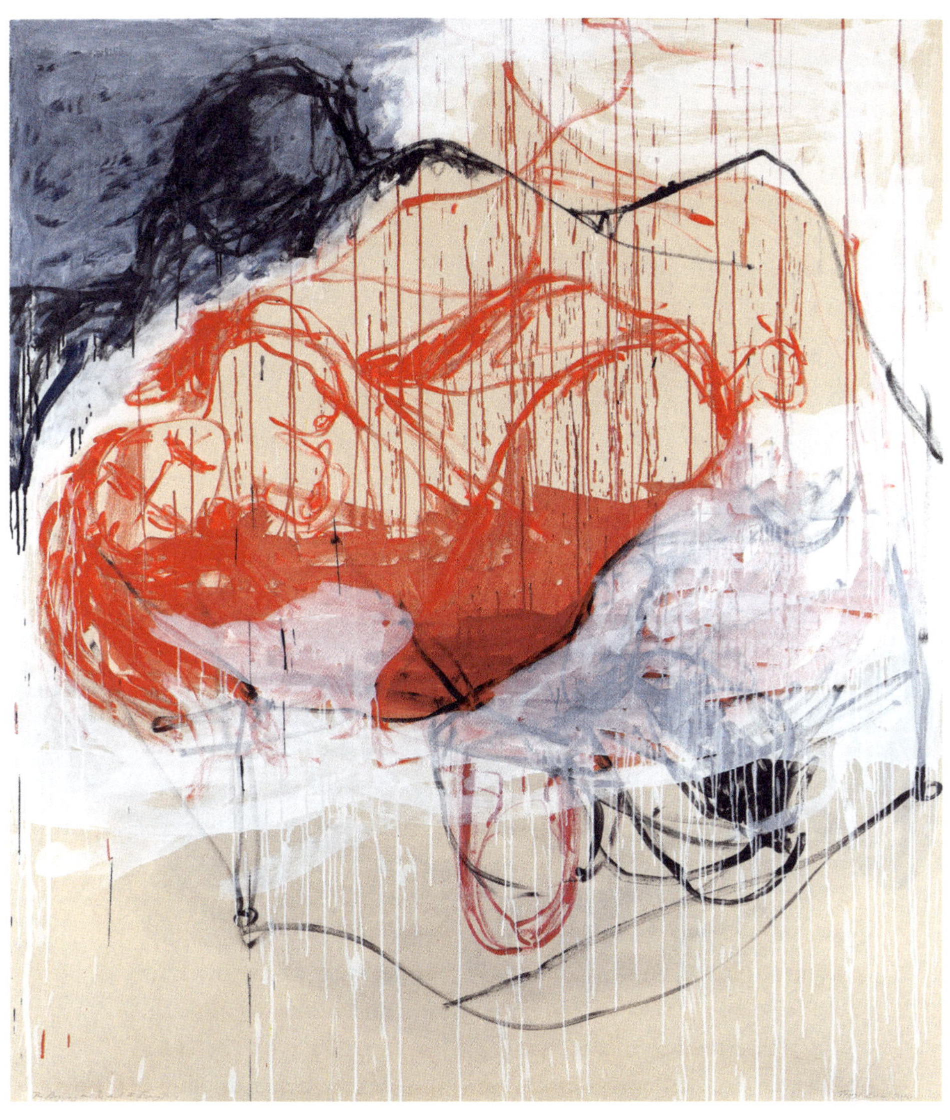

*The Beggining and The End of Everything, 2023*

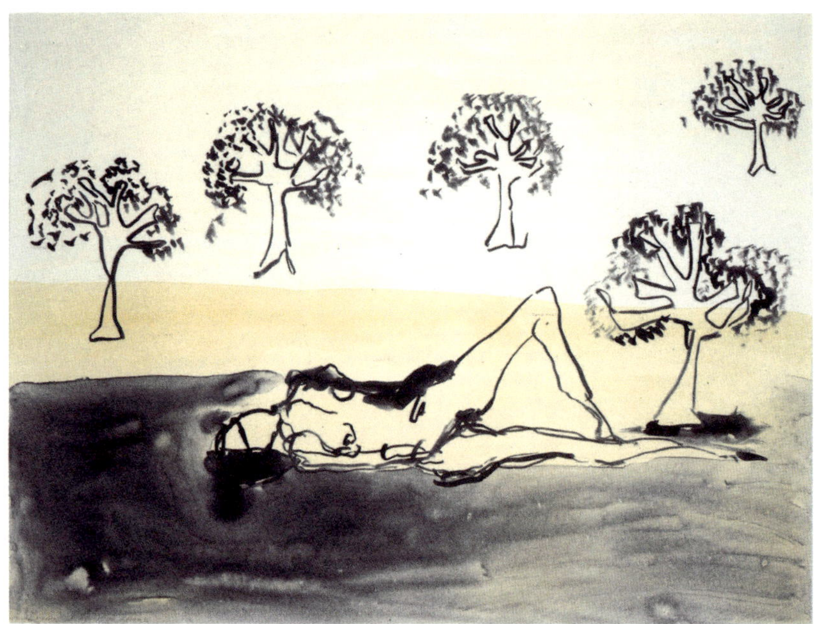

*Laying with the Olive Trees,* 2011

It's like we are growing these things that come out of us.
A few animals do something like that, make weird things
that come out of them. But essentially, it's pretty human.
It's what we grow. If we keep making these things, like
I do, then we will keep growing. Keep releasing and keep
growing.

MG  I once read that the way you can tell if a plant, such as
a tree, is alive is whether it is metabolizing. That means
whether it is taking in light, water, and nutrients and
transforming them into new cells, fresh energy. You could
call that alchemy: transforming substances into something
completely different. Perhaps a person, and especially an
artist, is the same. You take in new experiences every day
and out of that comes growth. That is how you can tell a
person is really alive: they're still metabolizing.



*A little cork tree*

**TE** Also, you have this trunk that gets bigger and bigger
and bigger, with all these rings, and all the leaves
and branches that come and go. It's always changing;
seasonally, it's always recreating itself. It gets older and
older and older, but it always revives, it always comes
back to life.

**MG** Before the cancer, you had already had quite a career.
You were famous, you had shown at the Venice Biennale …

**TE** Yeah, but that was not *my* career, not the career that
*I* wanted. The cancer changed all of that. I'm being really
honest with you. I even thought I might have died and
gone to heaven because what I have now is so different
from before I became ill. Think about how many people
are not doing what they are supposed to do. That is what
was happening to me.

I'd got into a way of doing something that I shouldn't
have been doing. I had to stop it. To stop and say no and
readjust. That's what cancer is pretty good for: it really
makes you stop in your tracks. It was brilliant for me,
because it made me value, *cherish*, look at everything
that I had. Cancer gives you lots of time, because every
moment that you have is more special. That sounds so
corny, but it's true. Most people, maybe 99.9 per cent
of people, think it doesn't matter what happens to them
when they become sick. I wasn't like that. I thought,
'I've got about six months; I've got to make the most
of every day.' I just got happier and happier, and four
years later, I'm still here, getting better. And I've got
this amazing career that I didn't have before. I didn't!

*

Painting is an ancient activity. It is so old, in fact, that we cannot really be sure when it began. The earliest paintings that we currently know about, on the walls of caves in Indonesia, are estimated to be around fifty thousand years old. But the earliest pigments and palette — ochre mixed in a seashell, discovered in South Africa — are around fifty thousand years older than that. Perhaps, then, painting is as old as spoken language, or even older. But when you stand in front of prehistoric pictures, as you still can in a few places in southern France and Spain, one thing is obvious. These pictures were made by people just like us. They still communicate directly. As do Tracey Emin's, and more and more powerfully in recent years.

**MG** It's twenty years now since the first time we had a conversation. It was in your first studio in Spitalfields. We talked about lots of things, and different kinds of work that you were making. But we never mentioned painting. In fact, I think the first time I saw a painting of yours was several years later.

**TE** I painted when I was at the Royal College of Art, but after I left in 1989, I stopped for a few years. I always drew, but my drawings and the monoprints were more like a diary. Every day, I would do ten drawings or so. Then, from 1996 on, I sort of painted, but I never showed anyone my paintings because, as we know, if you were a sincere, full-blown figurative painter in the 1990s, well forget it, it just wasn't happening. But then I started painting again properly around 1999, and I just carried on painting and painting and painting.

**MG** The first time we talked, you had a staff of assistants in your London studio. Nowadays, it's really just you,



*A little cork tree*

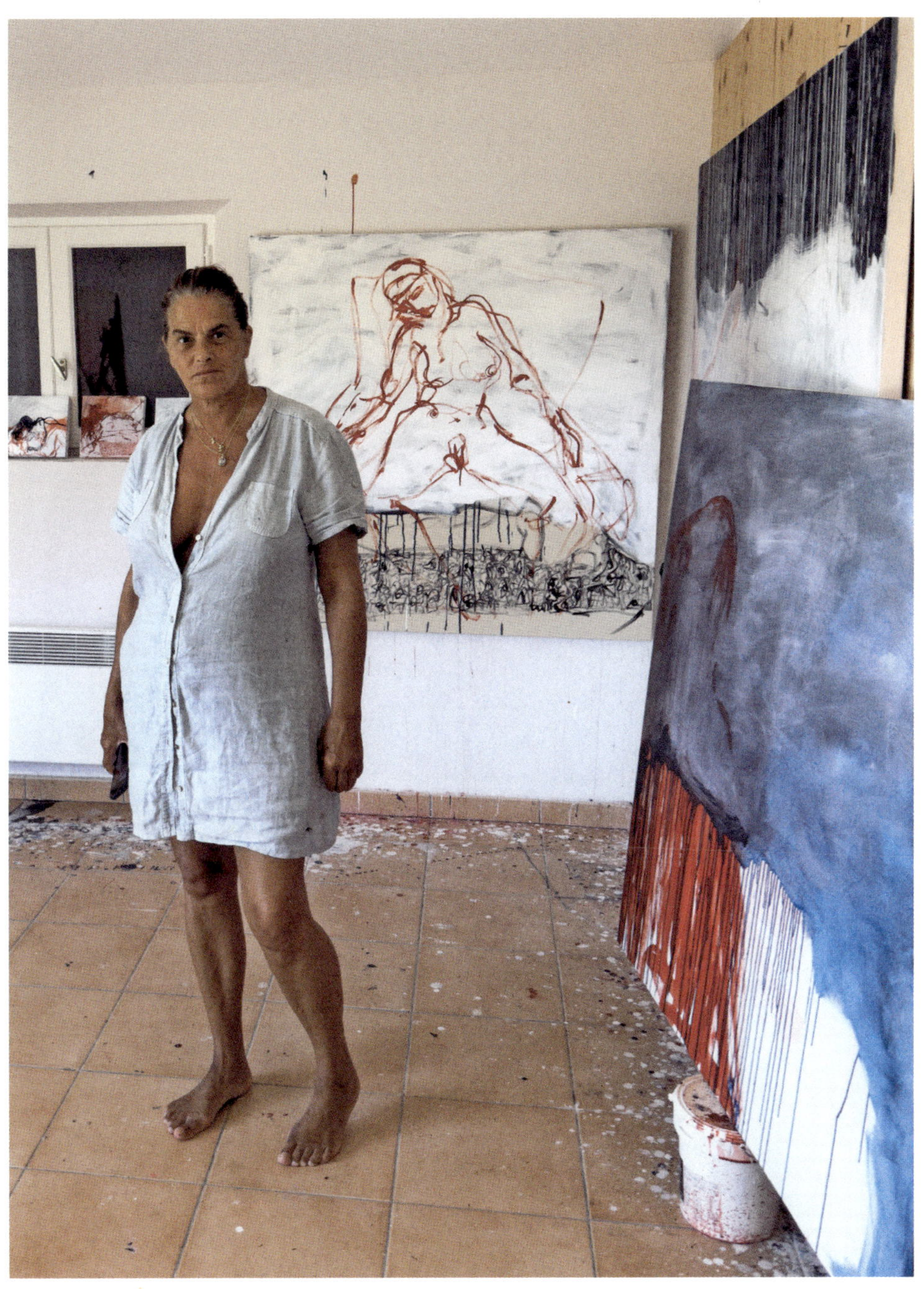

Tracey Emin in her studio in the south of France, June 2023

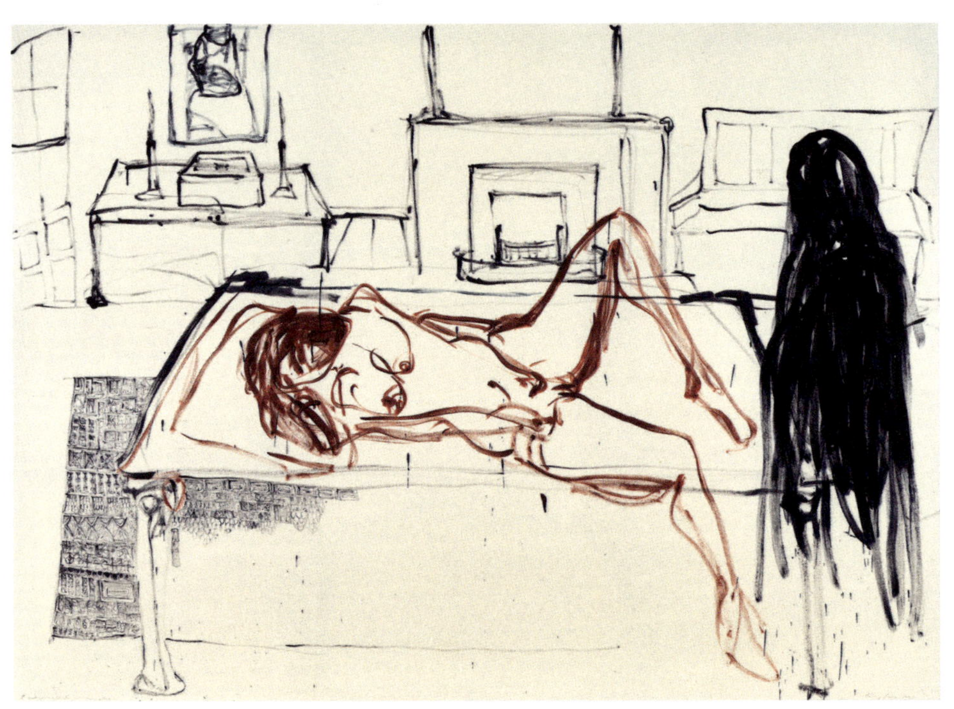

*I watched Myself die and come alive, 2023*

a person alone in a room with paints and canvases – like
so many artists before you: Edvard Munch, Francis Bacon,
Lucian Freud. When did that change happen?

**TE** It really started in 2016, when my mum died. Even
though I still had my studio in London with my office
and everything, I began to work mainly on my own
in France, and there I worked in a different way. Then
I decided that I didn't want a studio set-up, with an
office and this person and that person. I think all of
that – the office, the assistants, the stuff – is just a buffer
zone to stop you from working, to stop you from taking
the responsibility of being an artist, of being who you
are as a complete individual. That's what I am.

In the 1990s and early 2000s, I was in such a mess
with all these external things that had nothing to do
with me really. Nothing at all. Now I feel I've gone full
circle. I'm back home in Margate. I'm doing lots of work.
Teaching, reinvesting my knowledge back into art.
So everything feels as it should, balanced.

Art has many rooms. There are lots of reasons for
making art and lots of different kinds of artist. I know
what kind I am, and that is what is important.

2

*The power of paint*

Earlier that day in 2024, after I arrived in Margate, I walked along the seafront from the station up into the centre of town, and found my way to Tracey Emin's house and studio. It was not the first time I had visited her: we had talked quite a few times before, though not for quite a while. But it was my first visit here. Previously I had met her in Spitalfields – an area just east of the City of London that for a few years became an equivalent to what Montmartre and Montparnasse had been in early twentieth-century Paris: a neighbourhood where numerous artists worked within a short walk of one another. I first got used to walking down Fournier Street to knock on Gilbert & George's door; then Gary Hume and Emin moved their operations close by. But that was a long while ago. It was more than a decade since I had interviewed her – as opposed to chatting with her at openings and parties. I had never seen this new house and workplace in Margate, although I had read about it.

Almost everything Emin does makes news, and this move generated lots of coverage. So I knew a bit of the story: how she had occupied an old print shop and warehouses and transformed them into what the French used to call a *maison d'artiste*, a place in which to live and make art. I was about to discover just how spectacular that transformation had been.

I phoned Harry Weller, her mainstay, principal assistant, and the creative director of the studio, and announced that I believed I was outside. He appeared from a door some way down the street from where I thought the entrance should be

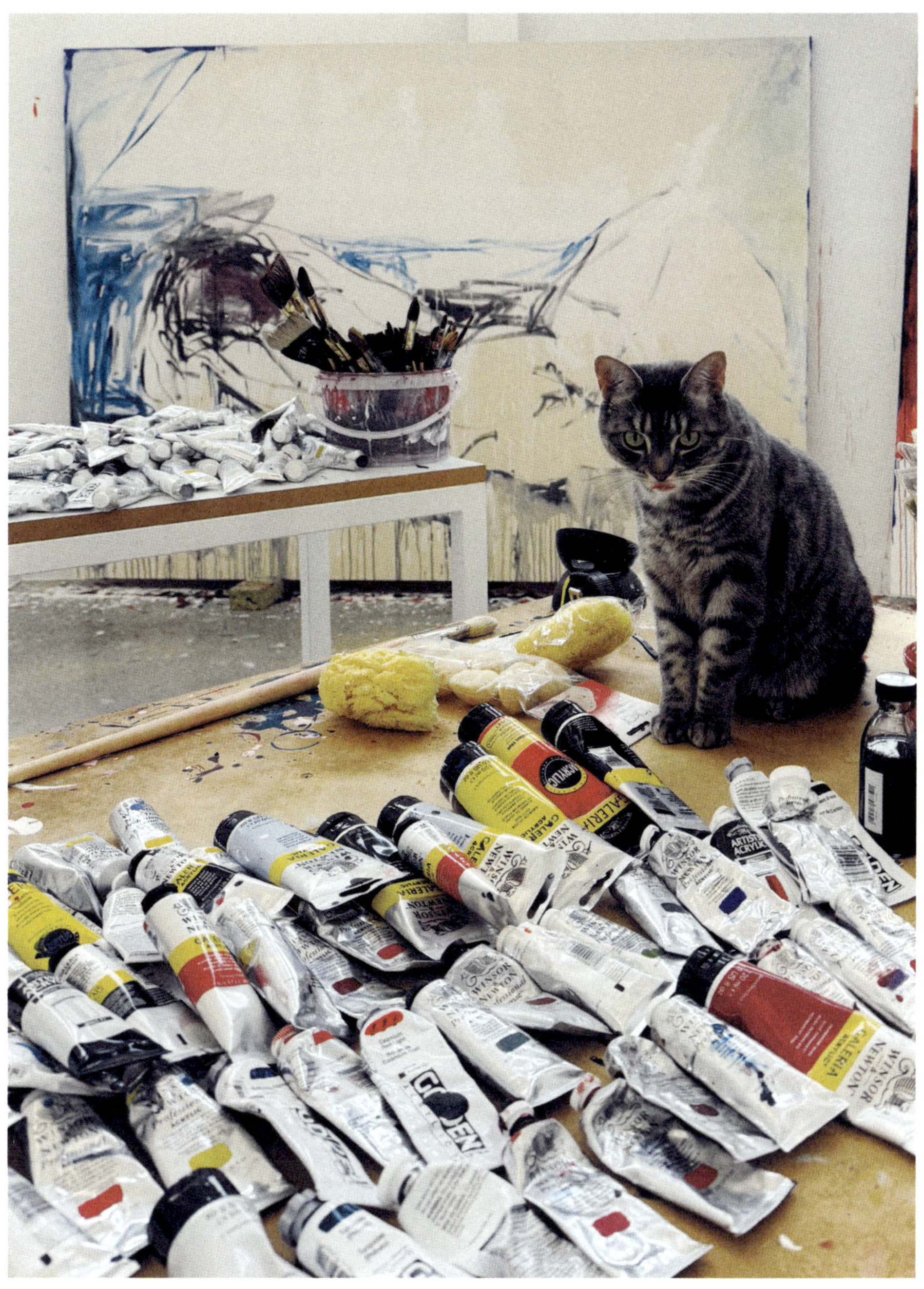

Inside Tracey Emin's Margate studio, 2025

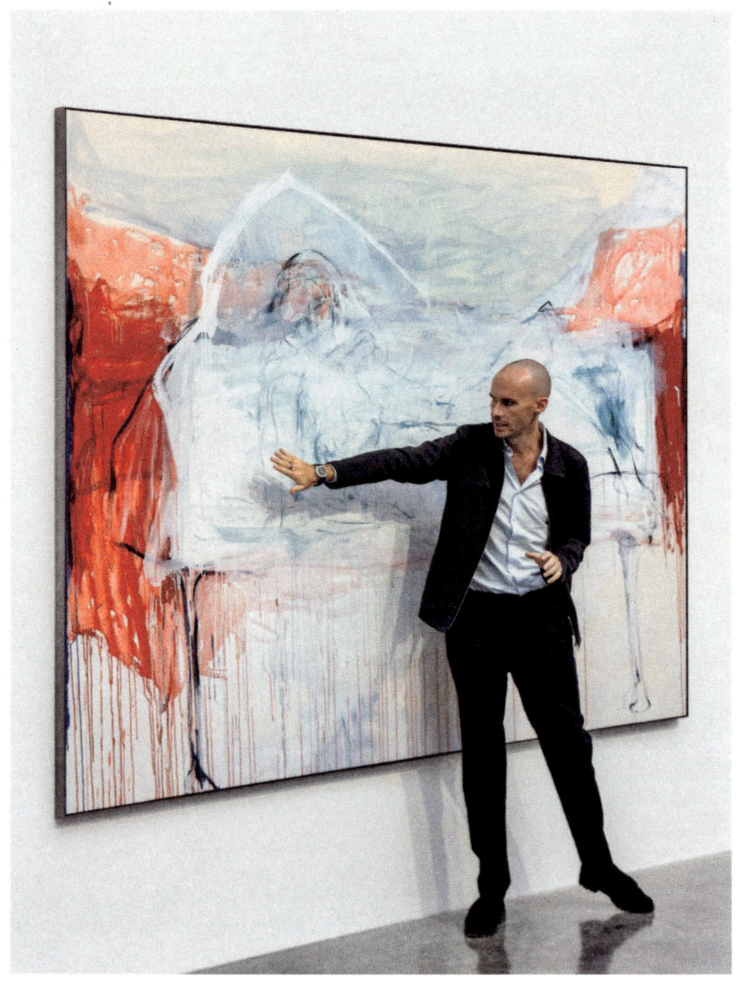

Harry Weller, creative director of Tracey Emin's studio

and led me inside, travelling up stairs, along corridors, and through a series of spaces filled with clear, bright white light. Anyone who based their ideas about an Emin interior on the crumpled disorder of her celebrated work *My Bed* would be astounded by these rooms. I was not one of those. On the other hand, the earlier Emin workspaces I had seen did not quite prepare me for the elegance, purity, and beauty of these ones.



*The power of paint*

As Harry started to explain, her illness had brought about a transformation not only in Emin's life, but also in her art – and how she thought about her art.

> We were talking about this yesterday. It's not that
> she was not satisfied with the work before, but this
> is where she wants to be now, how she sees herself
> as an artist: as a serious painter. Before, she took it
> for granted. Not that she wasn't serious, but she'd
> be the first to admit that she wasted a lot of time.
> When you look death in the face, it changes things.

Art history, like all history, is seen from a certain viewpoint. A couple of decades ago, few would have described Emin as a leading contemporary painter. For many years, she was famous as one of the so-called 'Young British Artists': a celebrity, an artist producing work in many media, but not especially as a painter. The 'YBA' category was one of the least descriptive tags in the history of such art labels (many of which, including 'Fauvism' and 'Cubism', were not originated or even accepted by the artists concerned). 'Young British Artists' was the result of an attempt to find a common denominator between the participants in a series of five exhibitions at the Saatchi Gallery between 1992 and 1995. Whatever else linked (or did not link) the people involved, they were unquestionably all young, British, and artists.

There were other common factors that were mainly social and educational. Many of the core group – including Damien Hirst, Sarah Lucas, and Gary Hume – had gone to Goldsmiths College in south-east London. Emin had been added to this category later on. But still I was surprised and intrigued when Weller told me, as we strolled from one studio to another looking at recent work, 'She doesn't consider herself a YBA:

she didn't go to Goldsmiths, she wasn't in [the exhibition] *Freeze*. When all that was happening, she was in the mountains of Turkey, painting goats.'

This was a rearrangement of the recent history of British art, and a rejection of what had long been a standard piece of journalistic and academic shorthand (though an absurd one, since the YBAs were now in their late fifties and early sixties). There was, however, a clear logic to what Weller was telling me. The Goldsmiths graduates worked in different media, but at least they shared certain influential teachers – such as the conceptual artist turned sculptor-painter Michael Craig-Martin. Furthermore, many of them had taken part in *Freeze*, put together by the young students themselves in an empty warehouse in the semi-derelict Surrey Docks in July 1988.

At that point, however, Emin was still a student at the Royal College of Art. Indeed, as we shall see, instead of taking a holiday, she spent that summer taking an intensive course in the technical aspects of oil painting. Almost the first thing I heard about her, from the critic Norbert Lynton at a dinner in the mid-1990s, was that the people who were teaching her at the Royal College thought that she was potentially an absolutely brilliant painter. Mentally I filed that information away, but as a matter of regret – since I love painting and want it to continue – because at that point painting was not the type of work that she was known for at all. It was not for a decade afterwards that I first saw a full-size painting by her (at the Venice Biennale in 2007). And it was not until twenty years after Norbert told me this unexpected information that I started to see paintings of hers that had the impact of truly major work; paintings that were unlike anything I had seen before and yet had the instant impact and lasting memorability of the best paintings.

While we were chatting, Weller and I were walking through a studio in which an entire exhibition was leaning against the



*The power of paint*

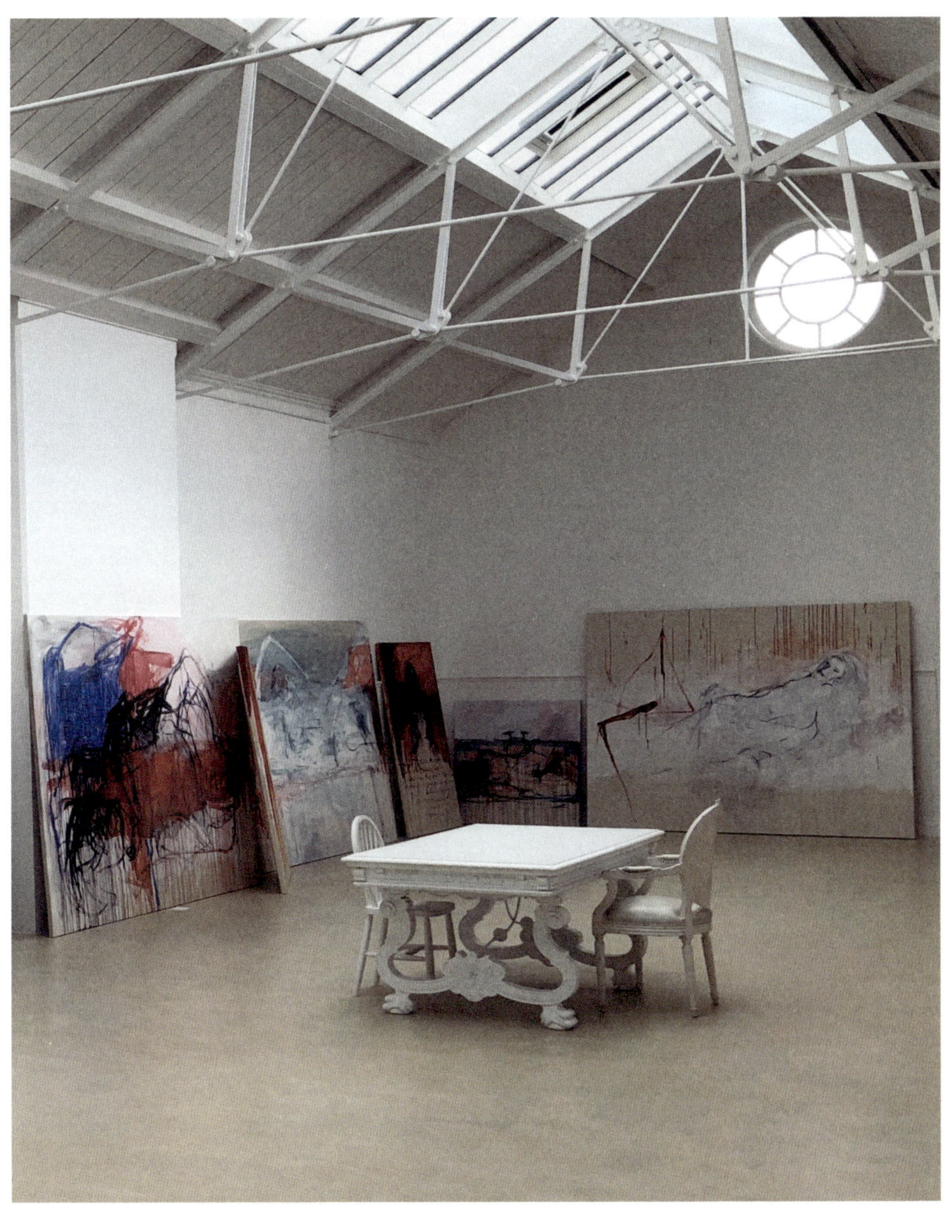

Inside Tracey Emin's Margate studio, 2025

walls, an extraordinary display, among other qualities, of sheer energy. He showed me a film that he had taken on his phone of Emin attacking a canvas with slashing brushstrokes, shouting and screaming as she did so (page 170). Obviously, she does not always work like that, or even often. But among other things, these paintings were demonstrations of sheer mental and physical vitality: of what I think of as 'the will to paint'.

I had seen a similar phenomenon earlier in the year when I visited the studio of Georg Baselitz in the foothills of the Bavarian Alps. He, in his mid-eighties and unable to walk unaided, had produced a sequence of big paintings, enough to fill a large gallery, without help, in about nine months. They were some of the strongest works of his entire career, which stretches back to the 1960s. One of their novel features was a new mark: the track of his Zimmer frame as he moved around the canvas on the studio floor. I asked him how he had done all this under such conditions. He answered, 'Basically, it's impossible.'

Weller explained that Emin, too, had to conserve her vitality. 'Since her surgery, painting takes a lot of energy and physicality, and often she is limited.' When that was the case, instead of brushstrokes powering across the canvas and paint cascading down the surface like rain or tears, he told me, she sat down and concentrated on 'intricate, delicate pattern-making'. Assistants perform different tasks for different artists. Some actually make the work. Others, such as Emin's old friend David Dawson with Lucian Freud, or Jean-Pierre Gonçalves de Lima and Jonathan Wilkinson for David Hockney, support and help in other ways. This is the case with Emin, as Weller explained. 'It's only her who touches the canvas, not me.'

There was another, internally imposed pressure: 'A painting has to speak to her and surprise her. She could paint a classical reclining nude with her eyes closed, but she has to challenge herself. Sometimes she flips the canvases over, erases the figures

          *The power of paint*

with white, and waits for the painting to speak to her. There are
never any preparatory sketches, ever – it's all immediate. If it
doesn't surprise her, it's not worth keeping.'

When we had finished looking at the new work, I was led
upstairs to a spacious, uncluttered, light-filled room where
Emin – who spends about three days a week in bed, recuperating
from her labours – was reclining. We said hello. Then she said:
'I wonder what you think of my work.' This is the crunch point
that is likely to occur in any studio visit. I decided that honesty
was the best course. I replied, 'I find myself liking it more and
more over the last few years.' She thought about that for a
moment, then smiled, and said, 'Me too'. And we began to talk.

# 3

## *Drawing, painting, and feeling*

One of the first topics that Emin and I talked about when we first met in her studio in 2005 was drawing. At that time, I was not aware of her painting, but I had recently had a short but instructive conversation about her drawing with Lucian Freud. He was examining her Christmas card of a robin on a branch and musing, 'She's got an individual line.' This sounded like a compliment. Individuality was a quality that Lucian rated very highly, and understandably so. Being able to make a mark with a pen, a pencil, or a stick of charcoal that is recognizably *yours* is quite an achievement. After all, people have been doing this same thing for tens of millennia. But somehow powerful artists find ways of doing it that is uniquely theirs. That is why scholars are able to attribute this sheet of sketches to Michelangelo but that one to Raphael (although admittedly they do not always agree).

So when Emin and I first sat down to talk twenty years ago, drawing – and specifically, drawing in a way that was like nobody else's – was one of the first topics I raised. Where, I asked, does that individual line come from?

TE   I spent seven years learning to draw, and in life-drawing classes, and I don't have to try to draw *weird*. If I draw as well as I possibly can, there's still this expressionistic line, this angst thing. Some people have an affectation of trying to be weird, trying to be different. They are just boring, affected people. Whereas me, I try to be as on time as I can; I try to be as respectful, as truthful as possible;

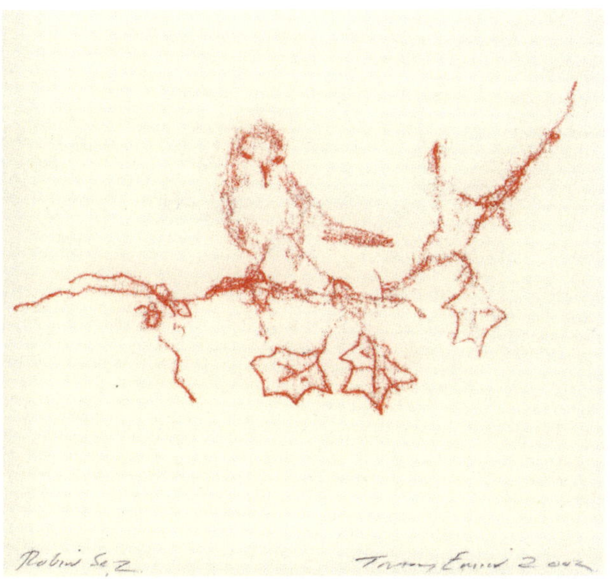

*Tate Christmas Cards: Robin Sez, 2002*

all of those things – and yet the result still comes
out chipped, crooked, not right. I still have this level
of eccentricity. Someone – it was Matt [Collishaw],
actually – said, 'Trace, you're going to have to face facts.
You and normal parted a long, long time ago.'

MG   You once said that if you were left alone on a desert island,
you would still have the need to draw.

TE   Yes, I would be drawing in the sand. I would always
draw. I *have* always drawn. I've never not drawn. And
I've always done figurative drawings, except when I
gave up art after I decided I wasn't very good at it and
should be a writer instead. Back in 1990 and 1991,

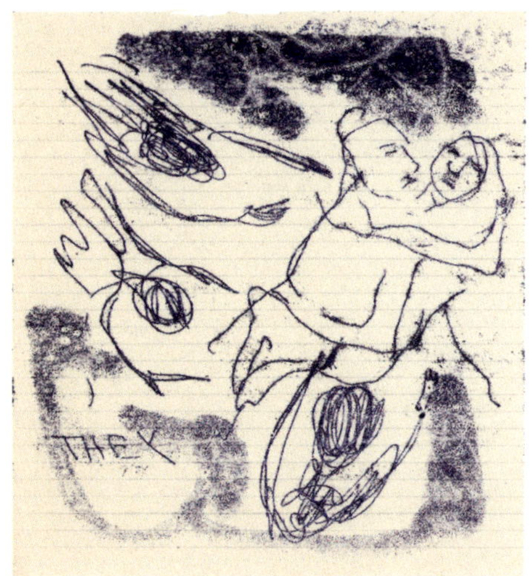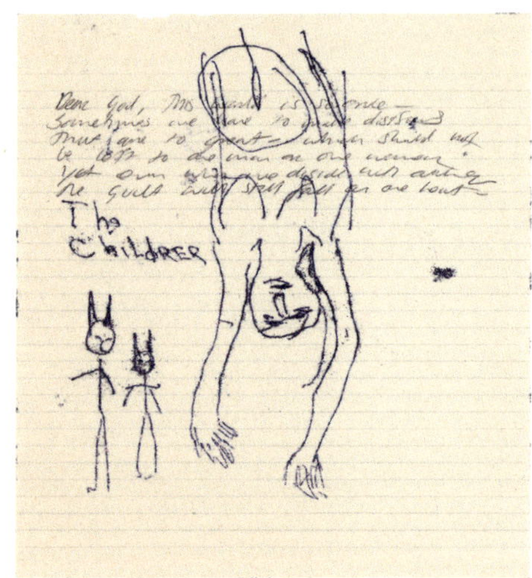

Two untitled sheets from the *Monoprint Diary*, 1991

when I had absolutely no money, I just sat at a table
drawing. I had no studio, nothing, but I could still draw.
To me, drawing is a natural extension of mental creativity.
It's like handwriting. Without drawing, I wouldn't
really exist.

Drawing for me is a lonely pursuit. I don't draw
with someone else. I don't masturbate with someone else.
These are both activities that are entirely down to me, and
how well they work comes down to my own imagination.
Drawing is meditative. It is an extension of the soul. You
have a vision in your mind, then it comes through your
hand, out onto the paper, and back into your mind again.
It's a very good therapeutic exercise. It's quite cleansing.
There's alchemy involved because of the switch-over from
your mind to the paper. My drawings are not me looking
at something; they're stamps of images in my head.

*

     *Drawing, painting, and feeling*

A few years later, in a feature about drawing for the *Guardian*, she revealed more about how she viewed it as a way of recovering past events and, more importantly, how she felt about them:

> I like to record the moment, the event of the memory.
> I remember an event from my childhood. I pull it to the
> front of my mind. My emotions force the drawing out
> of my hand – this explains why so many of my drawings
> are repeated images. It's not because I draw the same
> thing, but the same moment wants to be redrawn. I am
> the custodian, the curator of the images that live in my
> mind. Every image has first entered my mind, travelled
> through my heart, my blood – arriving at the end of my
> hand. Everything has come through me.

Emin also hinted that she had had to learn to appreciate her personal line and way of drawing, as opposed to a more natural-istic method.

> It took me years to understand the magic of drawing.
> For years, I tried to make things look how they are
> – instead of being what they are. Drawing is an alchemic
> language. Some of my favourite drawings I have done
> with my eyes closed – or so drunk I do not remember
> making them.

That, however, is not usually the method encouraged in life-drawing classes. So while we were sitting in her studio in Margate a decade and a half later, I asked how her years of learning to draw had been. Progress turned out to have been erratic, with an unexpected intervention by the railway workers' union ASLEF, who were involved in a depute with British Rail about something called 'flexible rostering'.

**TE** When I was young, fourteen or fifteen, I liked drawing
from my head. I would draw all these faces from my head.
I remember my teachers coming along and whispering,
'It's like Picasso!' Then when I studied fashion [at
Medway College of Design in 1981–2], we had to do
life drawing and I was really terrible at it, so-o-o terrible.
I got really bad marks.

In that same article in the *Guardian*, she remembered this dis-
heartening early experience: 'Nought for Design. Nought for
Life Drawing. Nought for Fashion Illustration. Nought for
Individual Flair. When I asked my teacher why, she said,
"Let's face it ducks, some of us have got it and some of us
haven't. And you just haven't."'

**MG** Some criticism you never forget, however long ago or
unfair. It's the same with reviews.

**TE** I was upset because I wanted to be an artist. You can
imagine, it was awful. Then I went to the opticians in
Margate and got some National Health Service glasses.
At the time, there was a train strike, which meant that
I couldn't go into college. But we had a shoe illustration
project to do. So I just drew my own feet in my shoes
with a sharpie pen and then I put a watercolour wash
on it. When we handed the project in, I got top marks.
The only difference was that I'd been wearing these
glasses. And when I went to life-drawing class – whoa!
– foreshortening, this, that, whatever! No problem,
because I could *see*. Before, when I'd been looking at
an arm, I couldn't see the muscles; I couldn't see the
shadow properly. Suddenly, with my glasses on, I could
see everything. Overnight, I could draw!

    *Drawing, painting, and feeling*

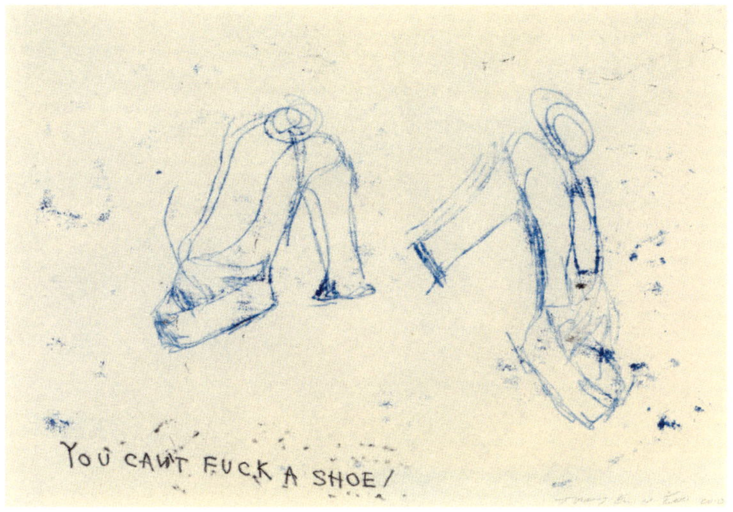


*You Can't Fuck a Shoe*, 2010

**MG** David Hockney once had a conversation with one of the attendants at the National Gallery. He wondered what the old masters had that was special. And the attendant answered, 'Very good eyesight!' It's true that clear focus is useful for drawing.

**TE** I am extremely short-sighted. Without lenses, I could only see four inches in front of me before things got blurred. But I never wanted to wear thick glasses because I was too vain. That's how I got lines on my forehead because I was always frowning. But when I had time to get glasses, although I hated wearing them, suddenly it was another world. I couldn't believe what I could see, and it made all the difference. Almost overnight I went from being really crap at drawing to being very, very good. I always had a good line, a bit like my handwriting.

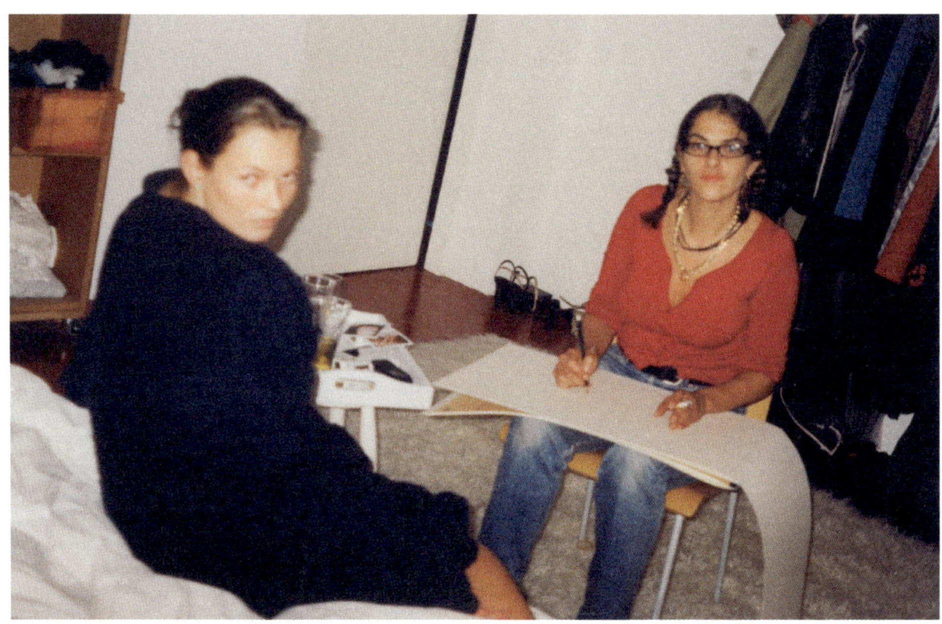

Tracey Emin drawing Kate Moss, 1999

Then my confidence improved, I dropped out of the fashion course and started going to all the life-drawing classes in art foundation.

When I went to Maidstone College of Art [between 1983 and 1986], we had life-drawing classes every week, and also intensive drawing courses. I would always sign up for them and I loved them. And at the Royal College of Art, I also did life drawing. After that, I took any chance that I could to do it. I did some in New York; and here in Margate, every other Monday we have life drawing. I've taught life drawing and I've been a life-drawing model. It takes me a couple of hours of drawing and looking to be able to do an academic drawing, but I can do it.

**MG** These days do you ever draw from a live model or subject?

 *Drawing, painting, and feeling*

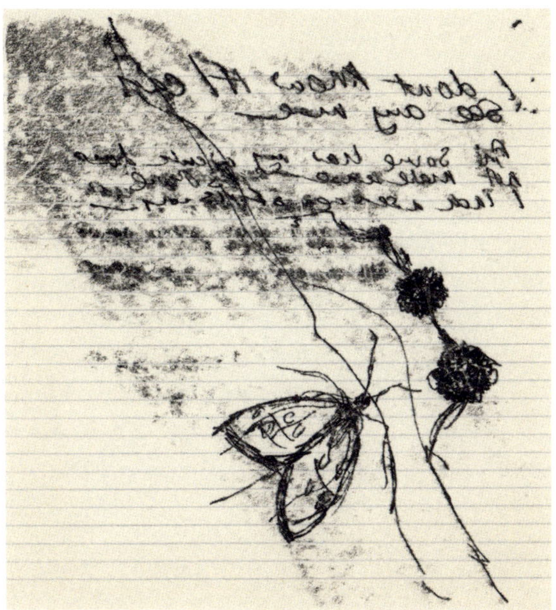

A sheet from the *Monoprint Diary*, 1991

**TE** I drew my friend's baby the other day, as a present, and often for charity I'll do a whole family portrait. But they still look like weird Tracey drawings; they still look like the family from my imagination. Some of the images in my early diaries are from a Ladybird book about insects. But nearly all the drawing I do is still from my imagination.

**MG** Bridget Riley talks about how her drawing classes as a student had helped her. Her teacher would ask, 'What is the model doing?', hoping for an answer such as 'She's standing' or 'She's sitting.' Then he would ask, 'Well, is your drawing sitting?' Although her later work was not representational at all, having learnt that intuitive sense of structure and stability helped her painting. Do you find that?

**TE** Yeah. If you are doing a painting, then you want to get a balance within the painting, an understanding of what's happening. It's understanding how things are, the weight of things. It's not to do with being able to draw something lifelike or realistic. It's about understanding how to look at things, how to balance things – and the connection that makes between your body, your hand, and your mind, and how it all works together. In one class, I tell people, 'You're going to draw someone sitting down, and you are going to sit in the chair they are sitting in.' When you sit there, you feel your bottom hitting the chair, you feel the pad of your foot hitting the floor, you feel your elbow on the chair. You're drawing an arm that's *weighted*. You're drawing a head that's heavy, you're drawing a hand that's limp. You're drawing someone who looks mournful.

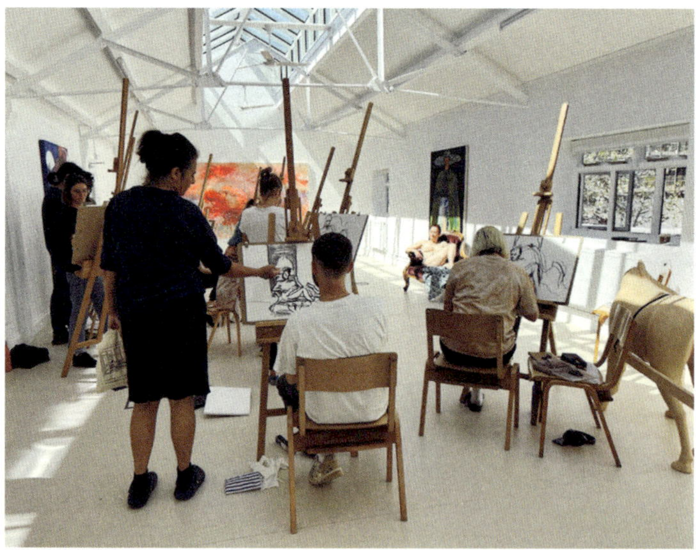

Tracey Emin teaching life-drawing at her Margate studio

    *Drawing, painting, and feeling*

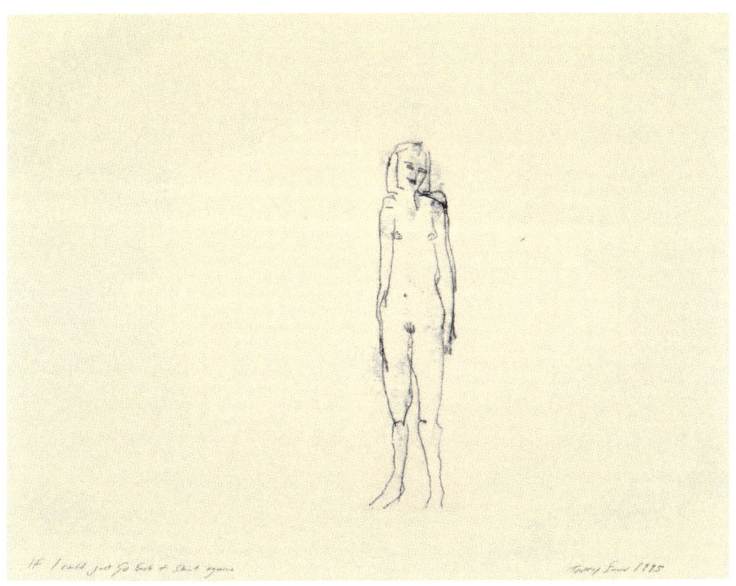


*If I Could Just Go Back + Start Again,* 1995

Another thing I do with the life class is after they've
been drawing away – drawing, drawing, drawing the life
model – then I say, 'Now, you are going to draw me *and*
the life model.' I'll sit at the end of the couch or whatever
it is. Afterwards, I say to them, 'Who do like best that
you've drawn, me or the life model?' They say, 'You'.
If I ask which they think is the better drawing, they say,
'The Tracey one'. So then I ask, 'Why do you think that
is?' Then I say to them, 'When you are drawing the life
model, remember she has a soul, remember she's a person,
remember she has skin. It's easy for them to remember
that I have all those things because I've been talking to
them. I've been explaining stuff, I'm moving, I've been
like this, I've been like that. Whereas the life model is
just like *this.* So often I get the life model to move around
and say something, so they understand that what they are
drawing is not just an object.

**MG** It sounds as if the lessons you teach are not only about structure and balance, but also about feeling and empathy.

**TE** Yes

**MG** I wonder about the connection between painting and drawing. Sometimes, with Rothko for instance, it's not so close. But in the work of other artists the drawing is the structure, the scaffolding you might say. I remember Leon Kossoff looking at Venetian painters such as Tintoretto and Titian and saying, 'They are drawing in the paint!' Is that what you do?

**TE** When I first started painting, I couldn't draw *with* the paint. I had to do the drawing first. At the Royal College, when I was younger, I would draw with a green pencil, then I would put a wash over it. But now all of it is drawing in the paint.

**MG** Critics talk about 'painterly' painting, meaning pictures that are brushy, not smooth, where you can see the paint marks, the texture of the material and the way it has moved and flowed. For painterly painters, the most crucial thing is what the material itself can do – its capacity to make marks of innumerable differing sorts, to flow, to drip, to sparkle, to absorb light and to reflect it. Manet was an archetypal example of a painterly painter, as were Jackson Pollock, Francis Bacon, Joan Mitchell, and late Lucian Freud. And we also talk about painters whose pictures come out of drawing, 'painter-drawers' you might say, in the way that Picasso was called a 'sculptor-painter' in the title of a famous exhibition. There are quite a few of those, for whom line comes before



*Drawing, painting, and feeling*

such qualities of paint as impasto or fluent brushstrokes;
Edgar Degas was a painter-drawer; Giacometti is another
example, so was the young Lucian Freud. Paula Rego
used to say that she was basically a drawer. An unusual
aspect of *your* work as a painter is that you belong to
several of these subdivisions simultaneously. Obviously,
you're a painter-drawer, but also you're extremely
painterly.

**TE**  My thing is painting *and* drawing – it's all *one thing*.
I've made these giant screenprints [following pages].
It takes half an hour to cover the whole screen. And you
are using a big brush, blocking out – and you can't see
what you've done underneath. That's pretty brilliant
because when it comes through the screen, you see the
drawing and the painting and everything, all one thing.
It's so exciting, the adrenaline and everything. That's
an extreme version of it. There's no linear image, no
painterliness; there's just the thing, the stuff of it.

**MG**  Do you have a set method of beginning a painting?

**TE**  I've got several ways of starting a painting. One of them
is to start off with a drawing, and paint over it. Another
is that I make a drawing, then just put a wash across it
and keep it as a colour-field drawing thing. Or I start off
by painting an abstract shape and just keep painting until
whatever I see comes to me and I put it in the painting.
Because I really want to paint, and to feel quite free with it,
I never, ever, start off with an image in my head. I don't
start off thinking, 'I'm going to make a picture of me laying
in bed with a teacup.' And if I make a big drawing, I never
know what I'm going to draw until I start drawing it.

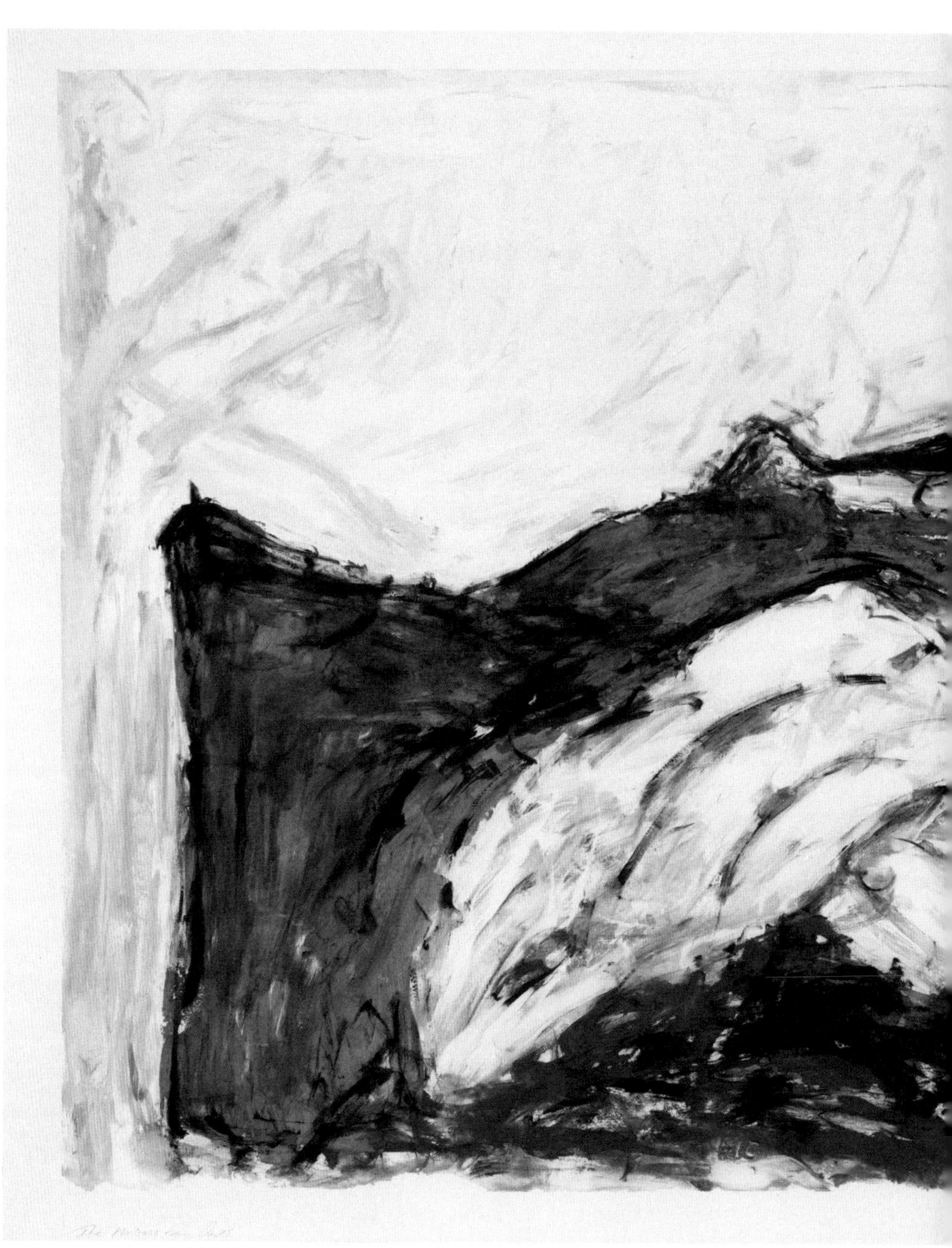

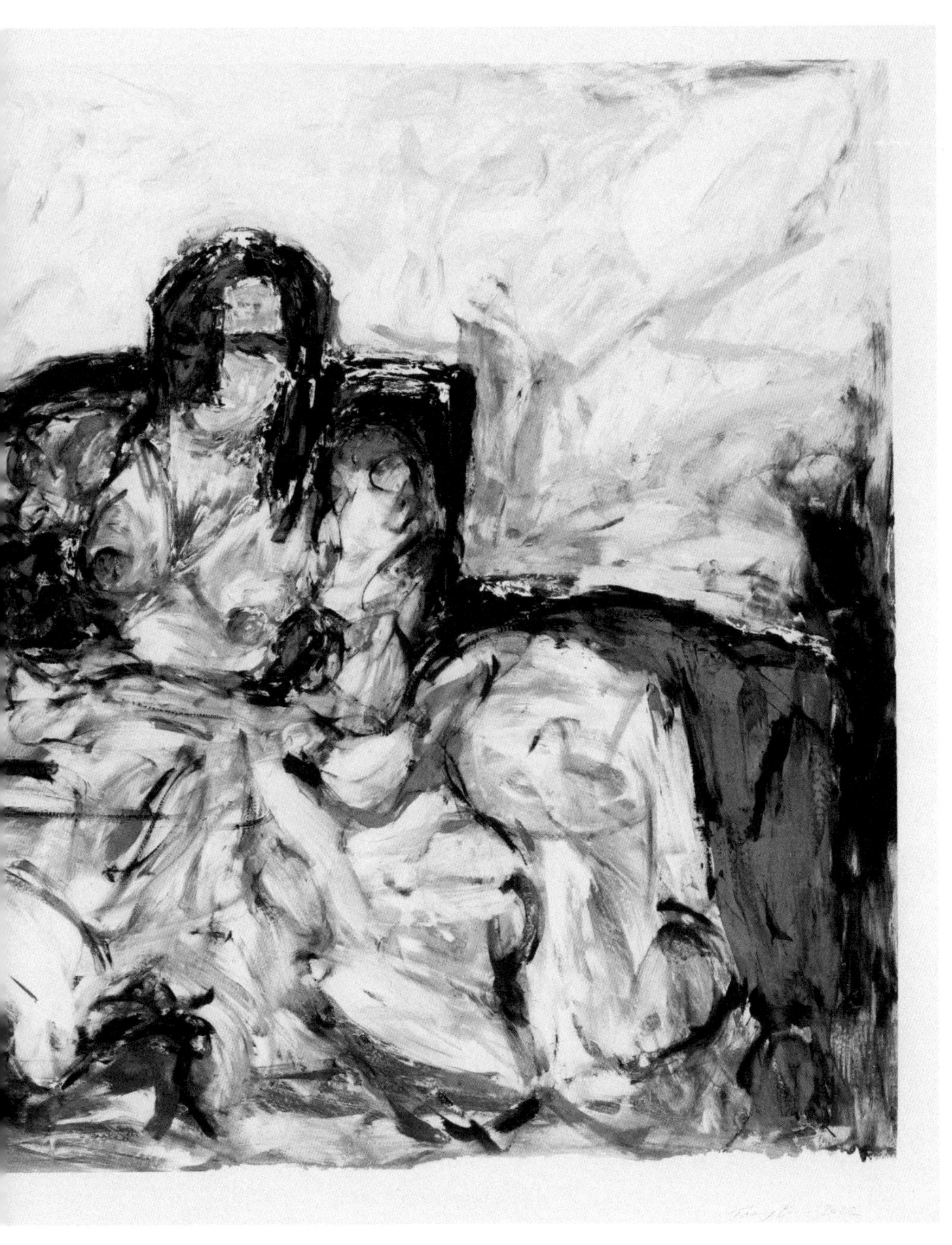

*The Mistress from Death*, 2022

# 4

## *David Bowie and Egon Schiele*

Original artists rearrange art history around themselves. They do so in two stages: first, while they are discovering (or creating) their identity, they select their own predecessors. Vincent van Gogh, for example, mixed his idiosyncratic idiom from a disparate set of sources, including seventeenth-century Dutch painters, mid-nineteenth-century realism, the Pre-Raphaelites, and Impressionist colour. At the time, this idiom looked wild and strange. In retrospect, it looks inevitable because Van Gogh himself has become part of the story, a reference point for every painter who came afterwards. (That's the second stage in a major artist's effect on history, when the sheer force of their work makes us change the narrative so as to fit them in.)

In Emin's case, her crucial guiding lights, the mentors who told her what art was and could be, were presented almost by chance. But her reaction showed that it was not really an accident but an example of what Goethe called 'elective affinities'. Or, as she would say, she discovered her team, her people, and instinctively recognized them. It happened like this.

**TE** I had a boyfriend in Margate called Simon, and he was a cool person because he went to Medway [School of Arts]. He was about eighteen and I was much younger, and I loved David Bowie. When the album *Lodger* came out, I said to Simon, 'What an amazing cover!' He said, 'It's taken from the Egon Schiele.' 'Who's Egon Schiele?' And he explained that he was this Expressionist painter.

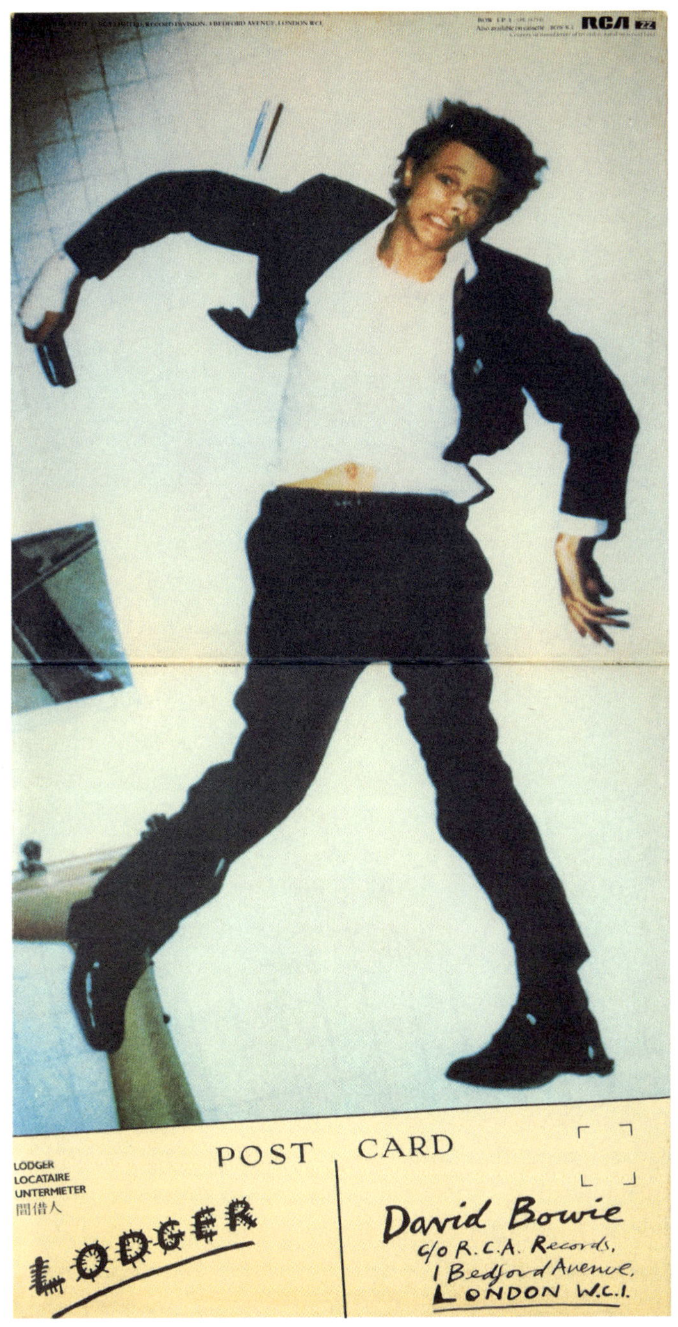



The cover of David Bowie's album *Lodger*, 1979

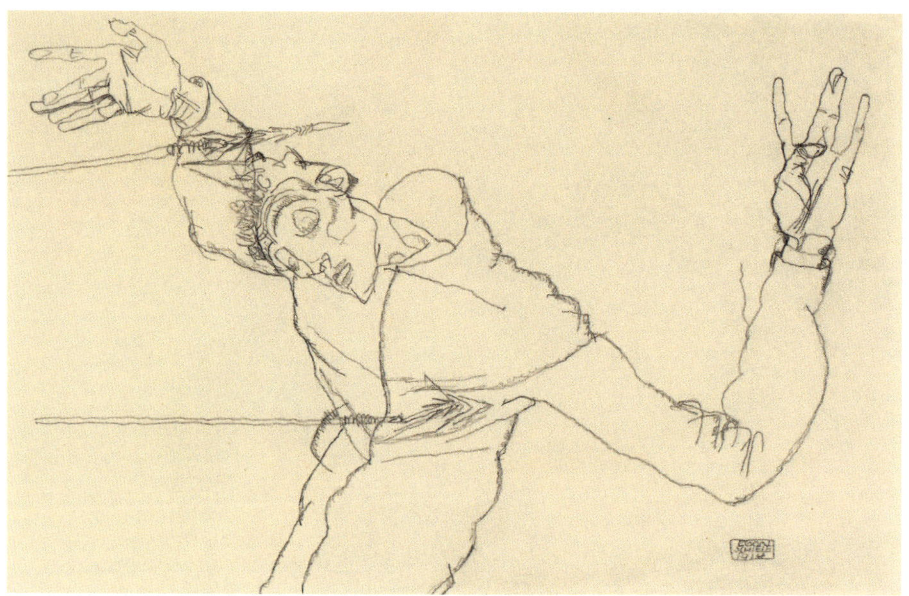

Egon Schiele, *Self-portrait as St Sebastian*, 1914

In those days, Schiele was a relatively unusual taste in
Britain. His work did not have the qualities most admired in
the British contemporary art world of the 1970s. It was not
cool, minimalist, conceptual, politically engaged, or ironic.
There were few, if any, of his works in British collections.
A photograph of Bowie from 1977 contains a copy of the paper-
back book on Schiele by Alessandra Comini, published in 1976
and the source from which many English-speaking people discovered him (I was one).

*Lodger* was released on 25 May 1979, which dates this incident. Assuming that Emin, as a keen Bowie fan, would have
at least looked at the album as soon as it appeared, she must
have discovered the art of Egon Schiele (1890–1918) early
in the summer of 1979, a little before her sixteenth birthday.
No sooner had she heard the name of this artist than she set
about discovering more about him.

　　　*David Bowie and Egon Schiele*

**TE** Up the street in Margate there was a bookshop, the Albion
Bookshop in Northdown Road. I went there and found a
book on Expressionism. I looked through it and saw one
small picture by Schiele. And there was Edvard Munch
and Käthe Kollwitz. I thought, 'Yes! These are my people!'

When I first saw the Schieles, I immediately
responded and thought, 'Yeah, this is it! This is what
art should look like. This is my heart, this is where
I belong with this torture, torment, emotion, expression,
feeling, angst, passion, sex. This where my heart lies
and my work. I understand this.' Suddenly in my life
a door opened for me and made it possible for me to
have an education and a direction.

I was fifteen then, so that was really enlightening
for me, and brilliant. Up to then, at school it was all
Andy Warhol and Roy Lichtenstein. Because at school
you had to learn about a living artist. (At one point, *I*
was the living artist that kids had to learn about, which
is really weird.) My mum bought me that book about
Expressionism for my birthday. She also bought me the
art of the Holocaust book, with drawings by survivors
that had been done inside the camps. So I was totally
affected by and interested in art that changed people's
inner emotions and gave people language and strength.
I wasn't interested in pop.

Of course, like Schiele, Emin too was not instinctively cool,
minimalist, conceptual, or ironic. So there and then she found
the kind of art that spoke to her, moved her, and that she wanted
to make herself. Almost the first thing she told me, more than
two decades later, was: 'I'm making work for people who are
emotional – sentimental, aggressive, angry, violent, jealous, all
those kind of things.'

One day, as a student – or so the story goes – Schiele called on Gustav Klimt, a celebrated older artist, and showed him a portfolio of drawings with the abrupt query, 'Do I have talent?' Klimt looked at them, then answered, 'Much too much!' From childhood, Schiele drew with manic fluency. His father, a syphilitic station master, was irritated to discover that a sketchbook, a gift to the boy intended to last for months, had been filled in less than a day. In 1906, at the age of sixteen, he sailed through the entrance examination to the Vienna Academy of Fine Arts to become the youngest student in his class. The following year Adolf Hitler ignominiously failed the same test (it is intriguing, if counterfactual, to wonder how history would have changed if Hitler had passed and gone on to become a mediocre painter rather than a genocidal dictator). As time went on, the Vienna Academy seems to have regretted letting him in. His teacher, the severely conservative Professor Griepenkerl, implored Schiele when he left, 'For God's sake, never tell anyone you studied with me!' The reason was that Schiele was simultaneously a prodigy and an *enfant terrible*. So, of course, was Emin when she burst onto the London art scene in the 1990s.

Schiele drew fast, always from the live model, and, according to his friend and dealer Otto Benesch, he never erased anything or made a correction. His line was spiky, tense, crackling with intensity. If a model moved, he either threw his drawing away and started again or simply drew new lines over the old ones. It is easy to believe that he worked at lightning velocity.

His figures were usually naked, definitely not the idealized, classicized thing, a 'nude'. The male figures are plainly the artist himself (even if he omitted the head, as he often did). Emin has explained why the faces are often omitted or crossed out in her own naked female figures: 'Because it's always my face, and it's not about me, is it? It's about everybody. It's not about "this is how I look"; it's about "this is how I feel".'

   *David Bowie and Egon Schiele*

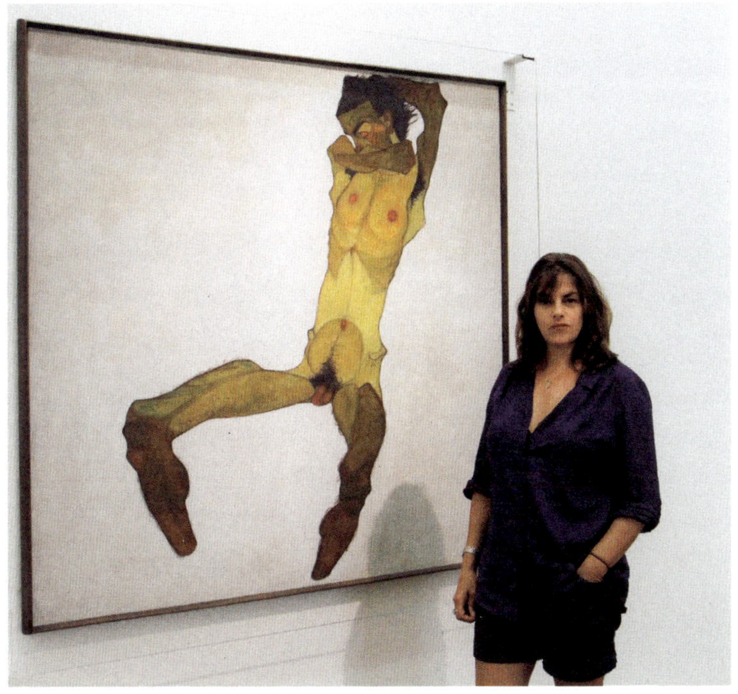

Tracey Emin with Egon Schiele's *Seated Male Nude (Self-portrait)*
at the Leopold Museum, Vienna, 2015

Schiele would probably have said the same. His people are gawky and extremely sexual, with careful attention to genitalia. The outrageousness of these works resulted in their being denounced as pornographic. Schiele was briefly imprisoned in 1912, and one of his works was burnt with a candle flame in the courtroom. After his death in 1918, prints derived from his works were seized by the police and apparently destroyed.

In 2015, some thirty-six years after she first discovered the Austrian artist, Emin held a joint exhibition with Schiele at the Leopold Museum in Vienna. There, in front of an audience

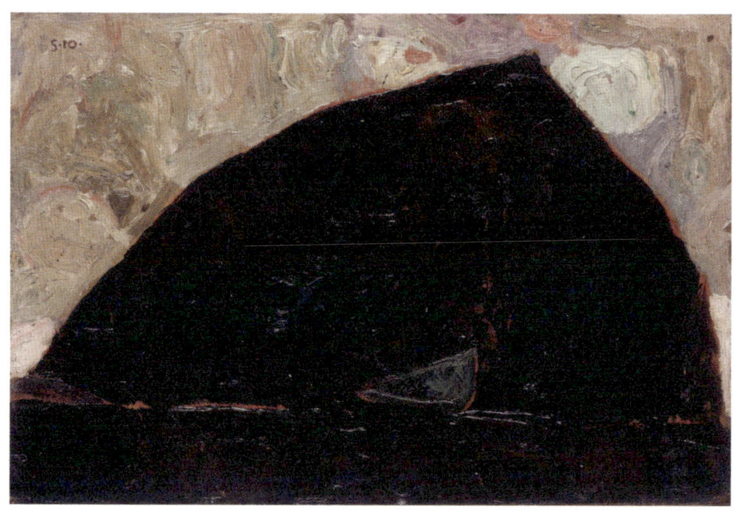

Egon Schiele, *Berg am Fluss* (Mountain on the river), 1910

in the museum's auditorium, she explained what the discovery of his work in that bookshop long ago had meant to her. There are plenty of connections between the two, but when she chose a work to talk about, she did not go for a naked self-portrait, or even any image of a person. Instead, she selected a landscape, *Berg am Fluss* (Mountain on the river) from 1910. And the way she spoke about it revealed a lot about how she feels about painting – and what it can do.

> I really love that painting. To me, it says as much about a self-portrait as a self-portrait does. When I look at that painting, I see a soul in it. I see something really melancholy. That yellow, orangey sun that looks like it's crying. It's such a sad painting. It resonates for me, it beats, it has real movement. I really like the idea that big is not always powerful. And I like the idea that that one painting can hold the whole wall [which is what this picture did in that exhibition].

Of course, as often happens when artists talk about other artists' works, Emin is talking also about herself. Her paintings, too, can beat and pulse with feeling, and dominate a wall even if they are small in scale.

One important difference between Emin and Schiele is in the shape of their careers. She has already done an enormous amount of work, been through various phases, weathered many crises, and won through to a tremendous flowering as a painter, which is happening right now in her sixties. Schiele's life, in contrast, was poignantly short. He was reaching maturity – as well as achieving financial success – at the point when he died in the Spanish influenza epidemic of 1918, aged only twenty-eight. What Schiele might have achieved had he lived into old age is a conundrum.

 I often wonder what would have happened to him if he
hadn't died in 1918 but had lived and gone to New York.
Say in 1938 he had said, 'Right I'm out of here because
I'm a degenerate artist and they are going to cut my
balls off.' And off he goes to New York. What would
his work have been like, among those skyscrapers and
big sheets of glass and all that energy, compared with
Vienna or that little village in Czechia where he worked?
He wouldn't have carried on making the same paintings
and drawings. In 1938, he would have been in his forties,
still quite young. Although when De Kooning went to
New York, he still spoke Dutch, in a way, he carried on.

**MG** You mean that he remained a European artist through
all those years of living and working in the United States?

**TE** Yes, which brings us back to Margate.

Emin, too, is an international artist, in that her work is shown and
seen across the world. During the recent time that we have been
talking, she has had exhibitions in London, Florence, New York,
and at the Yale Center for British Art in New Haven, Connecticut.
That is normal for her. But she has turned out to be grounded
in a certain place. More and more, her working life revolves
about Margate.

When they first set up the new studio in the town, Harry
told me, they thought visitors would want to come to her
London house. In practice, he added, everyone wanted to see
her in Margate. She has become a contemporary version of the
genius loci, or guardian spirit of the place. Would she work in
the same way in Paris or Seattle? It seems doubtful. Artists are
sensitive to their environments but, conversely, often carry the
imprint of the place that formed them throughout their lives.

# 5

## *The psychogeography of the Isle of Thanet*

Emin's internal landscape was formed in a gnarled piece of land that protrudes eastwards from the county of Kent. The Isle of Thanet, as it is properly (though inaccurately) called, has not been an island for a long time but was once separated from the rest of Britain by a narrow band of sea known as the Wantsum Channel. This silted up in the late Middle Ages, but Thanet still has a sense of separateness, and – because it is one of the closest parts of Britain to continental Europe – a richly eventful past.

Thanet, she wrote in her memoir *Strangeland*, thrusts, 'like a bent forefinger from the crazed knuckle of England'. Since that book was published in 2005, Emin has grown warmer about the place where she grew up. No longer does she talk about it as 'A Hades Paradise, famed for times long gone'. Nor as 'Planet Thanet, also known as the Last Resort'. She has developed a feeling that was probably always there but overlaid by darker emotions: an affection for her native place. When she was planning to return to Margate, she mused on the question of whether the change of place would alter her work. The answer was yes. 'I think it will. I worked for years with my childhood, using my childhood and bad memories. And I'm really wondering when I come back whether all the good memories will come through.'

And that is just what has happened. In the 1990s, when she was working in London, the urban topography of Margate, the scene of the traumas and dramas of her early life, appeared in her work. More recently, it has been the landscape that has surfaced from deep in her imagination. She talks about the town as an enclave, slightly separate from the rest of Britain, formed of maternal hills.

> I've got a picture of Margate High Street from 1705
> or something. It's just little thatched cottages with fields
> in the background. It makes you realise that the whole
> of Margate *undulates*, there's one great big wave of a
> hill, then it goes up again on the other side. In between
> was the Wantsum, which would have divided Thanet
> from the rest of England.
>
> The Isle of Thanet had a sort of sacredness to it.
> The Vikings came here, the Romans came here, it was
> the first place in Britain to have a Christian monarchy.
> So Margate has a lot of different kinds of history.
> I sometimes try to imagine what Margate must have
> been like when there was just the forest, the trees.
> Dane Valley with the forest coming up to the cliffs and
> the river going along King Street with mills along it.

Emin told Charles Schultz, interviewing her for the *Brooklyn Rail*, how it cropped up unintendedly in one painting, *I went home*. 'When I did that background, I wasn't painting Margate', she explained. 'I wasn't painting anything. I was just painting.' Her first thought was 'this is a bit like a Richard Diebenkorn' (a West Coast American painter whose work alternated between and blended abstraction and landscape). 'So I did my Richard Diebenkorn painting and left it for six months.' At that point she added a figure, then was struck by a thought. 'Fucking hell, it's the Isle of Thanet, it's Margate, it's where I live. I can see it. It's like this aerial view, looking down on Margate. And so for me, it was amazing because I've gone back to Margate where I grew up, and it's made me very happy.'

     *The psychogeography of the Isle of Thanet*

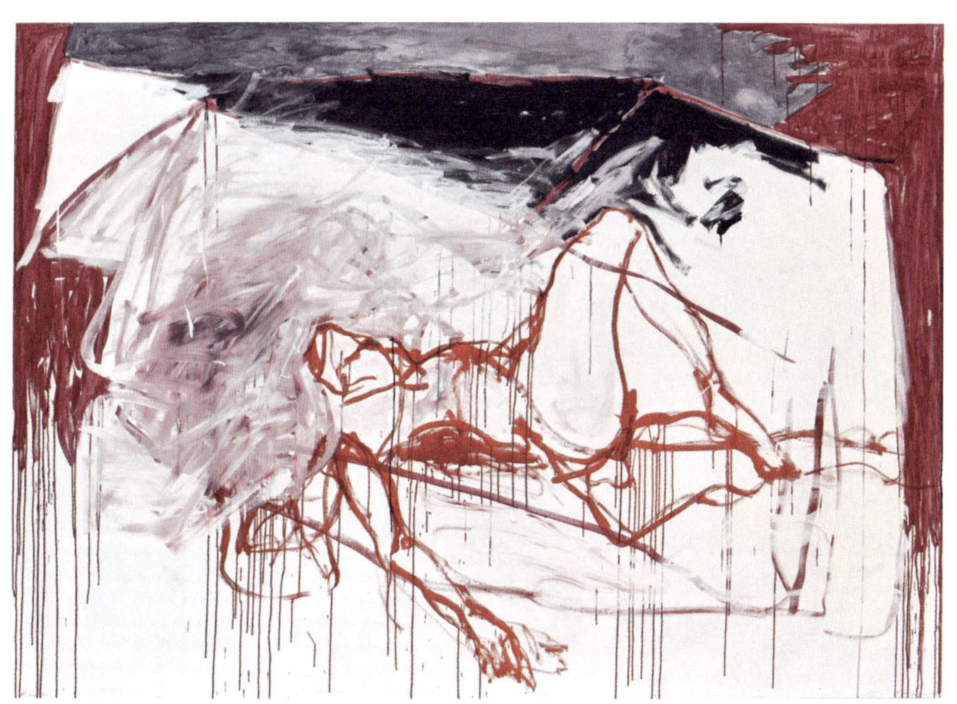

*I went home, 2023*

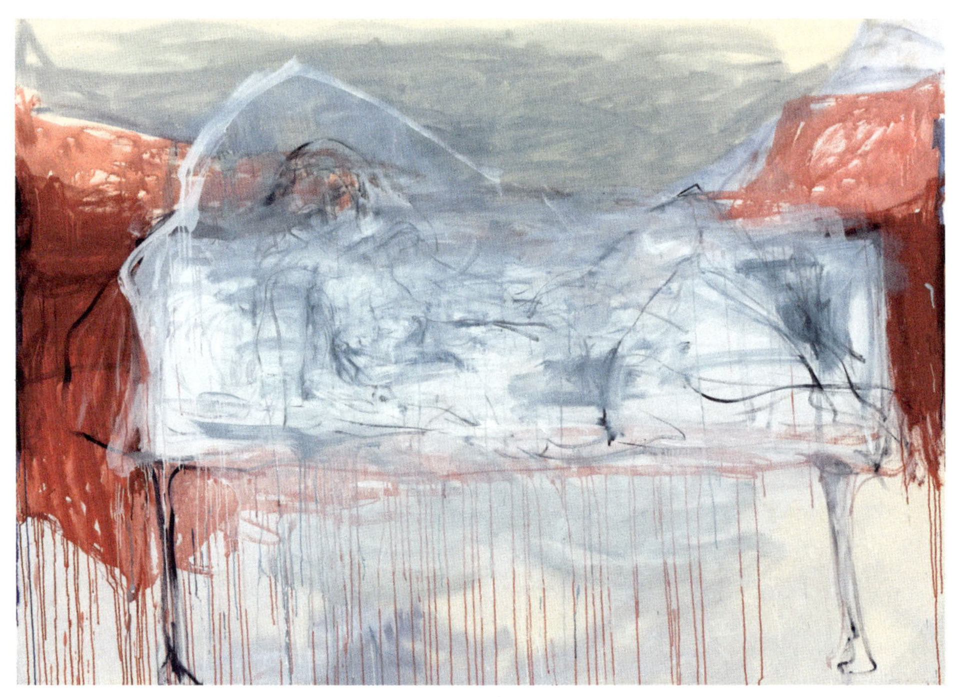

*The Bridge*, 2024

So either she unconsciously reproduced this topography or she instinctively recognizes it in a random shape, as in a Rorschach blot. The conclusion, either way, must be that this landscape is embedded deep in her mind.

While we were in the studio, Harry Weller pointed to an extraordinary painting, *The Bridge*, in which the figure (or perhaps figures) on the bed could be seen dimly through veils of overpaint. Below, in addition to bed legs, was a deluge of drips; above, an area of grey like a leaden sky. On either side there were masses suggesting hills or riverbanks, except they were red. 'This is called *The Bridge* because it reminds her of the Medway Bridge. It is an example of her erasing the painting but not painting over it completely. She loves the images coming through.'

The Medway Bridge is some distance west of Thanet, but in a way it functions like the Wantsum once did. It divides the south and east of Kent from the rest of the nation to the north and west. Any traveller to Margate from London, by car or high-speed train, is likely to pass over it (or rather over them: there are three bridges over the Medway here). Emin must have gone over these hundreds of times, always seeing the view over the water. The person (or people) in *The Bridge* seemed to be merging into topography, the bed becoming a viaduct between two blood-red ridges of land, the bed legs becoming piers holding up the structure. It is a painting that it is impossible to classify as landscape, or as nude or as surreal fantasy, or as anything. It is a Tracey Emin painting, only explicable in terms of herself, her origins, her evolution, what she is doing and thinking now. It is something new in the long, long history of painting.

Bridges, like the geography of Thanet, form part of the landscape of Emin's subconscious:

**TE**  The bridge thing is something I've always dreamt about.
You know how people have near-death experiences or

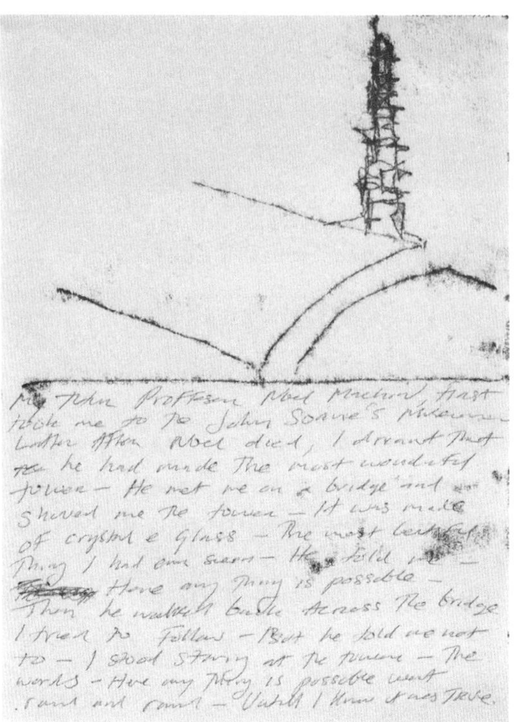


Untitled monoprint, 2010

experiences of the other world? Mine is a giant bridge, and on the other side of the bridge are these amazing crystal towers. This bridge is a thousand feet high and spindly. Always, when I dream about it, I am going across and my mum is coming towards me, and so is my dad. Once, I was almost across the bridge and my old professor at Maidstone, Noel Machin, was coming towards me, saying 'You can't come any further! You can't come any further!' I said to him, 'I want to see the crystal towers!' He said, 'You can see them from here. You mustn't come any further.' It was so corny, but actually he was dead by then; my mum and dad were both dead. Everybody I met on the bridge was dead, so it's not such a strange thing really.

A different version of the same dream is narrated on a monoprint from 2010, which also has a drawing of one of those towers.

*

**TE** When I was young, I did a set of Turneresque oil
paintings of the sea, from real life. They would really
stand up in any sort of Home Counties auction. People
would love them. Then from the age of twenty to thirty-
five, Margate was in my work a lot. The town was like
a character; the idea of it, its presence, was in my head.
Margate was home. Then along with Margate came
memories of my childhood, different events that were
psychological traumas. They appeared in my work.

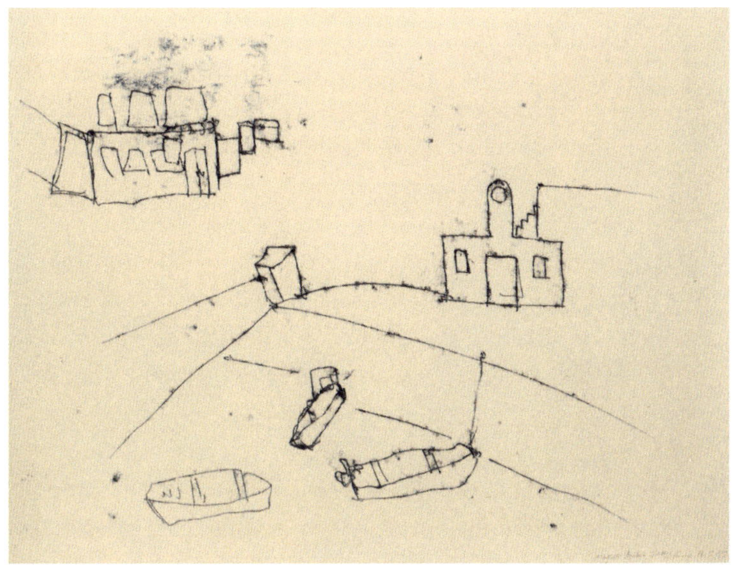

*Margate Harbour, 1995*

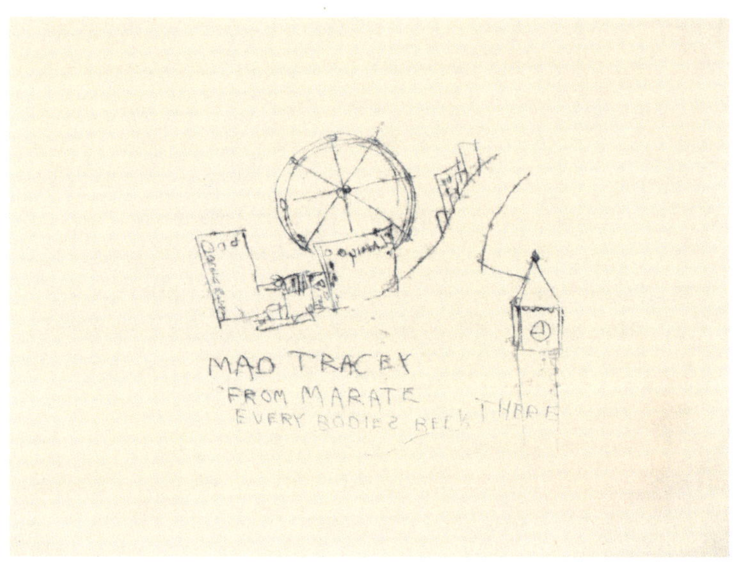


*Mad Tracey from Margate*, 1997

When I was thirty-two, I actually made many images of Margate. I drew the place, literally: the clock tower, the big wheel, the harbour, the seagulls. Then I did monoprints of Margate, from memory, but trying to make them as real as possible. And I made films about Margate, far more than people ever saw. I made *Top Spot* [a docudrama film written and directed by Emin in 2004], which was all about the town. It was like doing my own PhD on the place, my research on what I felt and what it conjured up.

Architecturally, the town of Margate is like a meal made up of various strongly flavoured but dissimilar ingredients. Its basic character is nineteenth century, with a ground note of late Georgian, an outbreak of 1960s concrete brutalism in the



*The psychogeography of the Isle of Thanet*

tower block Arlington House, and a punctuation mark of high Victorian in the Clock Tower, which sticks up halfway round the curve of the beach just where the road divides. The last was opened in 1889 to commemorate Queen Victoria's Golden Jubilee and looks like a miniature local version of Tower Bridge, slightly ridiculous but still proud of itself, the kind of structure that might have ended up on a postcard or biscuit tin. It is a spoke around which the seafront revolves. Behind is Dreamland, the music venue and amusement park that grew out of a Victorian funfair, founded in 1880 on the site of a disused railway station built on a salt marsh. In 1919, it was remodelled, freely, after Coney Island near New York. It dominates many of the monoprints that Emin made in 1995, drawing her home town from memory and imagination.

The technique she used to make these, the so-called 'direct trace drawing', involves covering a smooth surface with tacky ink, then putting a piece of paper over it and drawing on the topmost side of this with a hard pencil so the lower side is pushed onto the ink. This creates a reverse impression of the lines drawn with the pencil, but is also likely to leave a haze of ink elsewhere so the resulting image seems soiled or bruised.

In 1965, her parents, Enver and Pamela, opened the Hotel International, which overlooked another entertainment venue further along the seafront, the Winter Gardens. In a document entitled *Tracey Emin Curriculum Vitae Part I: November 1962 to December 1995*, she recorded that in 1968 after a spell living on the Black Sea coast of Turkey, the family returned to Margate. She 'went to Holy Trinity Infant School'. Then, 'Stopped speaking Turkish. Bit Mrs Man on the elbow and ran away. Spent the next five years becoming more and more strange.'

In April 2008, Emin wrote in her column in the *Independent* a lament to – almost an obituary of – Margate. The sad fact then was that the town was visibly decaying. Like most British seaside resorts, it had been unable to compete with inexpensive, sunnier rivals on the shores of the Mediterranean. The result was a slow, sad decline into the last resort:

> Every time I come here something has gone, something is missing. This time it's the scenic railway. Another time it's the big wheel. After the storms of 87 it was the pier. In the Eighties it was the entire Lido complex. Every single time I come something has been burnt, destroyed, fire bombed, boarded up, demolished or just completely forgotten about and left to go into a tragic state of disrepair.

Emin wrote that she wanted 'someone who is a giant to come along and treat Margate like their very own special model village'. This supersized saviour would bend down and with a

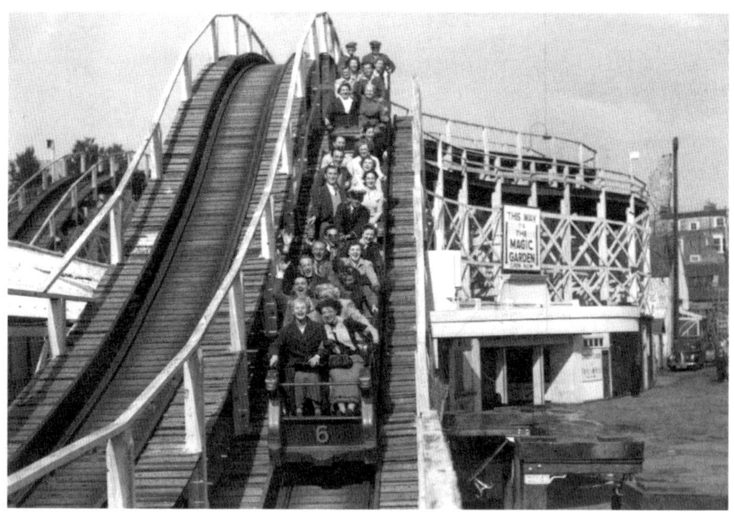



The Scenic Railway, Dreamland Amusement Park, Margate, 1951

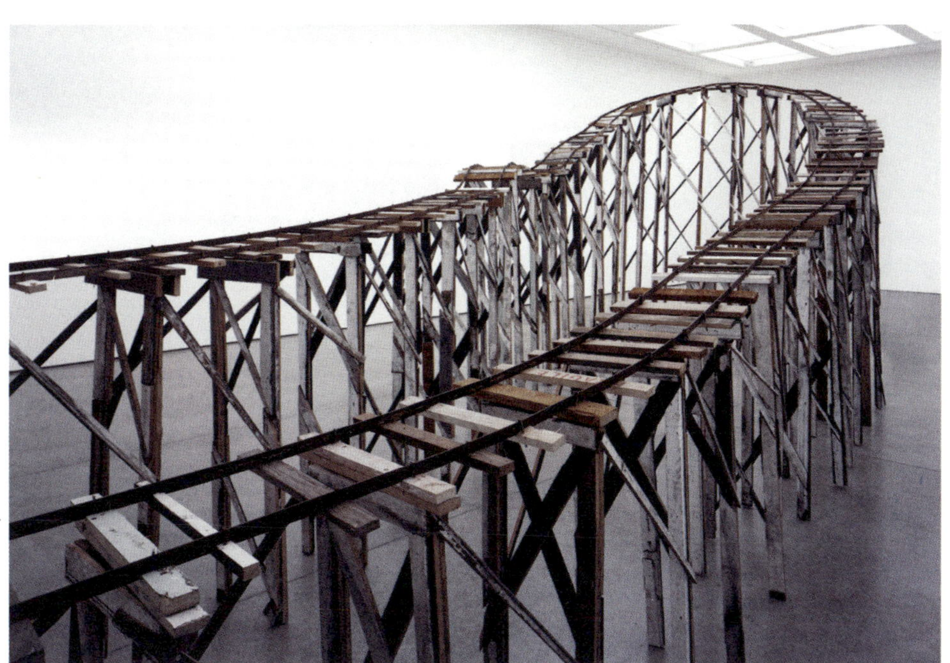

*It's Not the Way I Want to Die, 2005*

giant hand put back everything just as it was in the 1960s and 1970s, before the great decline set in. The giant would reconstitute 'the scenic railway and the big wheel' and 'make Dreamlands [sic] a place possible for teenage lovers to have dreams, the Teddy Boys to whirl on the wurlitzer and Mods to dodge with their girlfriends on the dodgems'. The Victorian iron railings would be restored; the giant would flick a switch and 'the summer lights would twinkle and dance between every guesthouse and hotel'.

Bit by bit, the landmarks from the geography of her early life were vanishing. During one phase of her career, she transformed the familiar landmarks of her youth into metaphorical structures. The Scenic Railway, pride of the Dreamland amusement park, became a rickety, perilous rollercoaster installed in an art gallery. An architecturally incongruous art deco masterpiece on the 'Golden Mile' of Margate's seafront, the Dreamland Cinema opened in 1935 as part of the amusement park. It features in a number of Emin's monoprints, its name serving as a description of this whole terrain of the imagination. At night, its illuminated sign rose vertically above the beach like a notice, as if the whole place had its name in lights.

Thus glowing letters have been part of her mental landscape since childhood. Perhaps there is no need to look further for the origin of her affinity with neon. For a while those letters went dark, but now they are shining again, ceremonially switched on by Emin herself in 2017. So in a way, Margate is returning to the way it used to be.

Emin has quite literally left her own mark on Margate. In 2010, she wrote a short and very public declaration of affection to the town across the facade of Droit House on the Stone Pier: 'I Never Stopped Loving You'. This little neoclassical building used to be the Customs House; now it is the visitor information centre. Like the town itself, it has been resurrected at least once. Tracey's declaration of affection for her native place shines brightly as the sunlight fades.

**TE**  The Margate I am in now is a completely different
Margate from then. The only thing that is similar is
the seascape, the beach, the townscape. Everything
else feels completely different. It's as if the town has
a different soul and a different energy. I'm sure that's
because I've changed as well. We've both changed.

**MG**  Have you altered it?

**TE**  Yes and no. Margate changed itself. It decided it couldn't
get worse, so it got better. That isn't just down to a
person; it's down to the bones of the town as well.

    *The psychogeography of the Isle of Thanet*

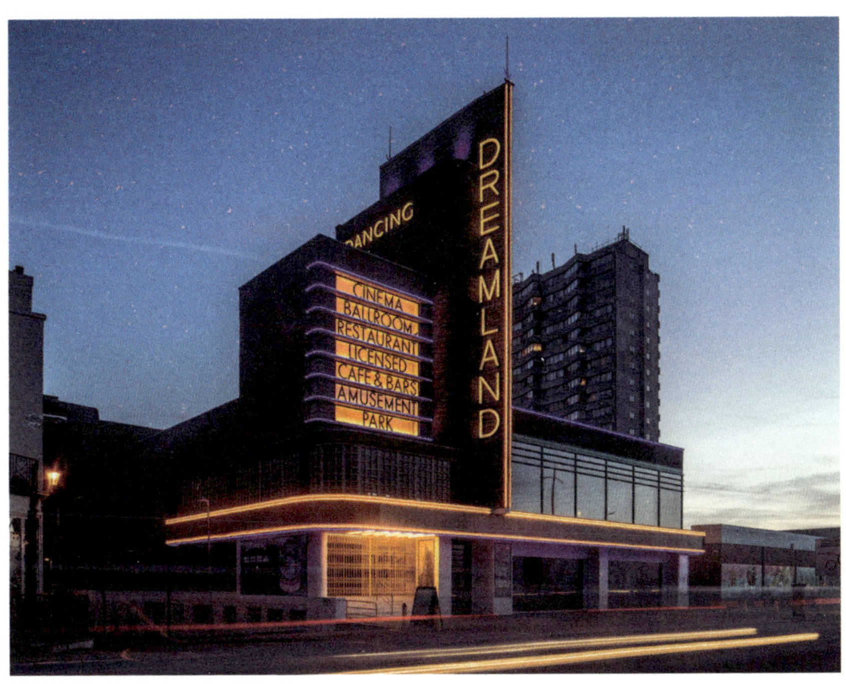


Dreamland Cinema, Margate, 2019

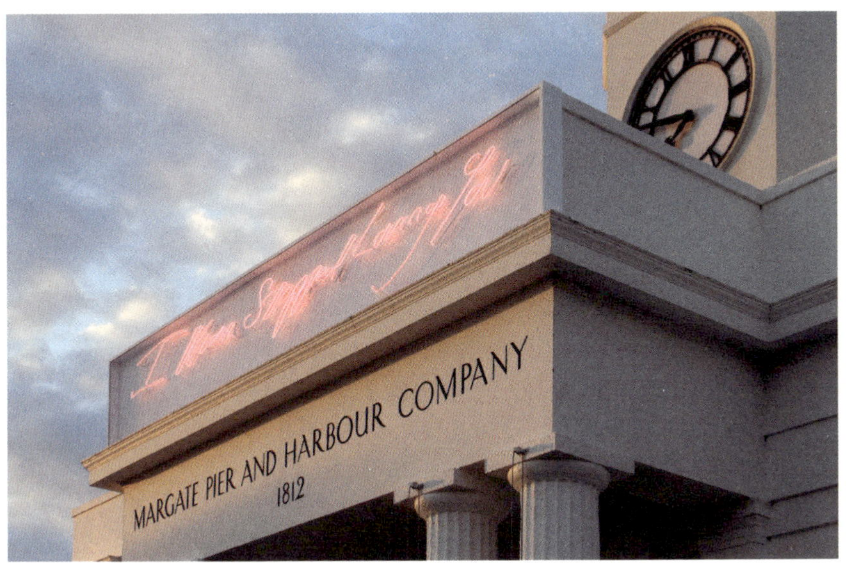


*I Never Stopped Loving You*, 2010, on the facade of Droit House, Margate

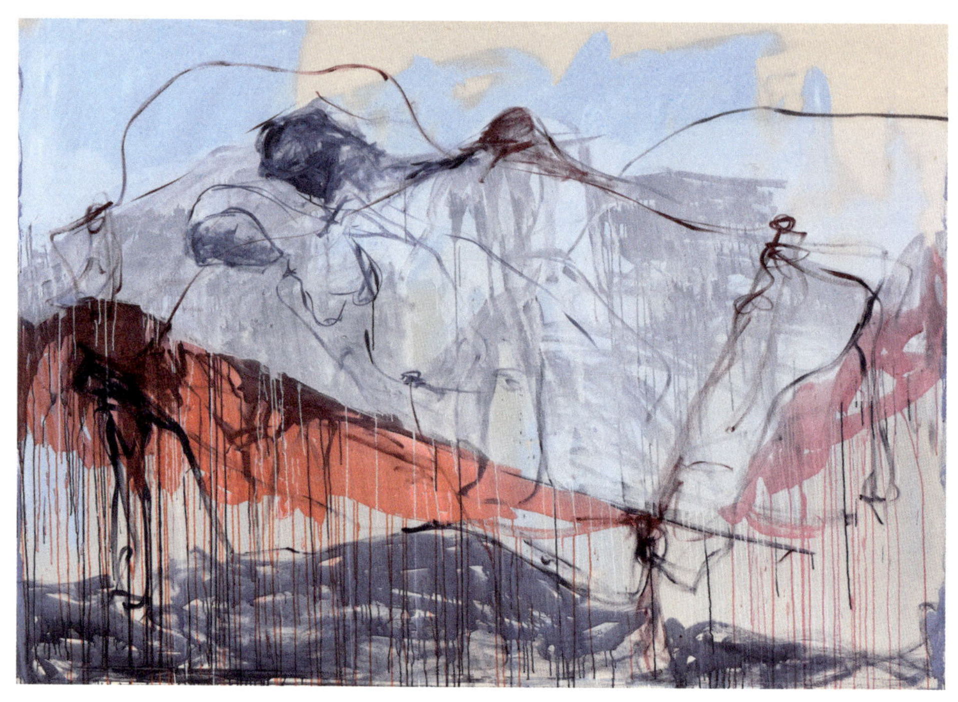

*The Saddest Tomb, 2024*

# 6

## *Tsunamis, swimming, and not drowning*

**TE**  I dream a lot about the sea. And often I dream about giant tsunamis, giant waves. I always have done since I was a little girl. So the sea is really *in* me. It's part of me.

Emin spent much of the first seven years of her life living in the family-owned Hotel International, looking out over the Winter Gardens and beyond to the chalk cliffs and the North Sea. So the background to her early childhood was marine: waves, distant horizon, and sky above. It is no wonder that these views and this powerful presence became lodged deep inside her mind, as she once wrote:

> Since I was little I've had the same reoccurring
> nightmare: that I stand by the edge of the cliff, the tide
> has gone out for miles, revealing the land mass below
> the sea, and as I look toward the horizon, a sound that's
> louder than any I've heard before comes with the moving
> sky, a tidal wave, a giant tsunami towering hundreds of
> feet high ploughs towards me. I have no escape, I turn
> towards the cliff and then I turn towards the wave, it
> splashes over me and through me and I'm left standing.

The sea is both majestic and terrifying, beautiful and lethal. As a sight and as a metaphor, it is endless. That a child with a strong visual imagination, living constantly with this force, should become obsessed by it is scarcely surprising.

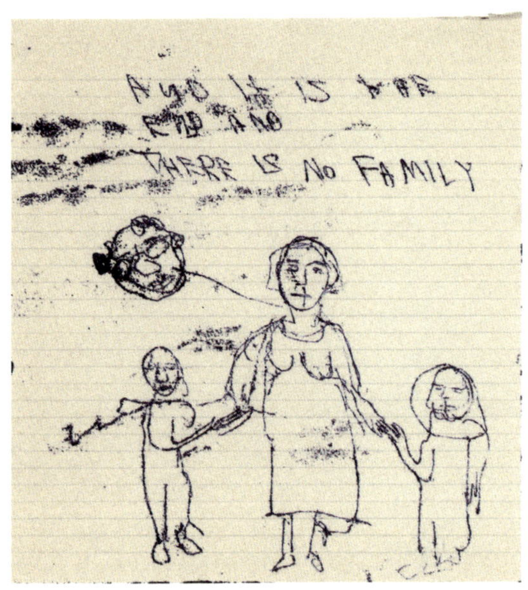


A sheet from the *Monoprint Diary*, 1991

When she was seven, her family's comfortable life in Hotel International was obliterated by a sudden catastrophe: her father Enver went bankrupt and lost the business, her parents split up, and she moved to a backstreet squat with her brother Paul and mother Pam. For a time, Enver disappeared from their lives. 'Dad was gone', she wrote in *Strangeland*. 'He had lost his money and lost the hotel. Suddenly we had nothing and we were squatting in a cottage which used to be the staff cottage.' At this point, she noted in her *Curriculum Vitae*, she 'became more and more afraid of ghosts – became thin, teeth rotted, wet the bed, and I hated to be alone. A very yellow-coloured child.' Perhaps this experience felt like a giant wave that left her shaken but standing. On the other hand, this was a marvellous spot to begin life, with this enormous, sparkling, surging element always nearby. It was an ideal background to the childhood of a Romantic artist (and romantic person), which, for all her telling of awkward truths, is in many ways what Emin is.



*Tsunamis, swimming, and not drowning*

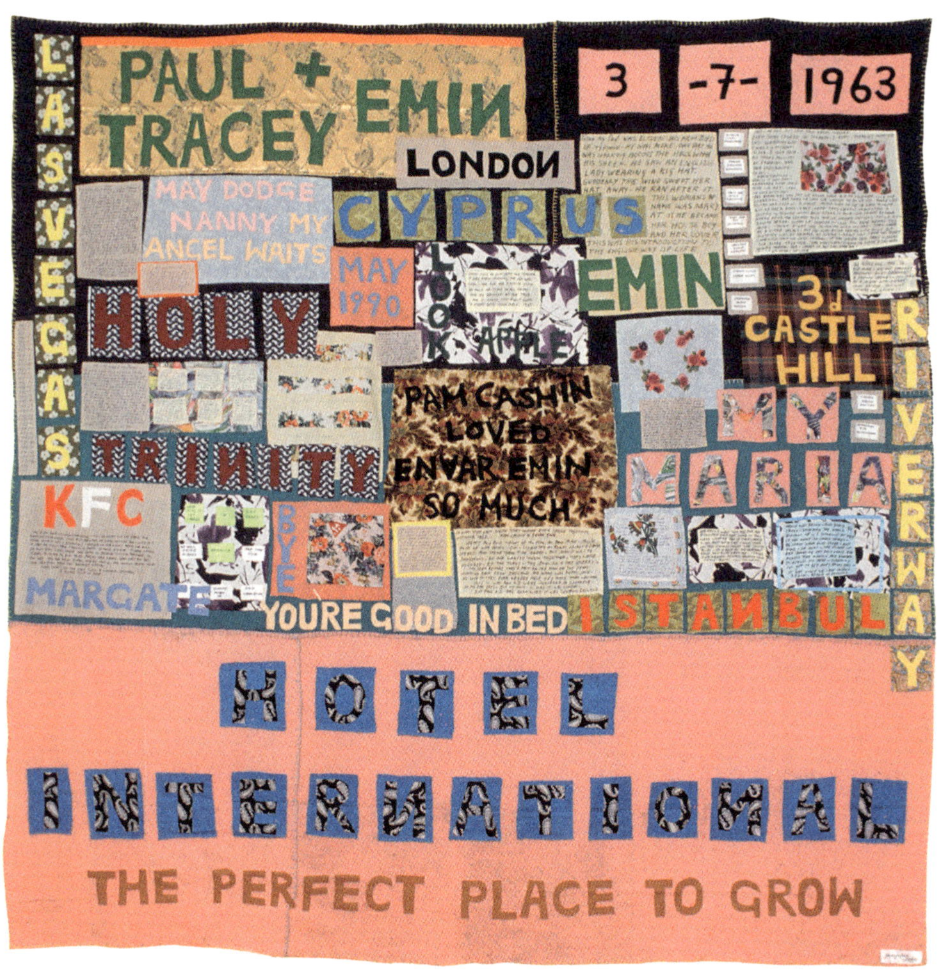


*Hotel International*, 1993

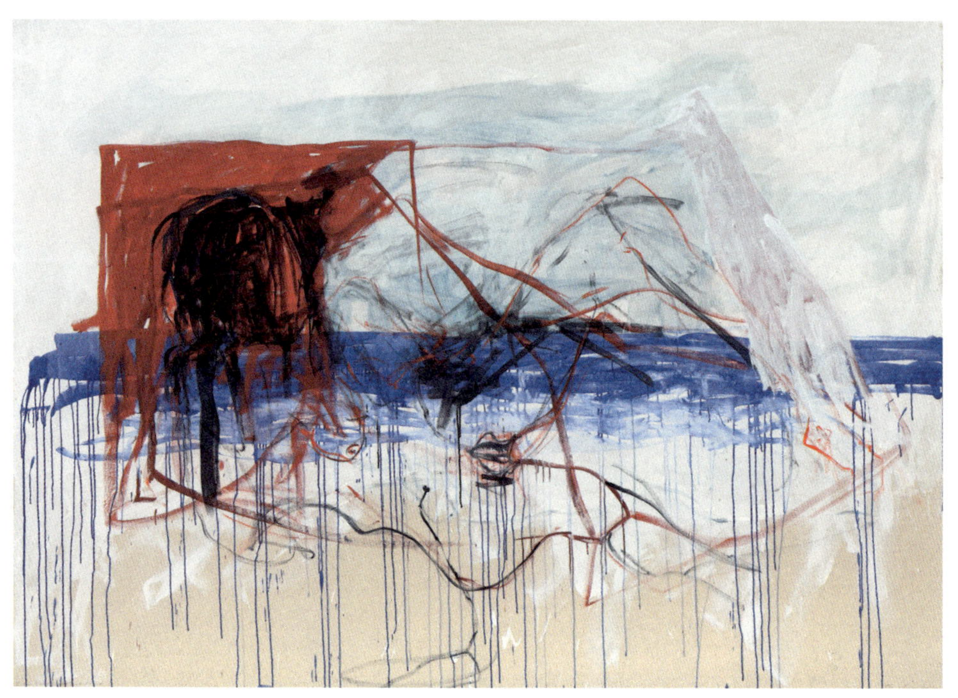

*I Saw you Coming like a Bird*, 2024

**TE** I think I'm really lucky that I grew up next to the
sea, and if I hadn't done, God knows what would have
happened to me. I might be dead by now. And I was
also fortunate enough to grow up with nature. A lot
of young people grow up with urban madness.

Seven-year-old Emin did not have precisely the same view
that middle-aged J. M. W. Turner had looked out on more than
a century before. But it was close. The Hotel International was
a little higher and to the north-east of the site of Sophia Booth's
boarding house where he lived between 1827 and 1847 (the
Emin family hotel was in fact made up of several boarding
houses knocked together, so basically it was much the same kind
of institution that Turner had stayed in).

Apparently, the landscape painter once remarked to his much
younger fan, and passionate advocate, John Ruskin that 'the
skies over Thanet are the loveliest in all Europe'. Many of his
late pictures of sunsets and sunrises are presumed to be scenes
observed at Margate – though it is often hard to be sure about
the location, and also whether it is a picture of dawn or dusk.

Whatever the truth about where Turner's pictures were set,
if anywhere except his imagination, and at what time of day,
there is no doubt that he spent a lot of time in Margate. Nor is
there any question that the town is in a remarkable position
for viewing sea and sky. It is situated on a small bulge project-
ing northwards from the knobbly Isle of Thanet peninsula,
which itself juts out from the Kent coast into the North Sea.
The result is a sea view that is unusually multi-directional.

**TE** Margate has the most beautiful sunsets in the world.
Turner said this and people laughed at him. I've said it
and people laugh at me. But it has, because although we
are on the north-east coast of Kent, Margate is facing *west*.

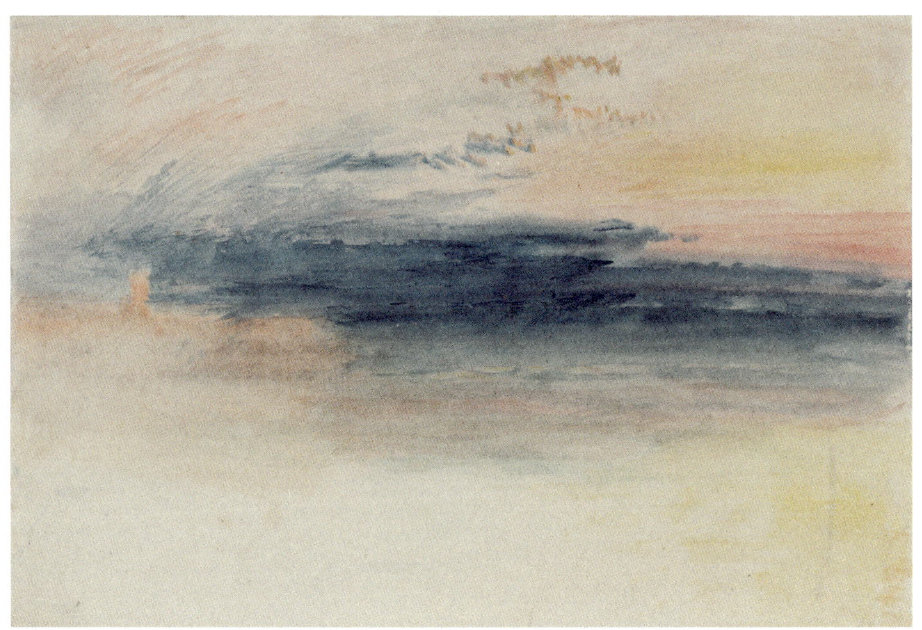

J. M. W. Turner, *Sunset off Margate Pier, c.* 1840–5

So the horizon is very close to us, and the sun is very, very big. It's like this giant orange ball that just *slip*s below the horizon and shoots out these effervescent rays of the rainbow. It's incredible.

*

TE  In the nineteenth century, Margate was like the French Riviera. It was one of the first places the train came to; there was a ballroom at the train station. Turner painted here, Sickert painted here. Van Gogh walked through here.

Walter Sickert and his wife Thérèse Lessore spent the summer of 1934 at Margate, living in a flat. Sickert rented a studio at 10 Cecil Square, a few minutes' walk from where Emin's house and studio are today. He gave a series of lectures

   *Tsunamis, swimming, and not drowning*

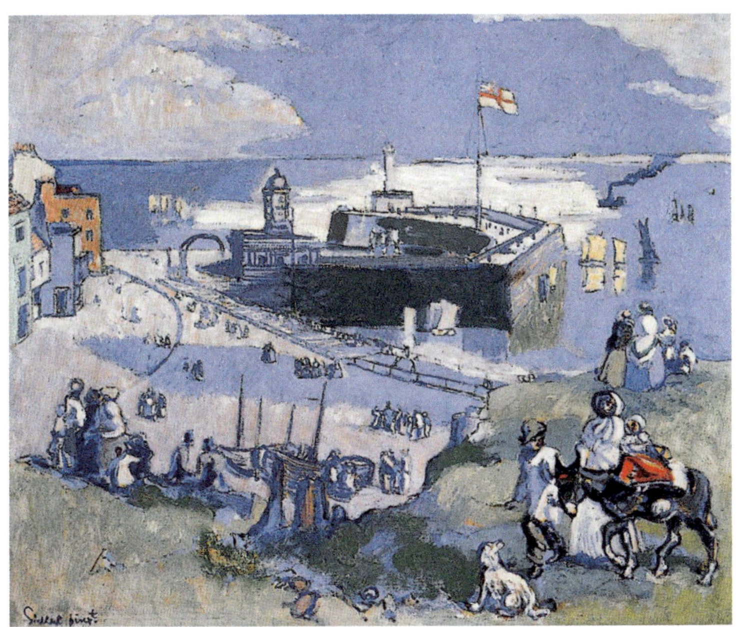

Walter Sickert, *Margate in the Time of Turner*, 1930

at Thanet School of Art, on subjects such as 'Underpainting' and 'Colour', that she might have found interesting. For him, the fact that Turner had painted here was part of the allure of the place. He did a picture entitled *Margate in the Time of Turner*, based on a Victorian print, which was exhibited in Margate in September 1934. It is not just an image of the town in Turner's time; it is pretty nearly Turner's view of the place, seen from a little above the site of Sophia Booth's guest house.

Although it is not recorded that Vincent van Gogh ever visited Margate, he may have done so, since in April and May 1876 he lived close by in Ramsgate, working as a preparatory-school teacher and going for long walks along the coast. He was not yet a full-time artist, although he did one sketch of Royal Road in Ramsgate and the sea. In his letters to his brother Theo, he described landscapes that he had seen. This one, for example, came after a walk to Pegwell Bay on 27 April 1876:

When we got there we had on our left a high, steep wall
of sand and stone, as high as a two-storey house, on top of
which stood old, gnarled hawthorn bushes. Their black or
grey, lichen-covered stems and branches had all been bent
to the same side by the wind, also a few elder bushes. The
ground we walked on was completely covered with large
grey stones, chalk and shells. To the right the sea, as calm
as a pond, reflecting the delicate grey sky where the sun
was setting. It was ebb tide and the water was very low.

Since Pegwell Bay faces south-east, the glow of the setting sun
on the water there would naturally be less spectacular than
around the point, in north-west-facing Margate. Van Gogh is
not the only artist who can *talk* a painting so vividly you can
almost see it. On the day we were speaking, in the spring of
2024, Emin was fresh from an evening of sea-viewing, and her
description of what she had observed was so visually vivid that
you might say she talked a painting too.

**TE**  Yesterday, I was taking photographs of the sea
     and watching the sunset from a van my friend has,
     with a little mattress and cooker in it, looking at the
     last bit of the sunset and the ships out at sea. There
     was a black line with the ships on top with their lights.
     I said, 'Could you imagine if that was a tsunami, and
     the ships were on top?' It was really late, half past nine,
     and the sun had set at about half past eight. But there
     was still this orangey, faded light. I was thinking this
     would be a pretty phenomenal thing to paint. It would
     be so-o-o abstract, but yet so real. The colours would
     be this dark, *dark* blue and this weird wash that's like a
     hole that you slip through. I was thinking how interesting
     it all was when you look at it for a long, long time.

     *Tsunamis, swimming, and not drowning*

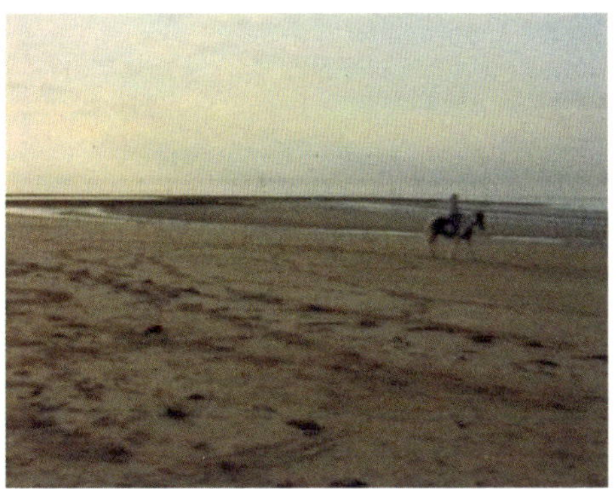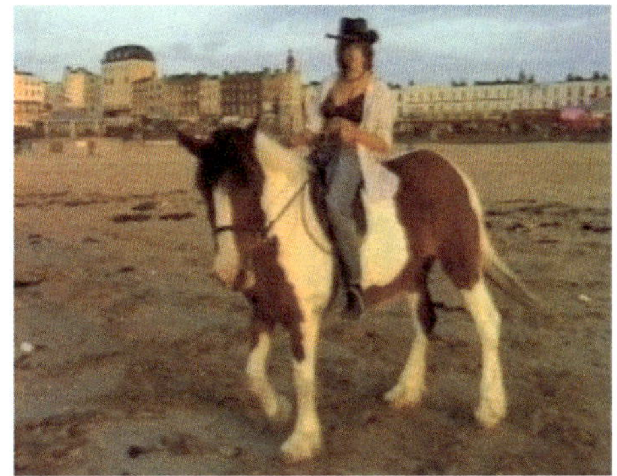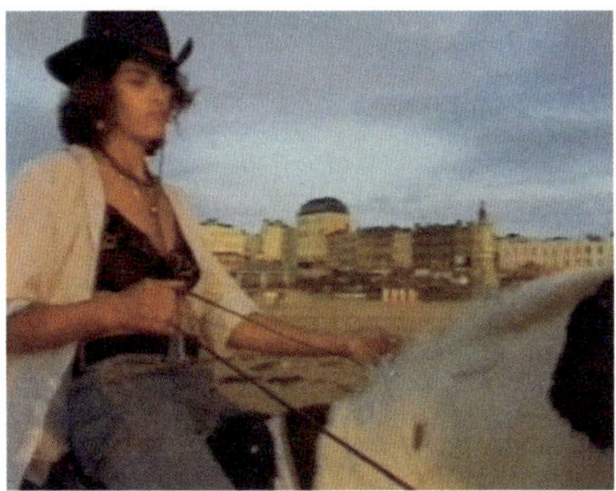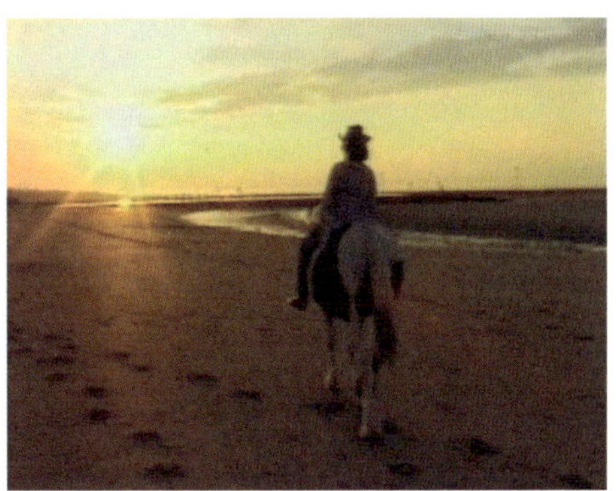

*Riding for a Fall,* 1998

David Hockney, another contemporary artist who is highly Turner-conscious, makes the point that photographs of sunsets are clichés (whereas paintings of sunsets can be very beautiful). Emin rode into a bit of a cliché in a wryly funny film work from 1998, entitled *Riding for a Fall,* in which she cantered across the beach at Margate in cowboy fashion, as the sun set against a pink and golden sky. As clichés often do, the image contained a truth. This is the location where many of the dramas of Emin's life have taken place, as risky in their way as any adventure in the Wild West. At twenty, in a state of emotional desperation, she tried to commit suicide by throwing herself off the harbour wall at Margate with a goodbye note (and a whisky bottle) in her pocket. Three years later, in 1987,

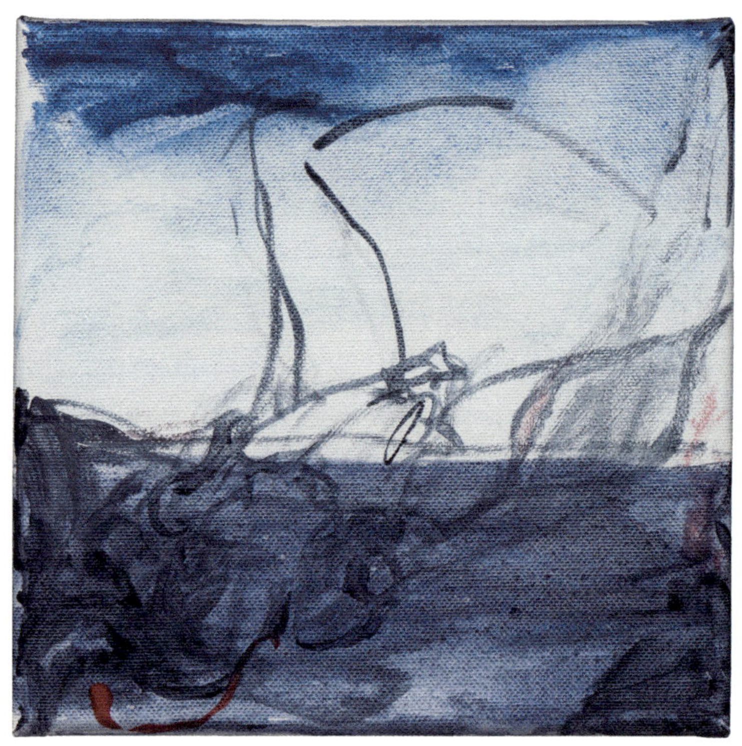

*I Kept Drowning, 2023*

in Turkey, she was saved from drowning by the Turkish fisherman, eighteen years older than her and married with four
children, with whom she was having an affair. The relationship
sounds like something out of Byron. She described him as
'wild, like a mountain man'. At one point, he tried to throw
her off a cliff into the waters of the Mediterranean, but on this
occasion he rescued her when she 'fell off a boat drunk, in the
dead dark of night, gently slipping under the blackness of
the sea'. She described how that felt to Stuart Jeffries of the
*Guardian*: 'It was a nice feeling. That's what makes you drown.
It's just like going to sleep so you don't feel anything.'

In 2004, Emin took part in the BBC radio programme *Desert
Island Discs*. In the course of the recording, she described how her
near-death experience in Margate harbour became a revelation:

> My feet went into the sand and then I came back up
> like a cork and I remember looking up and feeling
> stupid and really insignificant and really tiny, and there's
> all the stars. So what could have been a tragedy actually
> ended up being really beautiful, and I think that it was
> one of the first true times in my life that I understood
> about nature completely.

It is not surprising that the waves and dark waters permeate
her imagination and also flow into her paintings. Indeed, it
seems that the sea is deeply connected in her mind with art and
the kind of salvation that it can provide.

**TE**  I had stopped making art for a couple of years. I didn't
know whether I believed in it. And I really had no money;
I was so broke. I went down to Margate, and I took a
slide film in my bag. And as I went to get off the train,
I saw a blue plastic camera. I thought about handing it in,

but then I realized, 'Oh wow, it's got a slide film in it.
I'll take the slides then hand it in.' I went along the
seafront and started taking photographs. There was an
incredible spring storm with fifteen-foot waves smashing
over the sea wall. I took these fantastic shots, with a
crystal-clear blue sky with a few nimbostratus clouds.
Beautiful. I wrote 'I need art like I need God' on the sea
wall with chalk. 'Hmm,' I thought, 'that's a good title.'

And so it was, for an important exhibition of Emin's work that
took place at the South London Gallery in 1997.

TE  Then I thought, it's true, I really do. Whether I like
it or not, art doesn't leave me; art's like the best lover
I've ever had. Art can be really mean to me, but then it
comes back to me when I least expect it and it lifts me
up and takes me off.

Just like, it is hard not to add, the North Sea breakers that
crash into the beach and the harbour at Margate. In her show
*I need art like I need God*, plaster seagulls flapped across the
air of the gallery, each with the words 'I COULD REALLY HAVE
LOVED YOU' written in capitals across their backs and wings.
They were juxtaposed with the statement 'I need art like I need
God', written large on the wall behind. The birds constituted a
work entitled *I could really have loved you. In my family when
someone dies they are cremated and their ashes are thrown across the
sea.* That title, in turn, was a repetition of a statement that she
had made in an interview with the critic Stuart Morgan that
same year, 1997. The next thing she said was, 'I love seagulls.'
Then she added, 'I'd like to be one.'

Quite plausibly, the birds stand for the artist – or perhaps for
her thoughts and feelings. They have continued to appear in

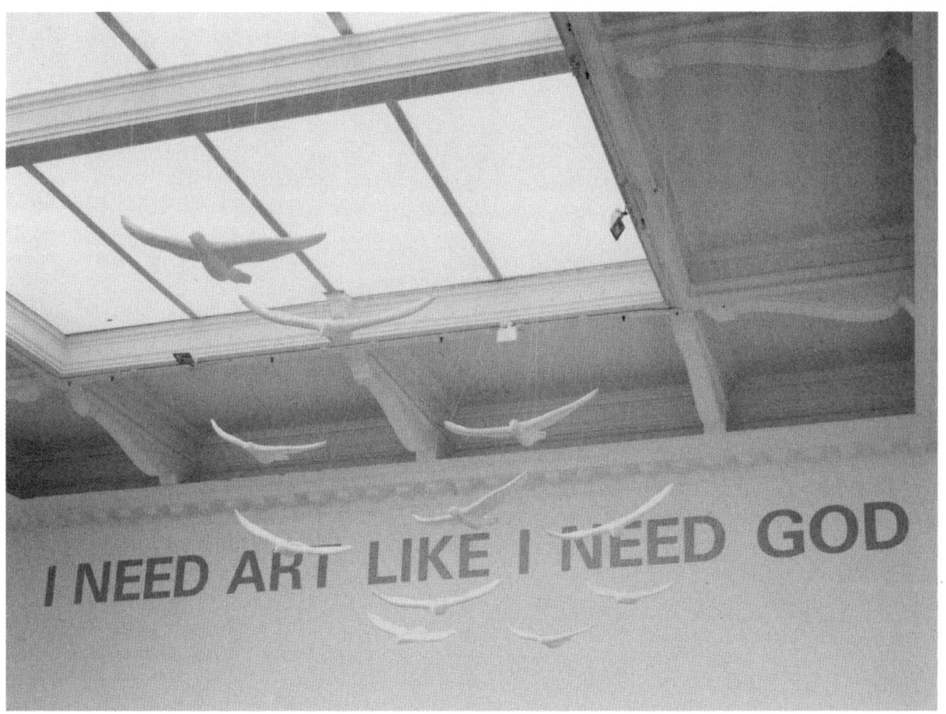



*I could really have loved you. In my family when someone dies they are cremated and their ashes are thrown across the sea*, 1997, installed as part of the exhibition *I need art like I need God*, South London Gallery, 1997

her works, in various media from time to time. It is not only their flight above the waves with which she seems to empathize, but also their motionless waiting, perched above the sands and the water. She remarked, when talking about her sculpture *A Moment Without You*, that she had 'always had the idea that birds are angels of this earth and that they represent freedom'. This piece is a deliberately unmonumental monument. She noted, rightly as far as the history of the form is concerned, that 'most public sculptures are a symbol of power'. Instead, Emin wanted to make 'something which would appear and disappear and not dominate'. In a way, it is a highly realist piece of work, consisting of five poles of the kind that often stand on shores

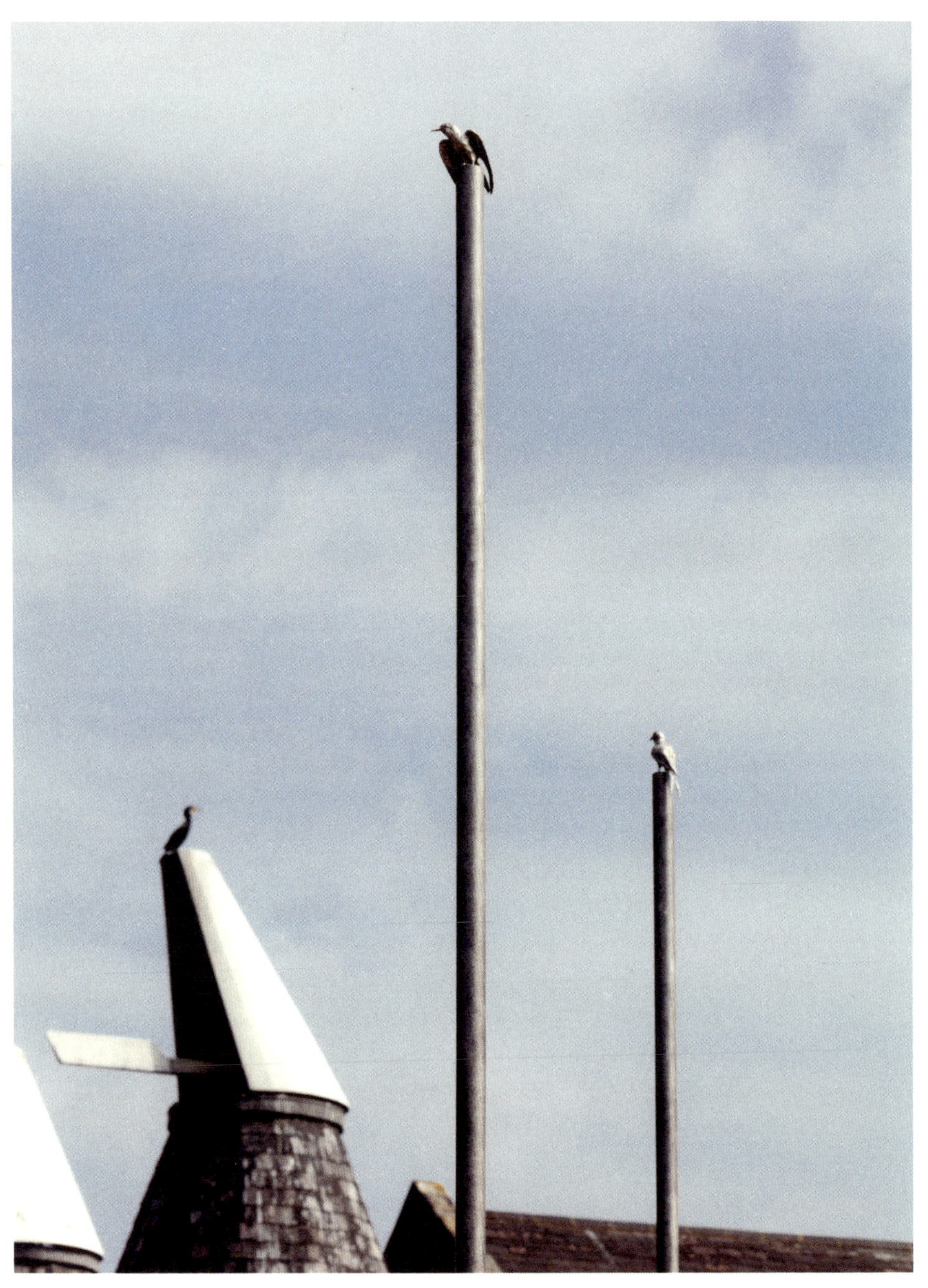

*A Moment Without You*, 2017, installed at Three Mills, east London, 2021

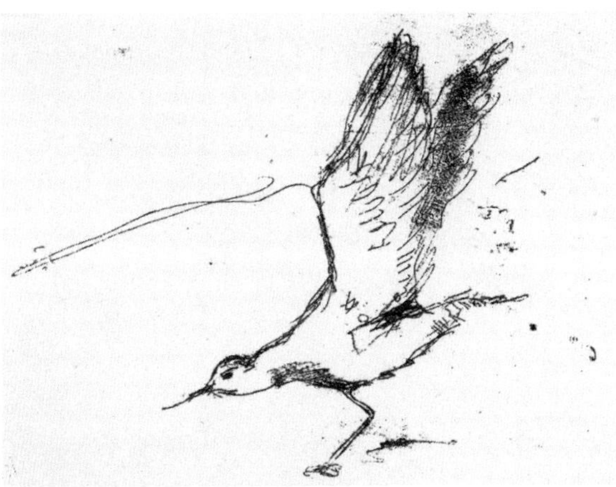

*About to Fly*, 2014

and in shallow water, with a small bird sitting – as they do – on the top of each one.

**TE** I like when things look as if they've always existed, like the tide-markers in Margate. As a child, I always loved them. I always wanted one, but I never knew what they were for. They always looked lonely and desolate in the sea. The seagulls land on them. They are poetic outposts.

After a particularly disillusioning return visit to a rundown and semi-derelict Margate in 2008, Emin wrote about the experience in her *Independent* column.

I'm like one of those people who sit in their car
with a flask and a sandwich watching the tide roll in.
It's so windy, the spring tides are rising high and a
crest of white foam rides on top of almost every wave.
The sea shelf is black in high contrast to the pale
blue sky with puffy Cirrus clouds. There is a slight
pinkiness to them and a slight pinkiness across the
sea to give a vision of a strange nostalgia, like looking

at an old tinted photograph. Seagulls flap around, dodging in and out of the wind, swooping and diving like a cliché from *Jonathan Livingston Seagull.*

As a child we had a plaque hanging up on the kitchen wall. It was blue with a white seagull flying high and below the seagull were the words: 'If you love something, set it free. If it comes back, it's yours.' At the age of 10 I always thought this quote from *Jonathan Livingston Seagull* was the most profound thing in the whole world, and I suppose to a certain extent it is.

Now, nearly two decades later, Emin has come back to Margate and sizable parts of it are quite literally hers. In 2023, she bought the Westbrook Bay Pavilion (sometimes called 'Westbrook Loggia') from Thanet District Council. This structure, probably dating from 1910, had begun with an air of late Edwardian

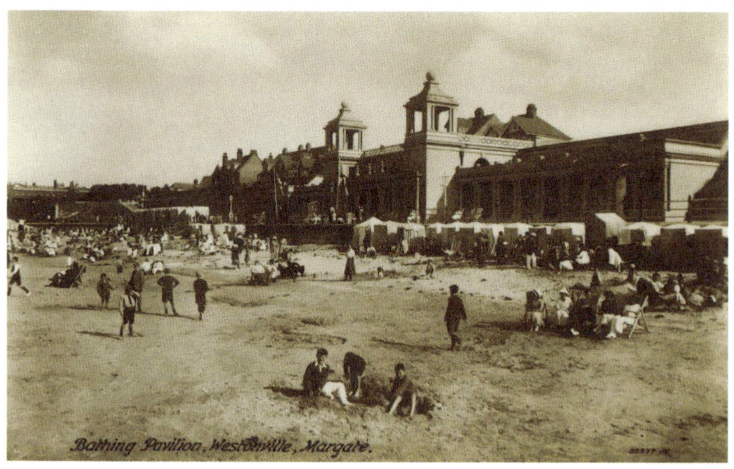


Westbrook Bay Pavilion, Margate, *c.* 1910s

opulence, then over the years its splendour had disappeared. First its towers went, then its colonnade, leaving a shell of bare cement. Emin has plans to transform the building into a place where you could not only bathe, but also live with the sea, work with it, make it part of your art.

TE  I've bought this great big building down on the
    beach. I was going to put in two huge studios, for
    artist residences. I wanted it to be for artists who
    paint the sea or use the sea in some way. But then
    I thought maybe it would be good for artists who
    *don't* use the sea, then you could watch what happens
    when they move there – if they start to make pictures
    with it. And maybe every few years, I would do a
    residency there myself and paint just one giant
    painting of the sea.

Despite the temperature of the North Sea off Margate, and her near-death experiences, Emin continues to swim. Her favourite spot is a place over which Turner looked out from the front windows of his lodgings. But it is a different, more surreal kind of painting in which she imagines she is immersed:

[The] cold green waters of the North Sea,
I find it romantic and dreamlike, I feel like I'm
swimming in a long-lost painting by De Chirico.
I like to swim along the harbour wall watching
the line of green algae disappear against the waves.
I like to swim against the tide, it makes me feel
strong, like I'm somehow invincible.

7

## *Beds and dreams*

Beds are the place in which most dreams are dreamt; and both beds and dreams are a prominent part of Emin's life and art. To her, it is clear that dreaming and painting are closely allied. When speaking, she can switch seamlessly from one to the other. Once when we were talking, she began a sequence of thought with the sea. Then she went on:

TE  One of my *best* tsunami dreams was that I was surfing on top of a giant wave of shit. I was surfing and having to balance, and everything below me was shit. I was surfing on the crest of this shitty wave. I think that is what life is like a lot of the time.

Then, without a pause, she smoothly moved on to art, which like dreams can be a form of understanding.

TE  You can be painting and it can all be going terribly wrong. Then suddenly – boom – something happens and it all goes into place. It all makes sense; the whole world makes sense.

One of Emin's ways of starting a picture is to begin with furniture, rather than figures, specifically with a bed. This is useful, she explained, geometrically and harmonically.

TE  Beds turn up in my paintings because of the golden section. Because once I draw a line across the painting

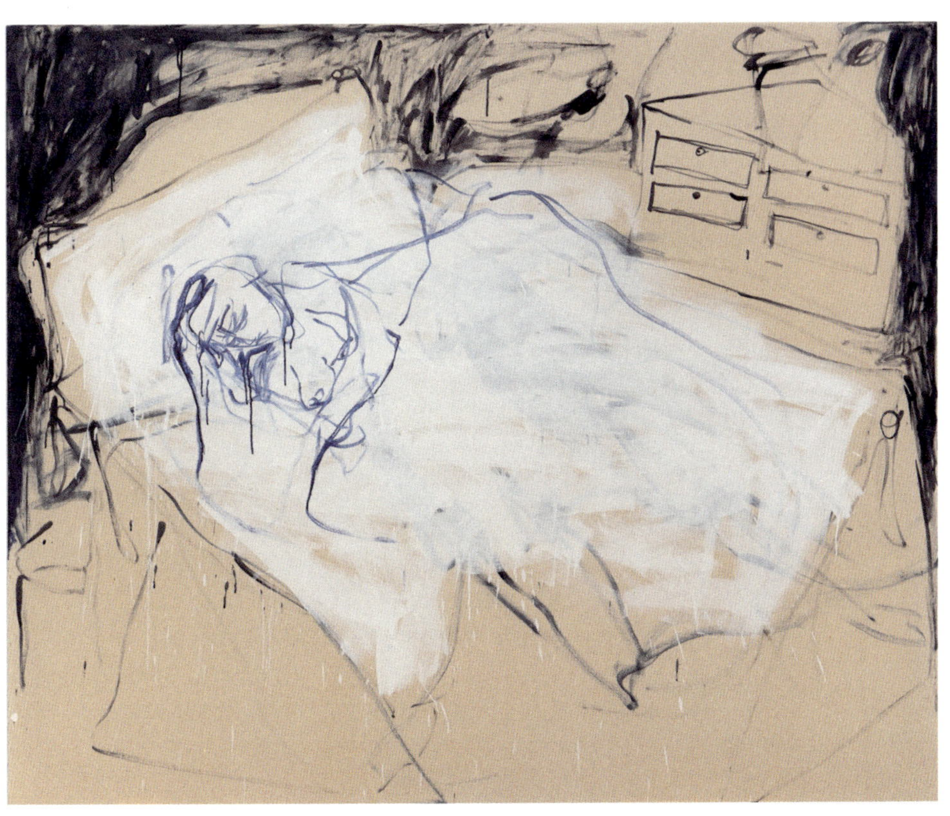

*Crying – Sleeping – Sleeping – Crying,* 2024

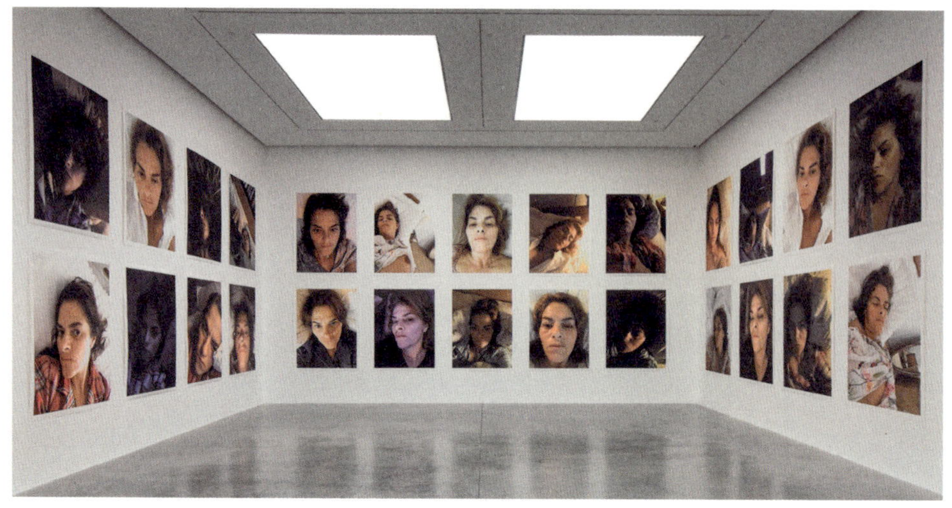

*Insomnia Room Installation*, 2019

and add an angle, which might be a leg or anything,
I can make anything work from that line in the painting,
anything I want. I realized that, actually, it was easy to put
a bed around that line at an angle. It then made it really
free for me to do whatever I wanted within that space. It's
just a device of a picture plane that I can spring from and
work from. So that's one really boring technical reason.

Then she moved quickly to a much deeper motive why beds
feature in her work. The bed is more fundamental to human life
than any other piece of furniture – a cupboard, say, or desks and
chairs (although Emin, as a painter of interiors, sometimes
depicts all of these as well).

**TE** We die in bed, fuck in bed, we give birth in bed, we read
in bed, we cry in bed.

Obviously we sleep in beds, but also – as Emin is perhaps
the first visual artist to stress – not always. Instead, many of



*Beds and dreams*

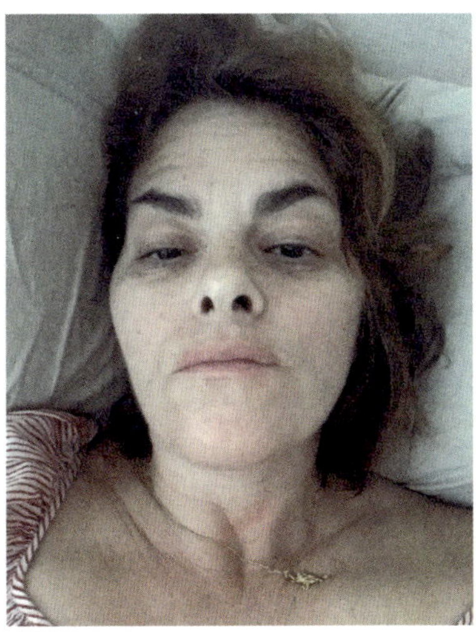

*Insomnia 14.39, 2019*

us often lie painfully, restlessly unable to lose consciousness. *Insomnia,* her sequence of photographic self-portraits from 2019, is an extraordinary record of a condition that might seem impossible to depict. She told *Wallpaper* magazine about her experience of sleeplessness:

> I had it [insomnia] in my early twenties in art school,
> but I loved it then, I could do whatever I wanted and
> it seemed that I had more hours in the day. As I've got
> older it's got more and more soul destroying. Insomnia
> is not an affectation, it's crippling.

*My Bed* (1998) remains perhaps her single best-known work. A few years ago, she told the critic Jonathan Jones that this work was actually a painting. Startling as this claim seems, it points to a truth that is often overlooked. As Jones concluded, 'It might seem to have nothing to do with old oil paintings, but you don't have to look long at Emin's paintings to see how *My Bed* fits into her own exploration of nudes, and their beds.'

It is a three-dimensional equivalent to a picture, the predecessor, setting, and subject matter for many of her canvases to come – and a counterpart of more that had been painted centuries earlier. In her emphasis on sheets, pillows, and mattresses – as in much that she does – Emin might seem an eccentric individualist. But then, the more you think about this idiosyncrasy, the more it reveals a hidden tradition of which we are oblivious.

Beds are ubiquitous in art, especially Western painting. In Titian's *Venus of Urbino*, the pictures of Sickert, Munch, Freud, and innumerable others, beds take up more space than the human bodies occupying them. If an industrious art historian performed the necessary calculations, it might well turn out that a greater area of classic Western painting has been devoted to beds and bedlinen than to the naked bodies that lie and/or embrace on top of them. Freud pointed out that he spent an enormous amount of time depicting floorboards, as opposed to the naked flesh for which he was much better known.

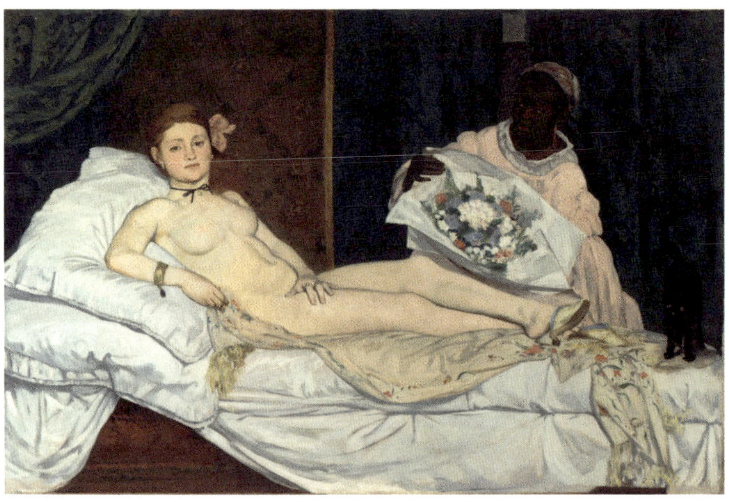

Édouard Manet, *Olympia*, 1863

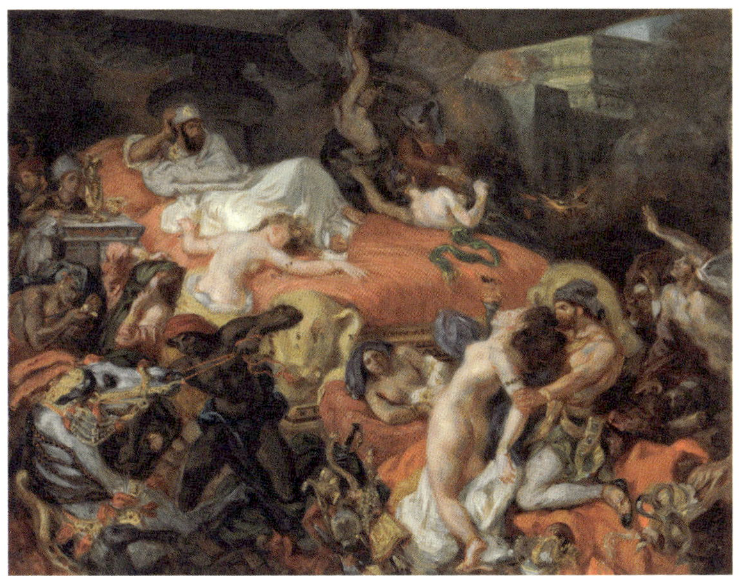

Eugène Delacroix, *The Death of Sardanapalus*, 1827

The same was true of sheets, pillows, and brass bedsteads. Édouard Manet's *Olympia* – the most scandalous picture of the later nineteenth century and one of the works in which modernism began – is, among other things, a painting of a mound of very comfortable-looking and beautifully laundered bedding. Understandably, bed-located paintings are often erotic. From Titian's time, the bed has been the native habitat of the female nude. But, as Emin pointed out, far more happens in beds than just sex. They are where the crucial processes of life take place.

Delacroix's *The Death of Sardanapalus*, another of the great rumpus-raising, Salon-disrupting masterpieces of the first part of the nineteenth century, is an epic drama set on an imperial Assyrian divan. You might say that just about every conceivable drama and melodrama is occurring on that bed. The doomed king reclines while around him everything revolves, a mêlée of death, sex, jewels, pearls, glittering daggers, naked flesh, frenzied horses, agony, despair, and violence.

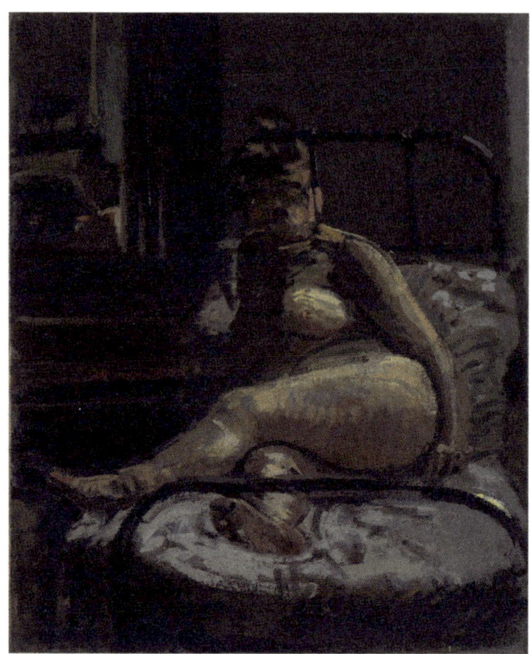

Walter Sickert, *La Hollandaise, c.* 1906

A good deal of twentieth-century British figurative painting features beds. Many (though not all) of Freud's 'naked portraits' are posed on an iron bedstead. Visiting his studio, I remember a delicate arrangement of feathers spilling out of a pillow that was 'posing' on the bed for several weeks, so nobody could walk too close in case a current of air disturbed them. Lucian himself posed on a rather similar bed for photographs to be transformed into paintings by his then friend Francis Bacon. That bed recalled another example that supported numerous Sickert nudes during his Camden Town period in the early years of the century, among them the strange and slightly scary *La Hollandaise*, who seems more of an apparition than a sex object.

Emin's own installation *My Bed* is more an updated version of the Delacroix than of the Manet. It is, you might say, *Sardanapalus* on a domestic scale. *The Near-Death of Emin*:



*Beds and dreams*

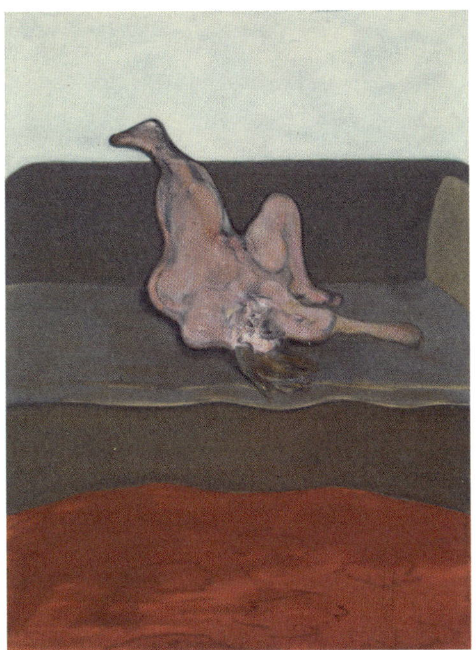

Francis Bacon, *Reclining Woman*, 1961

the location where she might have expired. She has recounted how, after the break-up of a relationship:

In 1998 I had a complete breakdown. I spent four days in bed; I was asleep and semi-unconscious. When I did eventually get out of bed, I got up, had some water, then went back to the bedroom and couldn't believe what I could see. This absolute mess and decay of my life.

The short version of the technical description of this work is as follows: 'Mattress, linens, pillows, rope, various memorabilia'; among the latter are listed 'crumpled tissues, period-stained clothing, cigarettes, empty vodka bottles, a pregnancy test, lubricant, and condoms'. *My Bed* looks like a tableau lifted from reality: lifted, as Emin put it, from her small flat and deposited in the white space of an art gallery. It was taken at the time as just that: a squalid display of bad housekeeping. But as we have just seen, it not only belongs in a gallery, but also fits into an art-historical context. Emin herself chose to reinstall it at Tate Britain surrounded by Bacon paintings. She pointed out how the swirling energy of the canvases was directly related to the chaos of the artist's private life: 'He drank whatever he wanted to drink, slept with whoever he wanted to sleep with.' One of the works by Bacon that she chose to hang beside *My Bed* was *Reclining Woman* (1961). This had, she said, 'these big undulating rolls of flesh and these things turning'. In a similar fashion, her bed 'is folding, the bed is turning, the bed is moving'. This introduces an aspect of *My Bed* that was missed by almost everyone when it was first exhibited in 1999: its formal qualities.

The art historian Martin Kemp, an Oxford professor and renowned expert on Leonardo da Vinci, raised the question of whether the bed was really a pure found object: the actual piece of furniture, together with accessories and detritus, removed from her bedroom and relocated to the Tate gallery. Instead, he suggested it was something rather different: a carefully contrived recreation of the original scene. 'When I say "My Bed",' Emin told the journalist Dalya Alberge, 'I mean it was the idea of the artwork. The bed has gone through many transformations. In a way it's a self-portrait.' It was not fixed. Kemp described the differences between various occasions on which the work had been exhibited and questioned whether the creases in the crumpled sheets and pillows had really been created by sweaty body and heavy head or rather carefully remade. 'Every time I reinstall the bed it will always be different', she declared. 'The bed is the physical ghost of my own existence.' So while it may seem paradoxical in the extreme to claim that *My Bed* is actually a painting, it is true to say that it has affinities with paintings; indeed it fits into a rich and complex sequence of



*Beds and dreams*

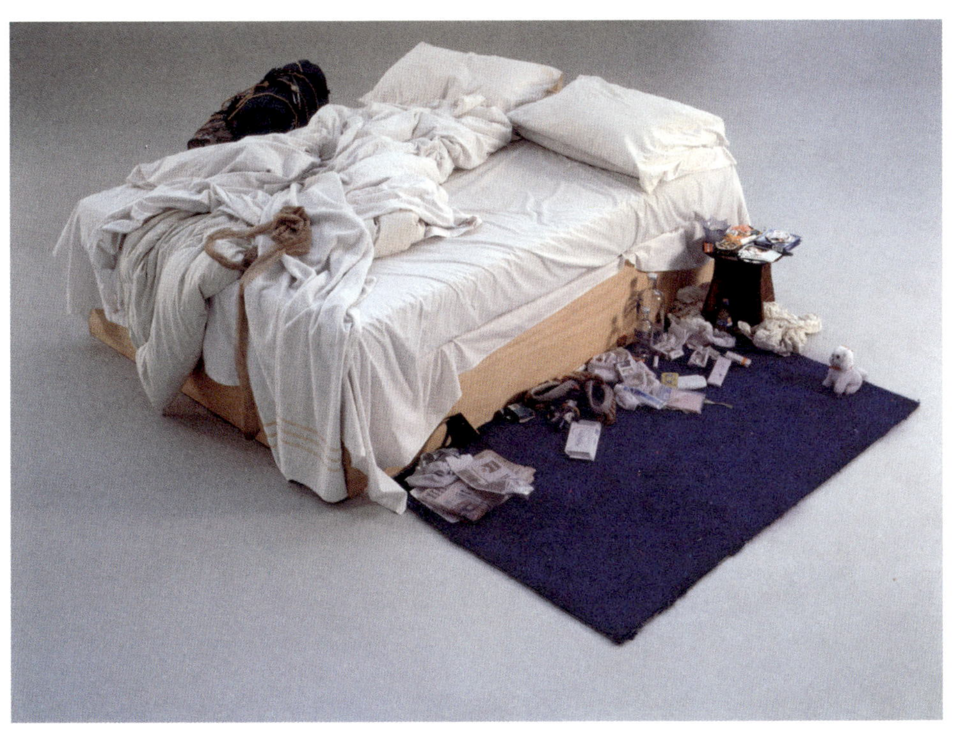

*My Bed*, 1998

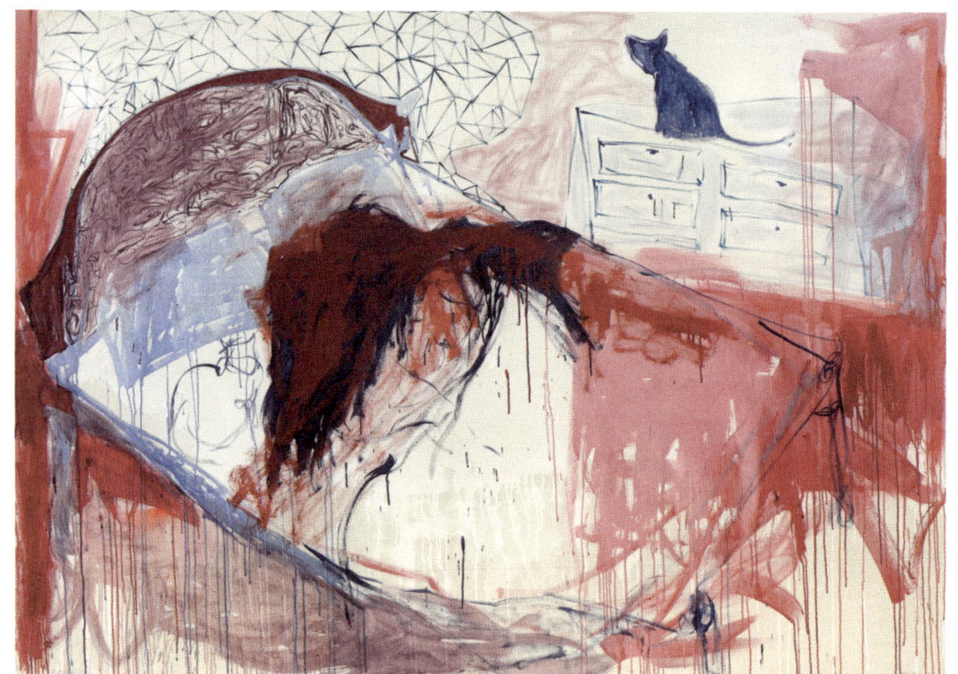

*The End of Love,* 2024

pictures going back to the Renaissance – and also that it has plenty of successors in paintings by Tracey herself.

These days, Emin often receives visiting writers and journalists while in bed. As she explained to me, while reclining comfortably among the sheets, it is an environment in which she spends a good deal of time when she is not at work. The bed she was resting in when we had a conversation in the summer of 2024 was very different from the one in her famous installation. It was almost as large as the divan on which Sardanapalus is lying in Delacroix's picture – but looked much more luxuriant.

TE  I lie in bed and I love it. And I have really, really
    mega-expensive thread sheets. They're cotton but
    they feel really indulgent and very soft. And I have

   *Beds and dreams*

really good pillows. I rest a great deal; I spend about
three days a week in bed, which is a lot, but I have to
because I get too tired. I just get knocked out. In my mind,
my bed isn't a negative place; it's a very positive place.
It's not where I retreat to hide; it's where I retreat to grow.

My friend refers to my bed as my 'boffice', because
I wake up very early and do lots of things in my bed on
my phone. And I always listen to relaxing piano music
as well. It's my little world before I *hit* the world, before
the world hits me. I have my cats, I have my tea. I like
the cosiness. My bed to me is a sanctuary, a place where
I feel safe.

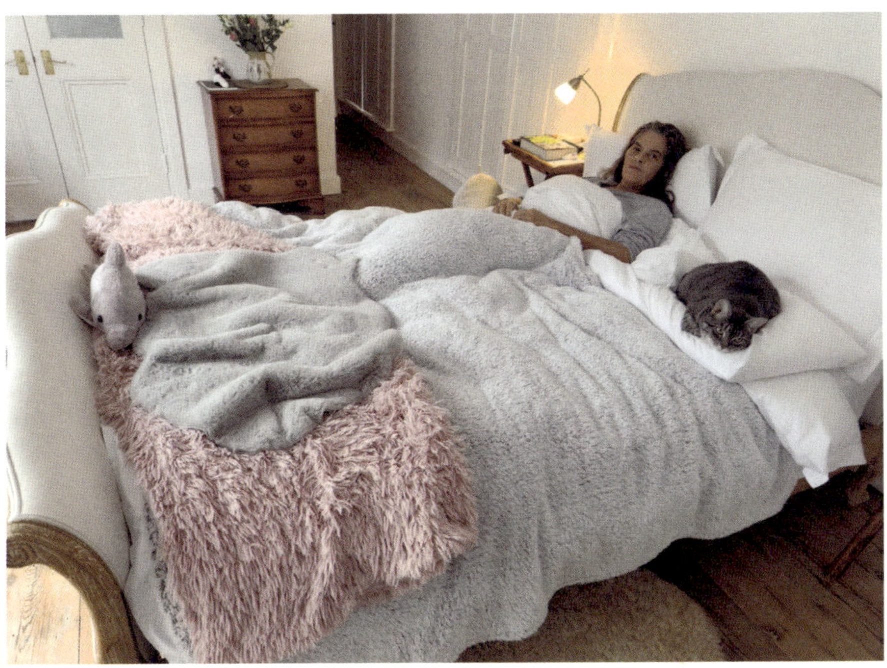

Tracey Emin in bed with her cat Teacup, Margate, 2025

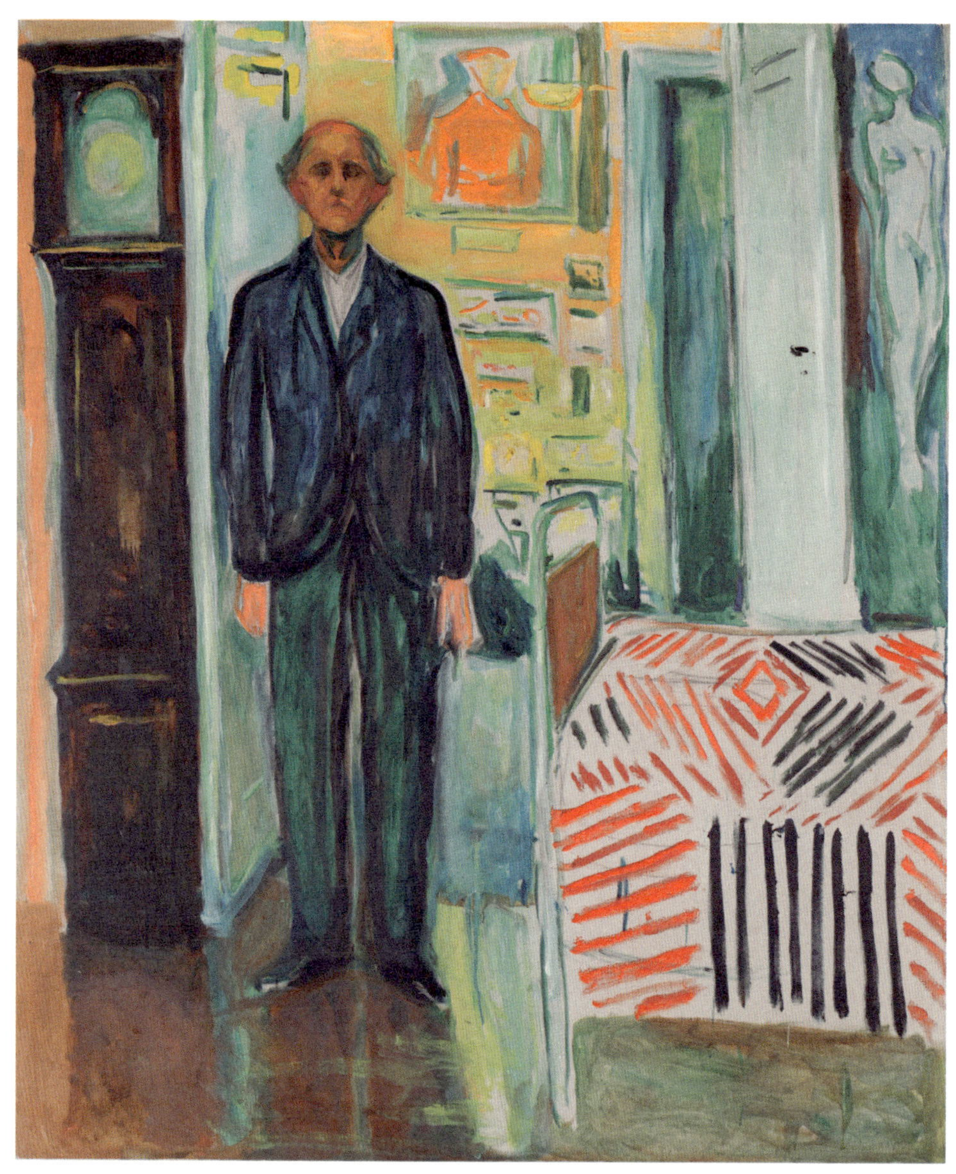

Edvard Munch, *Self-portrait Between the Clock and the Bed*, 1940–3

# 8

## *Edvard and Tracey*

In Edvard Munch's *Self-portrait Between the Clock and the Bed* (1940–3), the artist represented himself between a remorse-lessly ticking timepiece, on one side, and a bed with a painting of a female nude above it on the other: love, death, isolation, and passing time all expressed by a mundane array of furniture. Emin is doubtless aware of this masterpiece by a predecessor who means so much to her. As we have just seen, she has also painted many bedroom pictures, images that are at once psycho-dramas and emotional self-portraits. But her affinity with Munch is closer even than such resemblances would imply.

More than any other artist from the past, Emin has singled out Munch as an idol, role model, and alter ego. And more than that – she has confessed to having fallen in love with him early in life. The example of the great Norwegian helps her under-stand herself and her own art, as she wrote in 2020. 'When you find your kindred spirit, even if they're dead, and you look at their work, and their work is sincere and profound, and you link into it, it makes you feel better. You think: "Ah yes, phew."'

It is not unusual for artists to idolize forerunners. Vincent van Gogh felt like that about Rembrandt, Jean-Auguste-Dominique Ingres about Raphael, J. M. W. Turner about Claude. But even by those standards, Emin's feelings about Munch are unusually tender. When she talks about him, she can sound more like a lover than someone who just appreciates his work. In 2020, she told the *Guardian*: 'Munch's my favourite artist

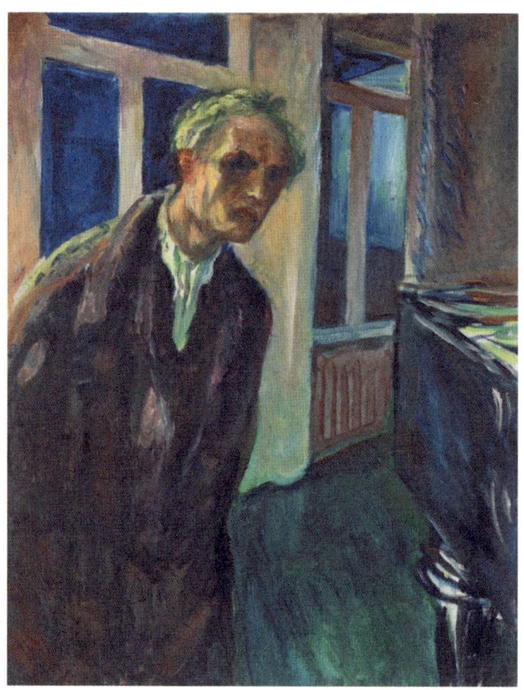

Edvard Munch, *The Night Wanderer*, 1923–4

in the whole world. He's gentle, he's emotional and he's just a really, really fantastic painter. He was spiritual, poetic, very, very handsome. And he worked really hard.'

The two of them, Tracey and Edvard, are now so closely linked across time that at points you could say they have pursued a joint career. She shared a two-artist exhibition with him at the Royal Academy in London and the Munch Museum in Oslo in 2021–2. Outside that museum's new building on the city waterfront, there is a large bronze sculpture by Emin entitled *The Mother*. It was a posthumous gift from her to him of something he lost early on: a nurturing parent. Munch's mother died of tuberculosis when he was five (and Emin had lost her own mother not long before she conceived this sculpture, in 2016).

*

 *Edvard and Tracey*

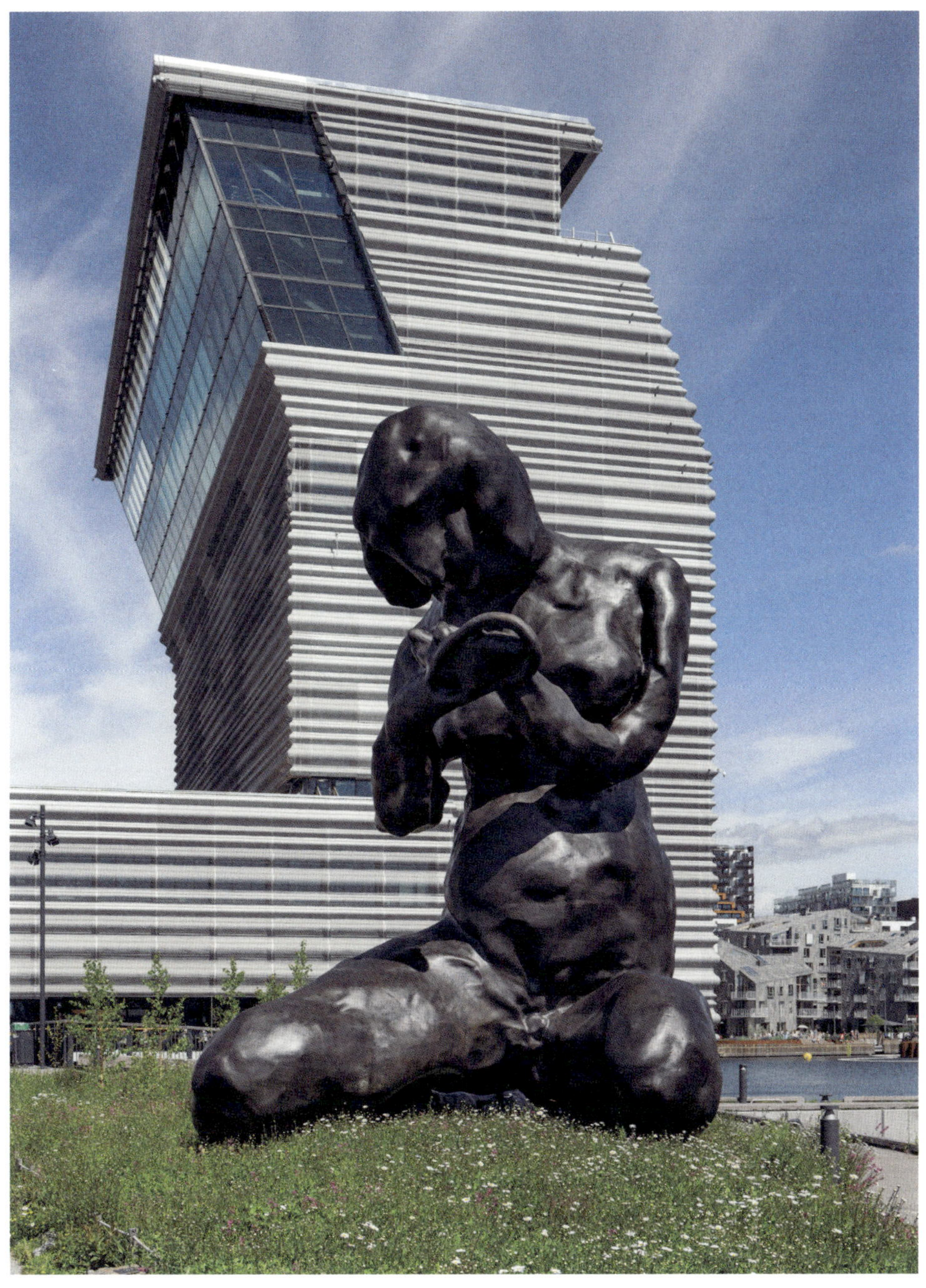

*The Mother*, 2021, installed outside the Munch Museum, Oslo

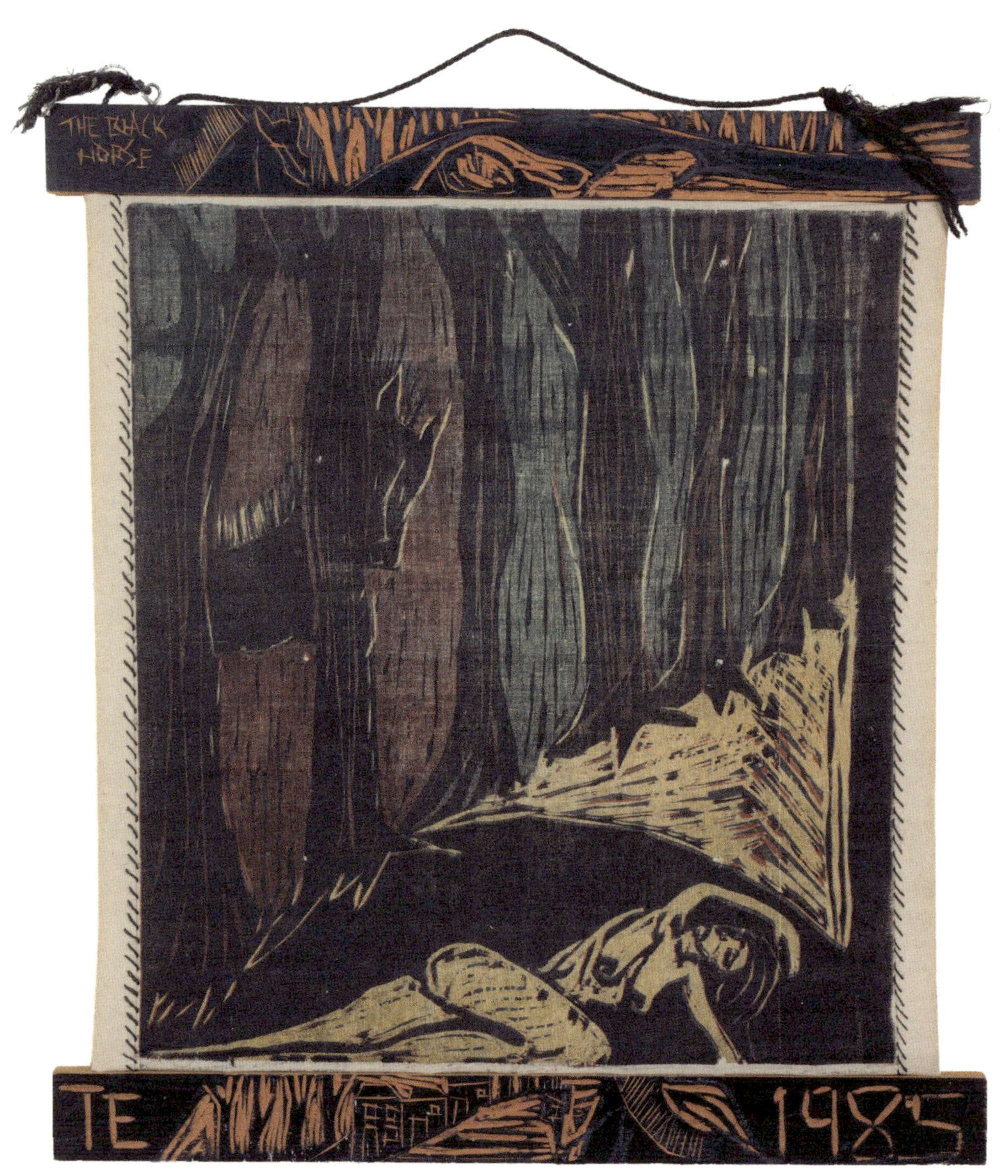



*The Black Horse*, 1985

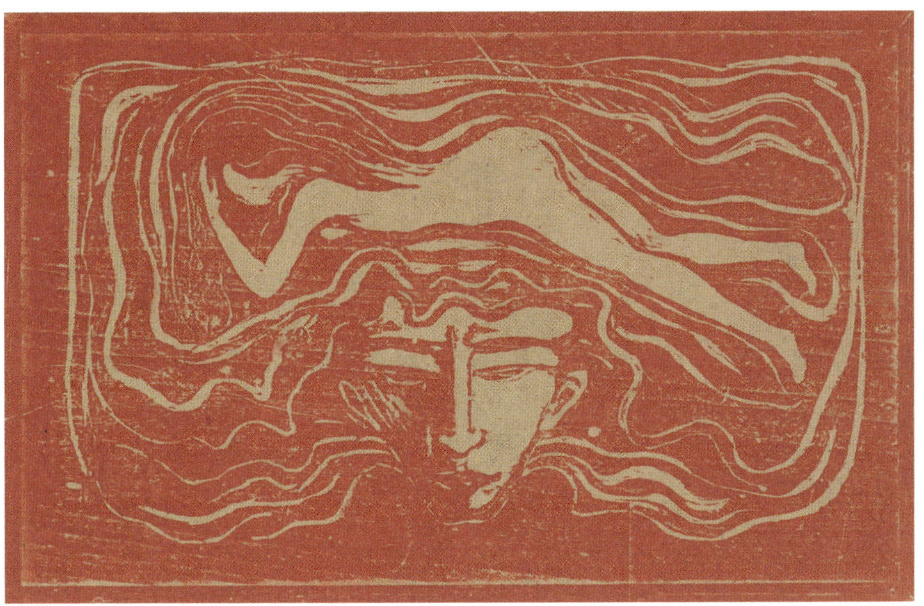

Edvard Munch, *In the Brain of Man*, 1897

Munch's work was the starting point for some of Emin's earliest surviving pictures, the prints that she made at Maidstone College of Art during the mid-1980s. At that point, she wrote: 'I began responding to Munch's work. I made homages to him. I made hundreds of multicoloured woodcuts. I made woodblock frames around my paintings. I copied Munch, for want of a better word, but with my own subject matter.'

Her choice of artistic idol was a highly unusual one then, and probably still is today. One reason is that, with the exception of occasional exhibitions, it is hard to see Munch's works in Britain. Almost all of his masterpieces are in Oslo, a rare destination for tourists. Another factor might be his emotional intensity. Munch has his admirers among painters (Hockney is one), but for every fan and artistic follower that Munch has in Britain, Van Gogh, for example, has dozens. Years ago, though, Emin told me firmly that she was not among the latter:

**MG** Do you feel any affinity with artists of the past such as Vincent van Gogh?

**TE** No, because he was male and rich and spoiled.

**MG** Whereas you grew up with none of those advantages?

**TE** That's right. So, no thank you to Van Gogh.

Munch and Emin, though separated in time, have much in common, biographically as well as artistically. One shared experience is a childhood blighted by deprivation and misfortune. She came from a broken family, reduced to near destitution when she was still a small child, and had suffered sexual abuse and rape by the time she was in her mid-teens. 'Illness, insanity, and death', Munch wrote, 'were the black angels that hovered over my cradle.' He was brought up in Kristiania – later renamed Oslo – by his father, a penniless army doctor. The family lived on the brink of outright poverty. As we have seen, his beloved mother died of tuberculosis when he was five; and his favourite sister Sophie perished of the same disease when Edvard was twelve. Munch himself very nearly died too in his boyhood. So much of his early life was spent in bed that in later life he preferred to sleep in a chair (this fear of beds was far from being his only phobia). Tracey and Edvard won through in spite of multiple problems, emotional, financial, and medical. Munch suffered from near-fatal lung complaints on several occasions in adulthood. But he was tougher than he seemed. He survived tuberculosis, malnutrition, Spanish influenza, many years of



*Edvard and Tracey*

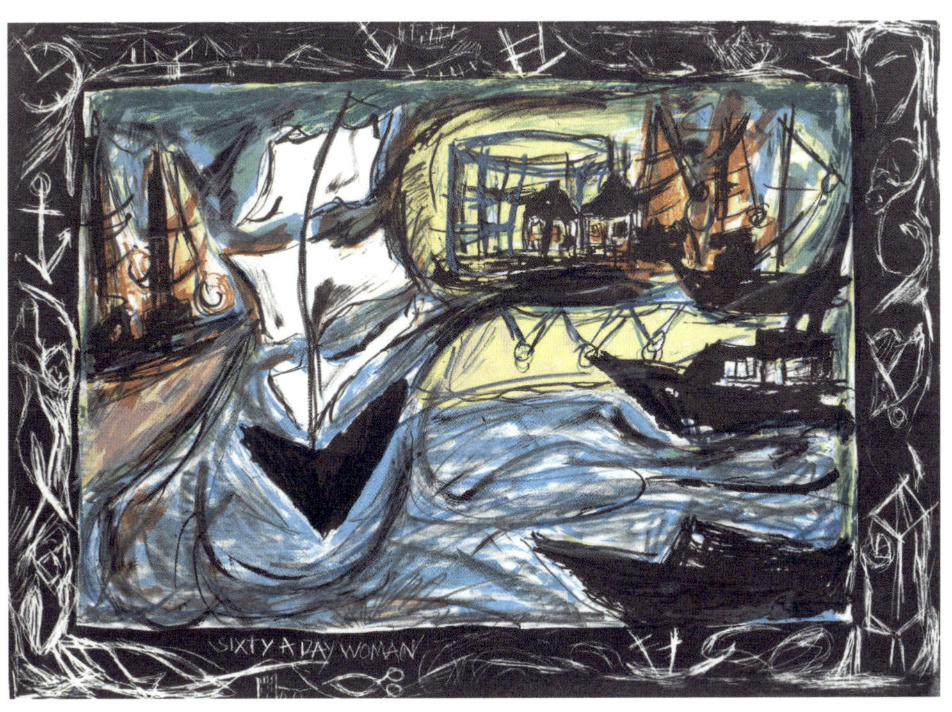



*Sixty a Day Woman,* 1986

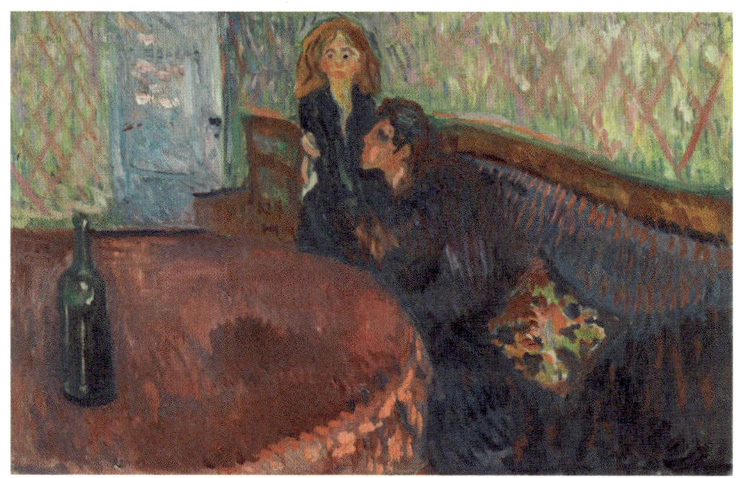

Edvard Munch, *Desire*, 1907

alcoholism, numerous fist fights, and a minor gunshot wound, to expire old and full of honours in 1944 at the age of eighty.

It would not be an exaggeration to say that loving Munch helped to make Emin the painter she is. 'As an artist,' she wrote, 'when you like another artist's work, you have a rapport with them; that's how you learn.' Her thesis for her degree at Maidstone was entitled 'My man Munch'. It was written on a ferry when she was travelling back from Amsterdam to Britain:

It was Sunday night, and it had to be handed in on Monday morning. So I analysed four of his paintings using the *Oxford English Dictionary*. For the painting 'Madonna', I used the argument 'Mad and onerous'. My conclusion being that you couldn't chop up Munch's paintings intellectually, morally or spiritually; they were about passion and emotion, and should be viewed as a whole. Plus, all the titles originally were in Norwegian, so it made no sense analysing them from the English dictionary, la-di-da-di-da. Professor Machin wasn't having any of it. He gave me a 2:2 and said I would



*Edvard and Tracey*

have got a first had I spent longer than two hours on it,
pissed on a ferryboat.

Perhaps Professor Machin had a point; but on the other
hand, this was a way of approaching the task that Munch would
have understood completely, one of several qualities that they
share. Indeed, there are many points of comparison between the
two artists. In their works, drawing and painting are inextrica-
bly combined, and, technically speaking, both paint *thinly*. For
her, and probably for him too, this is a matter of instinctive,
visceral feeling. Munch seldom uses even a single blob of
impasto. Both he and Emin depict themselves, their own bodies,
again and again, and both often do so naked. According to
Harry Weller, even the wallpaper that she sometimes adds to
bedroom scenes is related to Munch's interiors.

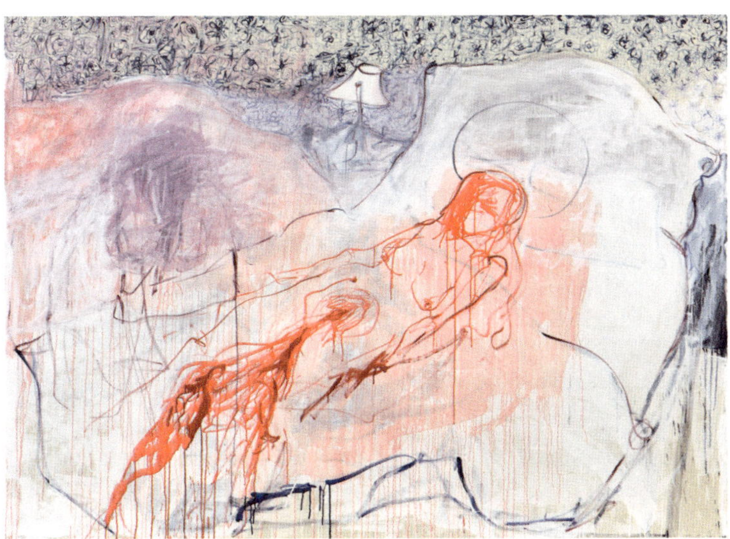

*Take me to Heaven*, 2024

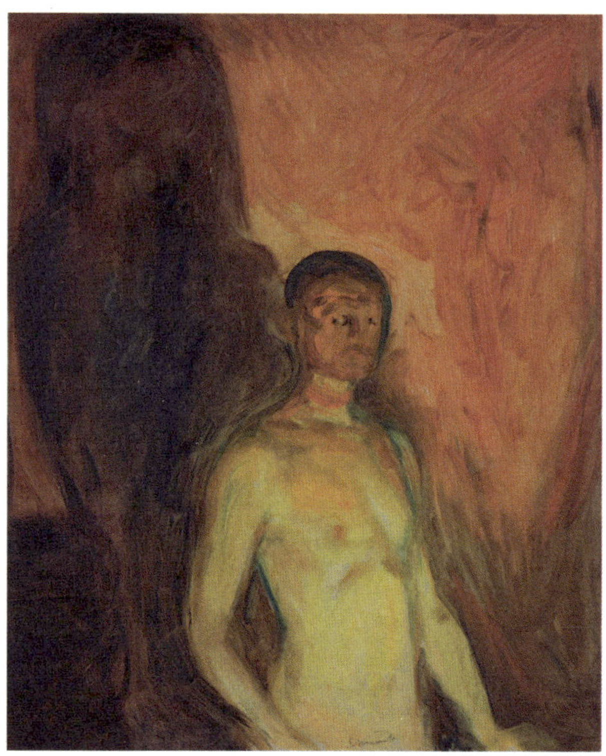

Edvard Munch, *Self-portrait in Hell*, 1903

While she was preparing the Emin / Munch exhibition, she had complete access to the archive of the Munch Museum, which contains everything he possessed at the time of his death, 'even' she pointed out, 'his hats'.

I went through all his works on paper, watercolours, notebooks, sketchbooks, his clothes, his old paints, his drinks cabinet, his furniture. Imagine being the number-one Munch fan and then having access to all that stuff. It was like a dream come true. I ran my hand along his sofa, and I thought: 'Oh god, that's so weird', because he must have done that 100,000 times.



*Edvard and Tracey*

In her mind, Munch and Emin chatted together. That, she added, was how he and she had been talking since she was seventeen. Ever since, she has spent a lot of time thinking about Munch's work – and him. Her conclusions are intriguing.

> I realised he was different from the other Expressionists. In fact, he wasn't really an Expressionist; he was more of a Jungian emotionalist. He made art about emotion, not about expression, and that was very different.

'Jungian emotionalist' is a thought-provoking – and novel – classification. Since Emin has regarded Munch as a model for so long, it probably tells us something about how she might categorize herself. Carl Jung (1875–1961) was the founder of analytical psychology. He was younger than Sigmund Freud (1856–1939), to whom he was close for a time before their ideas diverged. There are many differences between the pair, too many to go into here, but one that is not noted often in psychological literature was that Jung's ideas were much more *visual*. Freud was open to the fine arts. He collected ancient artefacts and wrote about Michelangelo's *Moses*. But Jung went further; he devoted a great deal of effort on making art himself, including paintings, sculpture, and illuminated manuscripts. The last time Emin was with Louise Bourgeois – another role model for her, but one whom she met in real life – they looked together at 'a great thick book' of reproductions of the psychologist's pictures. She described them as 'totally obsessive paintings, bordering on insanity, but really good, amazing'. It would be wrong to describe Emin as a Jungian artist, but she is evidently open to his thought. As we shall see, one of the reasons why she sought out Ken Kiff as a tutor at the Royal College of Art in the late 1980s was that she knew he was interested in Jung (which implies she already was herself).

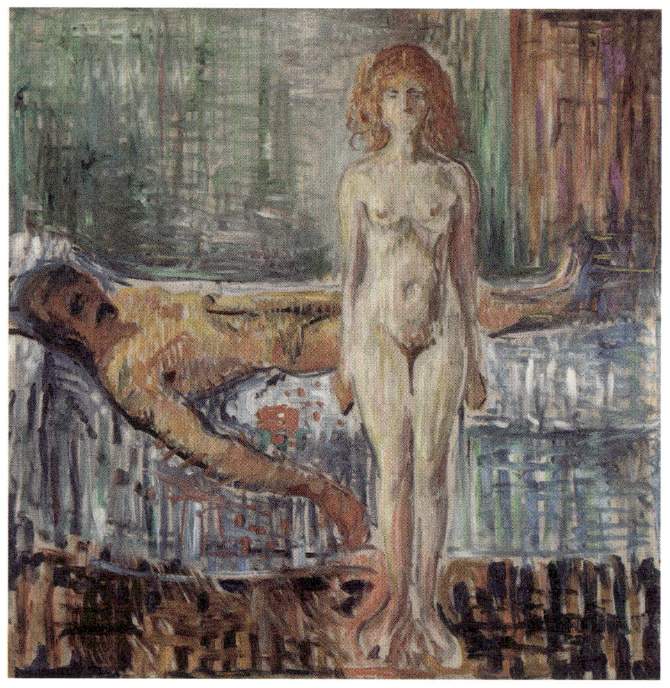

Edvard Munch, *The Death of Marat*, 1907

Several of Jung's ideas, whether you accept them or not, obviously lend themselves to visualization. The 'archetypes' that he postulated were universal themes and symbols in human minds. He gave examples such as the animal, the wise old man, the mother, the child. His terms 'anima' and 'animus' were inner gender opposites, the 'anima' being the inner femininity in a male psyche.

When Emin analysed one of the paintings that she had selected for their joint exhibition, a work from 1907 entitled *The Death of Marat*, she saw the picture in terms of psychological conflict. The carnage and the blood were emotional:



*Edvard and Tracey*

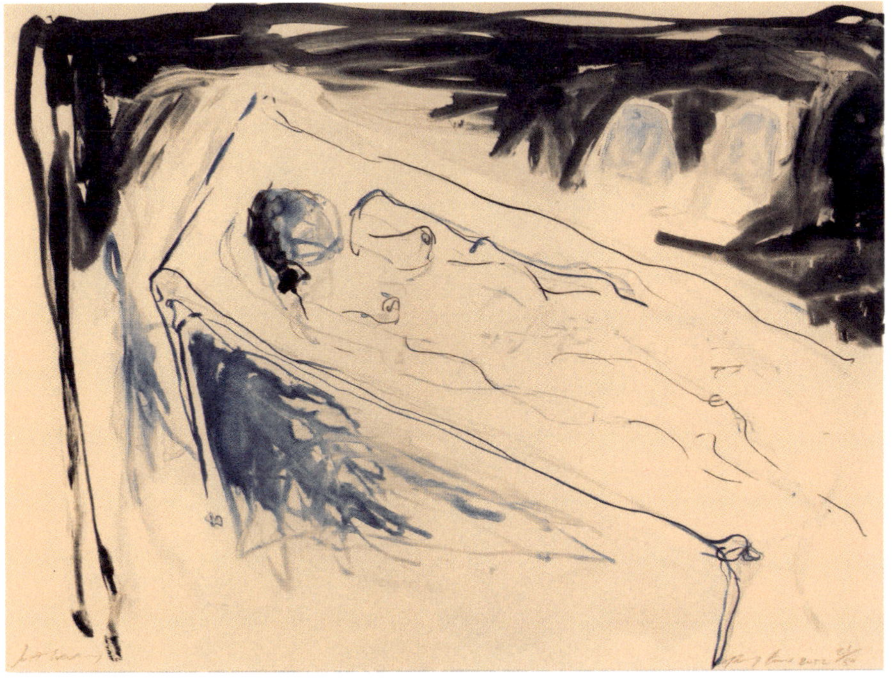

*Just Waiting*, 2023

It's like the death of the man, the male figure. It's about the woman killing the man. The woman having the control, the woman having the power, stopping him from living, from breathing, from his heart pounding. She's the one in charge. She looks so cold, she looks like she's cut off completely, like she's gone, she already left a long time ago. She has no emotional feeling whatsoever, unlike the dead figure who looks full of pathos, full of love, even a cuddle, which is really interesting – and she does, she looks stern, she looks angry. And his hand is almost going to touch her. There's this feeling of

wanting still, this love. She's turned her back on him
completely.

Munch and Emin are both entirely open about what and how
they feel, and there – in stereotypical terms – he was more feminine than masculine.

All of Munch's work was directed towards his emotions,
towards his vulnerability, which is fantastic for a man
back in 1890 or whatever. It's amazing that this man
just has his heart on his sleeve. So did Van Gogh. So did
Rembrandt. But Munch, I think, was the first person we
can really look at in the 20th century who was so open
about it.

Emin decided that the theme of the joint exhibition with
Munch that she planned would be isolation. Its subtitle was
*The Loneliness of the Soul.* In life, Munch showed a marked reluc-
tance – as people now say – to commit. Described as the
'handsomest man in Norway', he had in addition a fetching air
of aloofness, vulnerability, talent, and doom. However, he had
no happy, long-lasting relationship with any of his innumerable
mistresses – unless it was with certain models in his later years
(there, the evidence is missing). Essentially, his biographer
Sue Prideaux argues, he saw women as a threat to his freedom,
work, and peace of mind. In this darkly misogynistic attitude,
he would have been in accord with his sometime friend, the
Swedish playwright August Strindberg.

Emin questions such an analysis of Munch's feelings. She
concedes that he 'wasn't the best person at relationships' and
she agrees he was 'a bit sexist – they all were in those days'.
Nonetheless, she feels that, if he was not exactly feminist, his
work shows his positivity concerning femininity.



*Edvard and Tracey*

What I find incredible about Munch is the way that
he painted women. Women and girls, from the skinny
pubescent to the voluptuous Madonna, with her full
breasts, curvy hips, thunder thighs and rounded stomach.
For a man who supposedly had crap relationships,
he really did understand the female anatomy.

There was one exception to this empathy, in her view. 'He painted great breasts – but vaginas? Hopeless.' When he did depict these, she notes, he put them in the wrong place. This anatomical incompetence aside, she argues the pictures show that:

Munch had a really deep respect and regard for women.
He held them quite high on a pedestal. He was good
friends with the women he painted. For a long time,
I thought Munch was gay because his interpretation
of women is very romantic, and the sexual energy
behind the women is more archetypal – a femme fatale,
a Madonna, a mother or a sister. It's not about fecundity.

# 9

## *The education of an artist*

Once, a long time ago, I interviewed the philosopher and novel-ist Iris Murdoch about her views on art. While we were chatting about some Duchampian work (exactly what it was I have for-gotten), I exclaimed, 'But that just isn't art!' She gently replied, 'Remind me, what *is* art?' It was a marvellous put-down, the crowning touch of which was 'remind me' – and hers was, and remains, a good question. Decades later, I still do not have a ready answer, but it sounds as if Emin had the beginnings of a working definition while still at primary school.

TE  Already when I was little, I liked making things out
of nothing. Apart from drawing pictures, the first thing
that I really did at school was an appliquéd elephant.
I was about six or seven, and I cut the stencil of the
elephant out of this orange furry fabric, then I sewed
binding around it and did chain stitching round it.
To me, this thing was amazing. I kept looking at it
and I loved it. Because I had made it from the beginning
to the end. So at that age, I understood that making
something, creating something, wasn't playing. There
was something magical about it. You made it, you
created it. Without you, it wouldn't have existed.

It seems that Emin was behaving like an artist before she knew what art was. As she told Geordie Greig, in her world, 'Everything is visual. That's all I do. I've never been anything

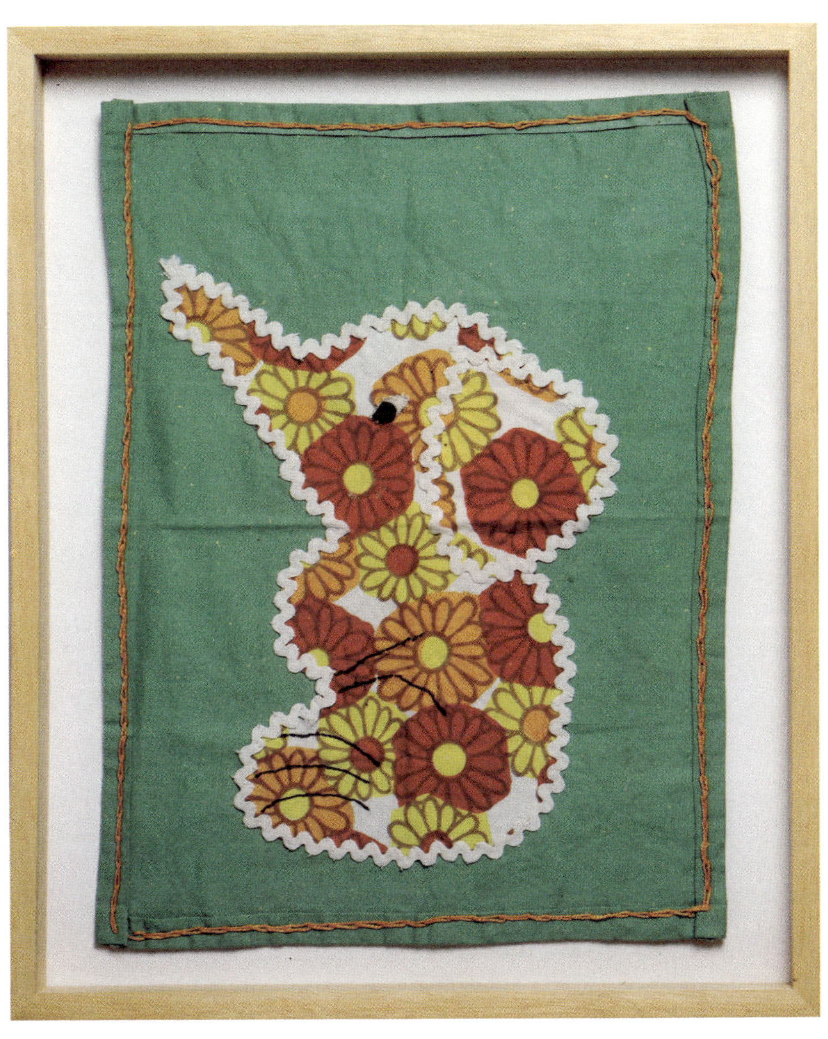

*My Elephant*, 1963–93

else but an artist, so it's all part of that. It's part of my mind, and how I think, and what my brain does.'

A few years later, she seamlessly translated an exercise in geometry into what sounds like an installation or perhaps a piece of sculpture.

**TE** My big break at school came when I was about nine. We had a maths class in which you had to make a little house using a compass, protractor, set square – measure it all, cut it out, fold it up. It was done with yellow card. That was in maths on Tuesday. On Friday afternoons, we had our free time at school, and what I did was make a little house, a little church, a little factory, and a little garage. And then I got a great big sheet of cardboard and put sawdust on it, and then trees. I made a whole village, a little town. This is what I did every Friday afternoon, and I *loved* doing it. I loved making this little world of cardboard houses.

I was never very bright at school. But there was a prize given to a person who had started something, carried on, and finished it. That was me. I won it for the little village that I made, and it was put out for show in the hallway. I remember feeling a sense of pride, not because I'd won this prize but because I'd created it from nothing.

Then I went to big school, senior school, but I stopped going when I was thirteen. I got sick of it for lots of different reasons. Then, by law, when I was fifteen, I had to go back for four months, three days a week, otherwise my mum would have been in trouble with the social services. But it was brilliant. I made millions of little clay figurines of my home life, of what it was like for me to be at home. I wish I still had them. They would have



*The education of an artist*

shown a lot of what I was going through. All these little
tiny clay figures, TV dinners, my bedroom, all the different
things in my house. Then I did tons of paintings on big
sheets of newsprint. I just loved it.

It is a shame those teenage Emins do not survive. They sound
intriguing, especially those clay sculptures of everyday life.
A sculpted TV dinner or a teenage bedroom would be a wonderful thing to see.

History relates many examples of famous artists whose
ambitions were opposed by their families. Michelangelo was
beaten by his father because he wanted to leave school, stop
learning Latin grammar, and join a painter's studio. John
Constable's father forced him to supervise a windmill instead of
studying at the Royal Academy Schools. Van Gogh's parents
tried to persuade him to enter a mental hospital rather than
begin his career as an artist. It might even be that the internal
strain of his frustrated artistic urge was causing some of
Vincent's problems. One of the first things that Emin told me,
in our earliest conversation twenty years ago, was that she
believed:

> If you have artistic talent within you – which not
> everybody does – but if you do and it is suppressed
> and dammed up and not allowed out, then in the end
> it will drive the person who has it mad. It can't be
> ignored; it's too powerful.

At this point in her life, unlike those famous predecessors, Emin
was not up against parental opposition. Her problem was the
bureaucratic rules of the British educational system. To become
an artist – or at least to get into an art school – you had to have
passed some exams.

**TE** I left school at fifteen with no qualifications, nothing, and
went to London. In London I stayed in a squat in Warren
Street. Everyone in the squat was going to St Martin's
or the Royal College of Art. They were all older than me.
So I thought I'd like to go to art school, and that was it
really. I put my mind to it and I did. But first I had to do
a foundation course. When I was seventeen, I came back
to Margate and went to the careers office. They said,
'What do you want to do?' I replied, 'Go to university'.
They said, 'Well you can't.' I asked, 'Why not?'

In certain people, such as those listed above, the urge to
become an artist is extremely strong – which it needs to be,
since the difficulties of being an artist, especially a good one, are
immense. Emin had little problem in blasting her way through
the barriers presented by the educational system, powered
as she was by talent, energy, and effrontery.

**TE** I called the Medway College of Design, got the forms
for the foundation, filled them in, and got an interview.
Got in on the spot. They said, 'Leave your certificates
with the secretary on your way out.' I said, 'I haven't
got any.' I just told the truth because I'd lied on the
forms, said I'd got O levels and stuff. So they couldn't
give me a place on the foundation course. Then they said,
'What have you got in that basket?' I was wearing clothes
that I'd made myself. I opened the basket and inside were
all sorts of mad clothes that I'd made. So they gave me a
place there and then to do a BTEC in fashion. But I didn't
want to do fashion; I wanted to do fine art.

Seen in old photographs, Emin's clothes are obviously the
work of someone with an eye and a knack for making things.

 *The education of an artist*

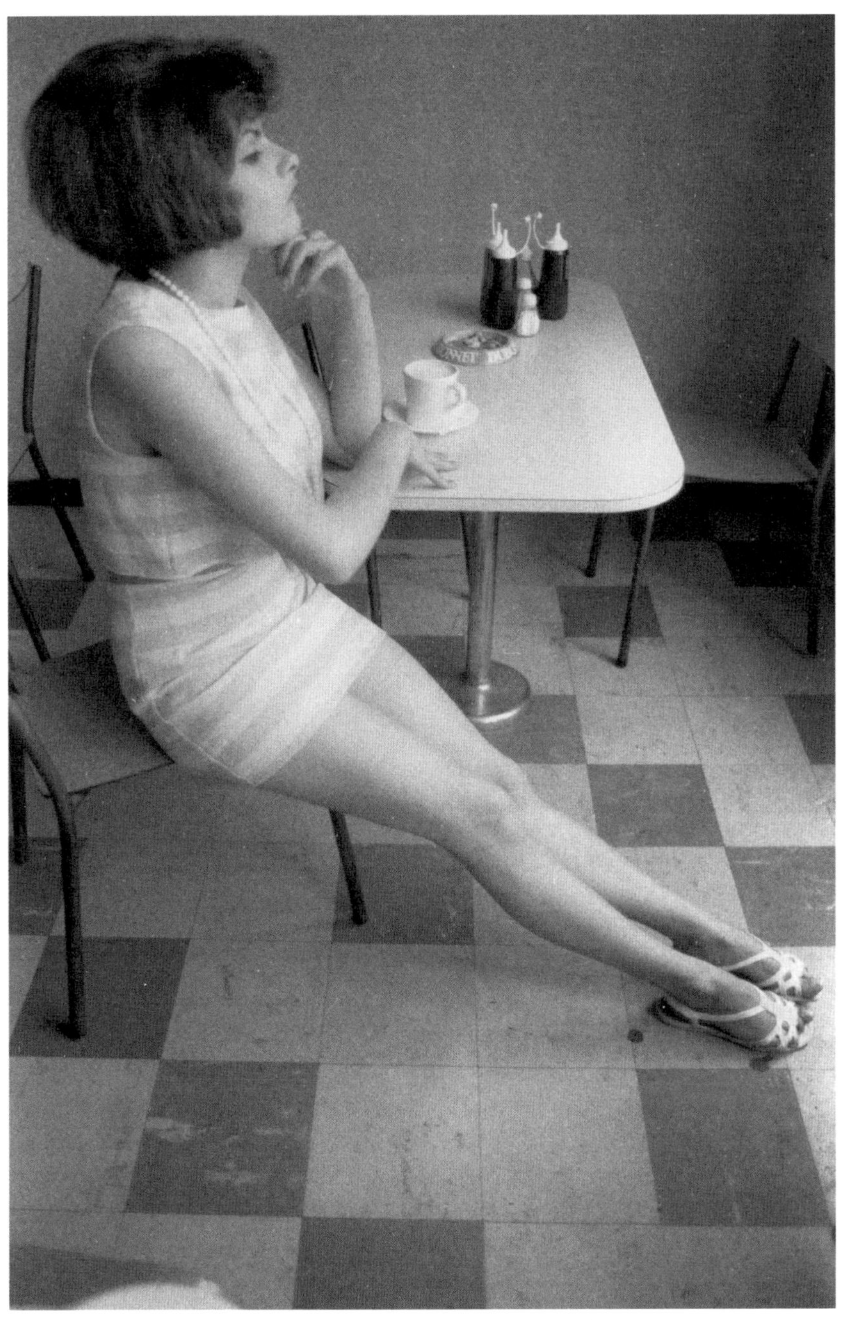

Modelling clothes made out of curtains II, 1982

But the pictures of her modelling them are better, like stills from a film. You could even claim them as performance art, especially her pensive pose in a café, which makes you want to know what happened next.

She described the next step in her progress towards becoming an artist in *Tracey Emin Curriculum Vitae Part I,* written in 1997: 'Dropped out after 1981–82 rail strike. Was advised to go and see a psychiatrist, as I was condemning myself to a life on the dole.' After a crisis in her personal life, she attempted suicide ('Weight no more than six and a half stone', she reported in *Curriculum Vitae,* 'Have to see analyst and do this 'til 1983'). But then she returned to art education by following up a random piece of information.

TE  I heard on the radio someone from The Clash talking about the Sir John Cass School of Art, and how you could do a foundation course there that only cost a pound to do. You just turned up with your portfolio and they go, 'You're in!' and you pay your pound. So I went and did it, got in, and started doing the three-day-a-week foundation course. But I found it *really, really* boring.

A regular feature of Emin's early career was that when she managed to get into an educational institution, somebody quickly spotted that she was immensely talented. The Cass School of Art was no exception.

TE  There was a printmaking course there, so I started going to that two days a week instead. I got together a really good printmaking portfolio. By this time, I was nineteen. The head of the printmaking department there said, 'You're wasted. You need to do a degree.' And he wrote me a really amazing reference.



*The education of an artist*

I had to go to either St Martin's, Goldsmiths, or
Maidstone College of Art, because I was living in Rochester
and I had to be able to commute. I flipped a coin and
decided St Martin's instead of Goldsmiths, but I didn't
get in anyway. When I went for the interview they said,
'We want you to know that you are the only person we are
interviewing without the necessary qualifications.' Instead
of thinking, 'Oh wow, that's amazing!', I went completely
the opposite way and thought, 'Fucking hell, I'm not going
to get in.' They said, 'Take a seat', and I said, 'No thanks,
I'll stand.' Before I had the interview, I'd gone round the
studios looking at what all the students were doing. And
everybody did giant flabby abstract paintings, *flabby, flabby.*
This was in 1983, probably the height of flabby abstraction.
Everybody I spoke to said that they were really happy to get
in, and they were all really posh, I thought.

It is not clear whether it was the bourgeois manners of the
St Martin's students or their flaccid abstract paintings that put
her off the place. Certainly, the latter would not have helped.
Any picture that was lacking in urgent feeling would be uncon-
genial to her. From this story, one can deduce that she had
already developed strong ideas about what painting should be.
Her response to the next college she tried was the reverse of her
response to St Martin's.

**TE** Then I had my interview at Maidstone and loved every
single moment of it. It was fantastic. I got there at eight
in the morning because I didn't have the money for the
fare and had to get a lift. I was sitting at the wrong gate
and the dinner ladies came along and said, 'Come with
us and have a cup of tea.' So I sat with the ladies from the
canteen and they gave me some breakfast.

Then I went for my interview for painting and got in. But then they said, 'Your portfolio's full of prints. Maybe you'd like to do printmaking instead?' So I had an interview for printmaking as well, and got in for both. At that interview, I'd painted all my long nails and stayed up all night making myself a dress, so I'd got it all wrong for art school. I really didn't know. I remember them saying in the printmaking interview, 'What do you think of feminism?' I said, 'I don't even think about it. I just do what I want to do.' Apparently, that was one of the things that got me in.

It was a wonderful answer, and very characteristic. Once I told David Hockney an anecdote about a jazz musician. He did not know anything about the musician or his music, but he immediately diagnosed from one reported remark, 'That sounds like an artist speaking.' You might make the same deduction about Emin's answer at her interview. Indeed, it is similar to Lucian Freud's response when asked how he felt about attaining the age of eighty-one. 'I don't think about age. I just think about what I want to do.' What Emin wanted was to be a painter, but – perhaps unlike the flabby abstractionists she had reacted so vehemently against – she was already aware that creating a truly powerful and original painting is a stiff challenge. Making wood-cuts, etchings, and lithographs seemed a more attainable goal.

**TE** Weirdly enough, I chose printmaking because I loved the alchemy of it. I loved the machinery, the old-fashion-ness of it, the smell of the ink – all that stuff. And I liked the fact that I was one removed from it. Because I always felt that painting was really difficult because there was just you and it, there was no middle man, whereas with printmaking there was this barrier. So I did a printmaking degree with painting as a second subject.

*Jaw Wrestling*, 1986

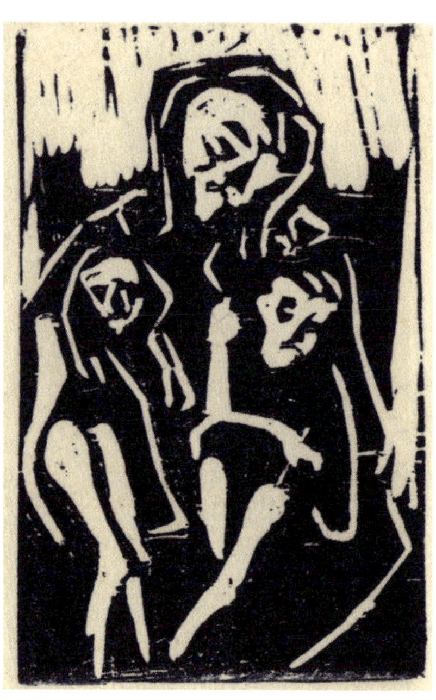

*Untitled* (mother and two children), *c.* 1987

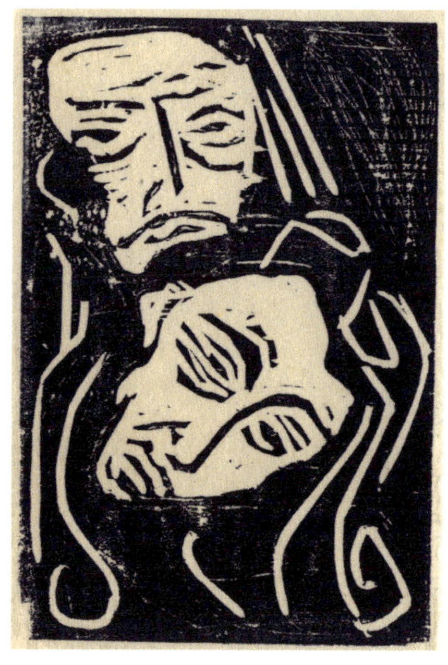

*Untitled* (two faces), *c.* 1987

**MG**  And you wanted to make prints like Munch's?

**TE**  Yes, totally. And Käthe Kollwitz's. That's why I did
printmaking. That was the art I liked. The Expressionists
were all printmakers. That's what they excelled at. And
I found it was easier for me to express what I wanted
through printmaking than it was through painting because
I didn't know how to paint. And I had no knowledge
of art history whatsoever, only what I'd picked up and
learned myself. Most people who go to art school have
done a foundation course or they've done A-level art.
They've learnt lots of history. They've looked at lots
of things. I'd only seen what I'd liked, and so I only
wanted to emulate or be part of what I liked, which
was Expressionism, because I wanted to express myself
through my art. Printmaking was a really good way for



*The education of an artist*

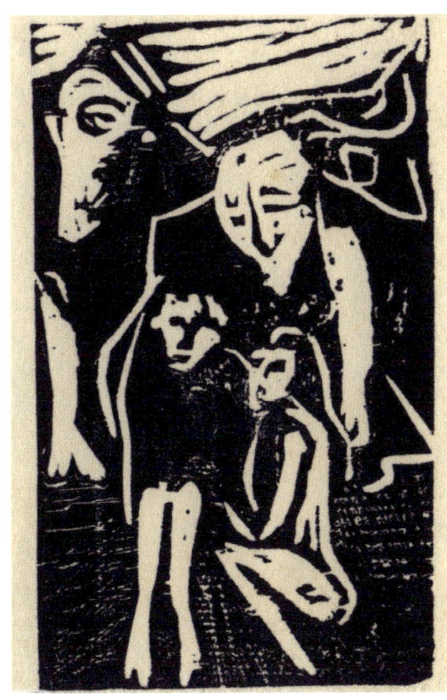

*Untitled* (mother, father, two children), *c.* 1987

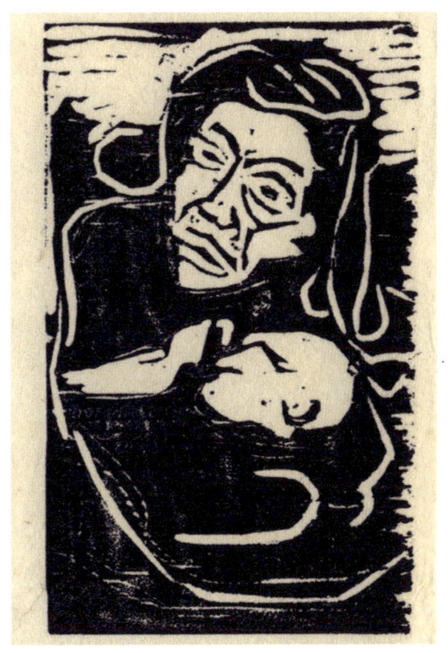

*Untitled* (mother and baby), *c.* 1987

me to do that. At that time, painting did not have that
magic for me. I didn't understand that there could be an
alchemy in painting. Now, of course, I totally understand.
There's something so magical about painting, it's
incredible. I love the otherworldliness of it, and I often
talk about the alchemy of art itself. It's magical, it's
otherworldly, but it belongs to us. Colours are alchemic.

MG  In the nineteenth century, people were always talking
about Rembrandt being a magician, until it became a
cliché. But it's true in a way.

TE  It's making shit into gold, isn't it? Something out of nothing.

## 10

## *Tears at the Tate*

**TE** I didn't go to the Tate until I was twenty-two. It was
in 1984. I know that's late, but I didn't even know where
it was. It wasn't as if I was taken there as a child. I had to
find it for myself and work it all out. The first time I went,
it was to look for the Munch. On my way, I came across a
yellow and pink painting. It was an abstract painting.
I didn't even like abstract painting. I liked Expressionism,
I liked Munch, Egon Schiele, Käthe Kollwitz. But I just
stood there and looked at this painting and was kind of
breathless. I sat down and stared at it. I started to cry and
cry and cry. Big emotional sobs. I couldn't stop crying.

I didn't understand why I had been affected by this
painting. It was like the whole thing was vibrating.
Afterwards, I looked at the label to see who the artist was.
It was someone called Mark Rothko. When I got back to
college, I went to the library and I looked him up. There
was a book with the history of his work. There were all
these figurative, religious paintings. I absolutely loved
them. My God, they are so beautiful! Then I continued to
look through and it got to his abstraction.

Rothko was born Markus Rothkowitz in 1903 in Dvinsk,
then part of the Russian empire, now Daugavpils, the second
largest city in Latvia. Dvinsk was one of the great centres of
eastern European Jewish life. Half the population of the town
was then Jewish, among them the Rothkowitz family.

Mark Rothko, *Untitled, c.* 1950–2

They emigrated to the United States while Markus was still a boy. But shortly after they arrived, Rothko's father died of cancer, leaving his wife and children in the position of poor relations. Mark, highly intelligent, won a scholarship to Yale University, but he was a misfit and dissident there and left without a degree. It was not until 1924 that he discovered his vocation as a painter, and not until the late 1940s – when Rothko was in his mid-forties and after the full horror of the Holocaust in Nazi-occupied Europe had emerged – that he developed his mature style: the floating oblongs of colour.

As he grew older, his health, both mental and physical, worsened and his work became darker. On 25 February 1970, he killed himself, cutting his wrists and taking an overdose of antidepressants. Though Rothko's work looked very unlike Rembrandt's, he shared the same aim as the great Dutchman: 'a maximum of poignancy'. In an interview he insisted, 'I am not interested in any relationships of colour or form or anything else':

> I am interested in the basic human emotions –
> tragedy, ecstasy, doom, and so on – and the fact that
> lots of people break down and cry when confronted
> with my pictures shows that I *communicate* with those
> basic human emotions. The people who weep before
> my pictures are having the same religious experience
> I had when I painted them.

According to a friend, Rothko was so fascinated by viewers' responses to his work that, during his first retrospective exhibition at the Museum of Modern Art, New York, in 1961, 'he would follow them around, eavesdropping on their conversations'. He would have been delighted by the youthful Emin's response. From his perspective, she was an ideal spectator.

Emin is so visually orientated, she reports, that for her reading a novel is like going to the cinema. In her mind, each episode in the plot, every character and conversation, is automatically translated into pictures. It is a reaction that many people would probably recognize. For example, perhaps most of us – though not all – have a mental image of how a character in a novel looks. Perhaps the better the writing, the clearer that image will be. And possibly the same mechanism works in reverse: the better the painting, the more strongly it will transmit feelings and thoughts.

On the other hand, as we have seen so far in this book, she is someone for whom the emotional charge of a work of art is crucial. And in this case, she concluded that Rothko's anguished feelings had been transmitted to her.

TE  When I read that he had committed suicide, I was in a state of shock, because this yellow and pink painting was so sad; it was crying and crying. I couldn't understand why I was feeling that way in front of it, but when I read about him it was obvious. I felt his emotion through that painting. I knew nothing about Rothko, I knew nothing about abstract painting. I wondered whether it was the effect of going to the Tate and being overwhelmed by being where I wanted to be. But it was the first thing that I saw that was, to me, really emotional and true, true art, and it just stopped me – it got me. As I'm telling the story, I'm still seeing this twenty-two-year-old girl sitting there crying, looking at this painting. It was amazing to have an experience like that from looking at a painting.

Emin's reaction to Rothko's picture at the Tate must have been triggered by the way that it was painted – the colours, the brush marks, the scale – because there is nothing else.

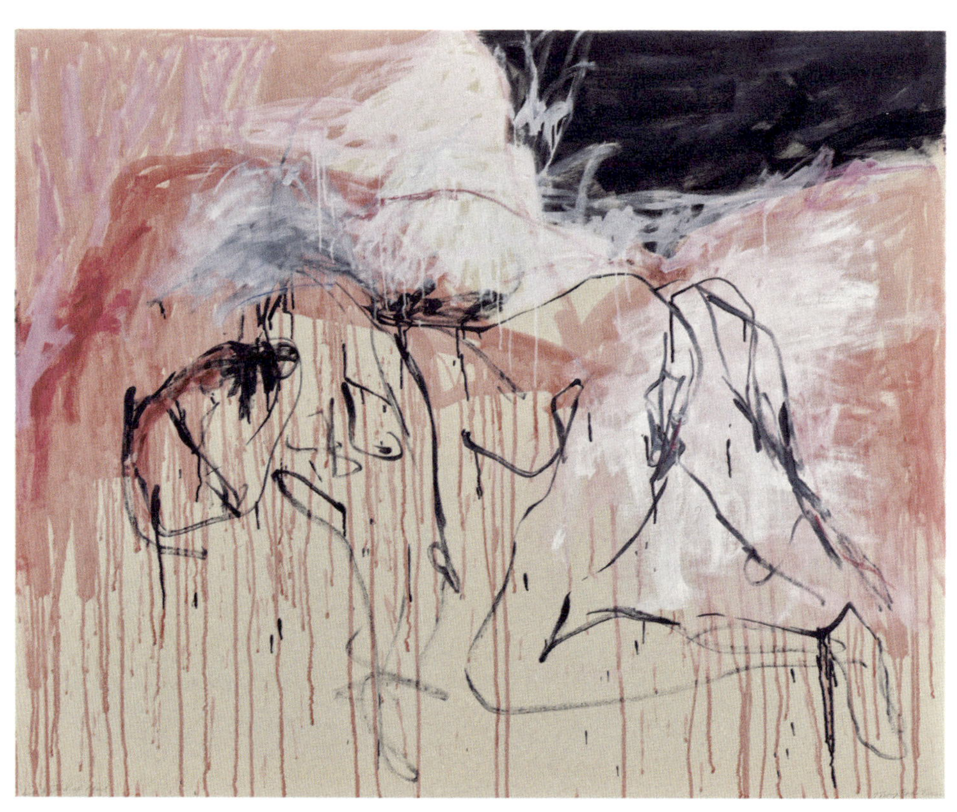

*Like a Cloud of Blood, 2022*

Once, talking about a late oil by Titian, Frank Bowling said it was all about the 'stirring up of the paint'. Emin's paintings have that, but they are done with acrylic paint that sometimes looks almost like watercolour. All truly individual painters are likely to have personal preferences, likes and dislikes, concerning the materials they work with. Many like the physicality of the stuff itself. Lucian Freud, for example, loved the *smell* of paint (and he was not unusual there). Gary Hume has described how he enjoys the whole process of painting. 'I love being alone, I love being in my studio, I love wearing my artist's clothes.' Naturally, painters also have equally powerful negative responses. And these will also affect their work. A painting is the result of numerous decisions – a mixture at once aesthetic, intuitive, and instinctive. Some painters revel in thick impasto; others find it viscerally distasteful. Both inclinations have implications. With each, certain possibilities open up; others are excluded. Rothko worked in veils of colour with results quite unlike, say, the flying skeins of paint in a Jackson Pollock.

TE  I've realized that I am a 'thin' painter. I paint with very, very thin layers of paint; I've tried to paint with thicker layers and I don't like it. It makes me feel sick. It's alright if it's an accident and the paint happens to be built up like that, but intentional thick paint doesn't make me feel good.

I was also a thin painter when I used to paint with oils, although back then I did sometimes put areas of thick paint on. At the Royal College of Art, I used to paint with lots of turps and lots of linseed oil. I used to build up a really slow gesso ground, for the background, so it could take all the oil and the linseed and everything. They used to look like giant watercolours. And I realize that light is important to me. I used to use lots of washes with linseed oil. So you have all this gold. I really liked it.

Rothko used oils; Pollock painted with an eclectic mixture of materials including oils, but also enamel, household paint, and others. Again these choices fundamentally affected the results.

**MG** Why did you change to acrylic paint?

**TE** When I was pregnant, I couldn't stand the smell of oil paint or turps. So I stopped using them, and then I stopped painting altogether for quite a long time. When I started again, I didn't go back to oil paint. I used acrylics instead. All my paintings are acrylic.

There's also another reason that I use acrylics: oil is considered the king of materials, while acrylic is like the pauper. But that's just snobbishness because, number one, a lot of acrylics now are really fucking expensive; and number two, you can wet acrylic paint and manipulate it just like oil paint. The other thing is that I don't know many people who can use acrylic paint like me. My use of it is intentional.

**MG** That thinness has consequences, but I take it that these are not unintended. The drips that shower or trickle down your canvases are not just an accidental by-product of the way you work. The paint often runs down your canvases like rain or tears, and to do that it has to be very diluted. You must want that to happen. After all, it's very beautiful and expressive. The drips are intentional, controlled, and give energy to the paintings.

**TE** If I load the brush up with very thin paint and run it along the canvas, I know there are going to be drips, but I can control them. I love it, actually, when we put canvases up in the middle of the studio and my cats watch the drips come down and then run and *pounce* on them. So I get this double pleasure from it. I enjoy the drips too, and the bold slashing brushstrokes that often start them flowing.

Much though he emphasized the emotional nature of his work, Rothko gave the impression that ultimately a painting was mysterious, even to its creator. According to his friends Barbara Novak and Brian O'Doherty, when Rothko was seated in front of his work, he subjected it 'to his habitual hypnotic stare, he studied how the waxing and waning light veiled and unveiled incident, content and moods that appeared like so many chimeras. He gave the impression, as one watched with him, that the painting, particularly if it were a dark painting, was unknowable.' There, too, Emin and Rothko are in agreement. Or at least, as we shall see later, she believes that, to have real power, a painting has to have an ingredient so hard to define that she calls it 'the thing'.

# II

# *Learning how to paint*

TE   What I did at the Royal College of Art was that I learnt
how to paint. And I was dedicated and focused while
I was there. But I was also distraught because it was
all so alien to me, everything about it. The year that I
applied, which was 1987, was a double-application year.
Two thousand people applied for twenty places, which
was crazy. You had to send in a portfolio with works on
paper, twenty 35-mm slides, and up to seven sketchbooks.
So I, with my forty sketchbooks, wondered 'Which ones
should I put in? Maybe this one, maybe that one.'

In the end, I made a selection of seven sketchbooks and
sent them in. Apparently, when the tutors [Adrian Berg,
Alan Miller, and Professor Paul Huxley] saw these, they
said, 'We've found one! We've found one!' So I got an
interview. Adrian Berg told me later that when they
walked into the room with my paintings, they thought
– each one of them thought – that they had never seen
such bad paintings in their entire life. Their disappointment
was incredible, because the sketchbooks and works on
paper were amazing. Of course they were, because I could
draw really well and I had done printmaking. They
asked, 'Why are the paintings like this? I explained it
was because I painted with screen inks because I didn't
have the money for oils, and I worked just on wood or
whatever I could find. So they said, 'Why do you want to
come here? I answered, 'Because I want to learn to paint.

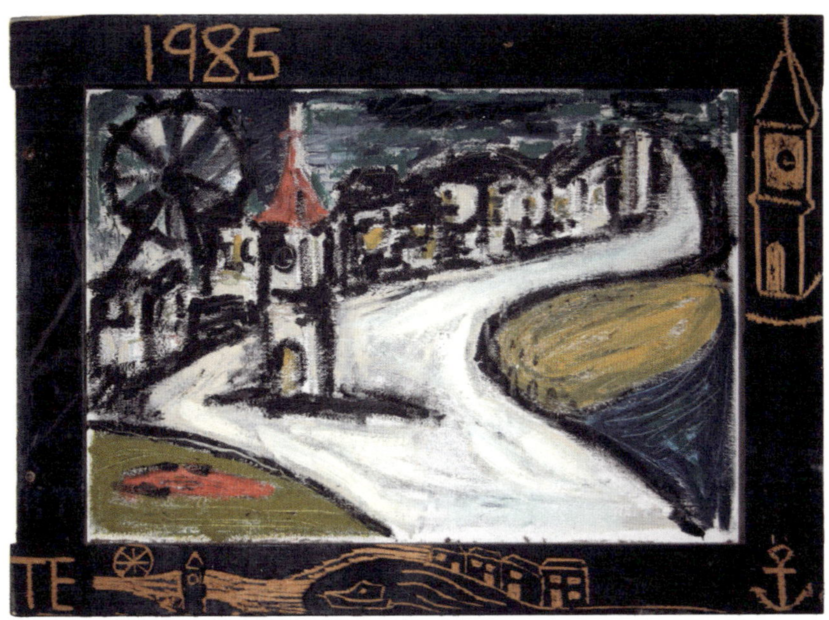

Untitled Margate painting, 1985

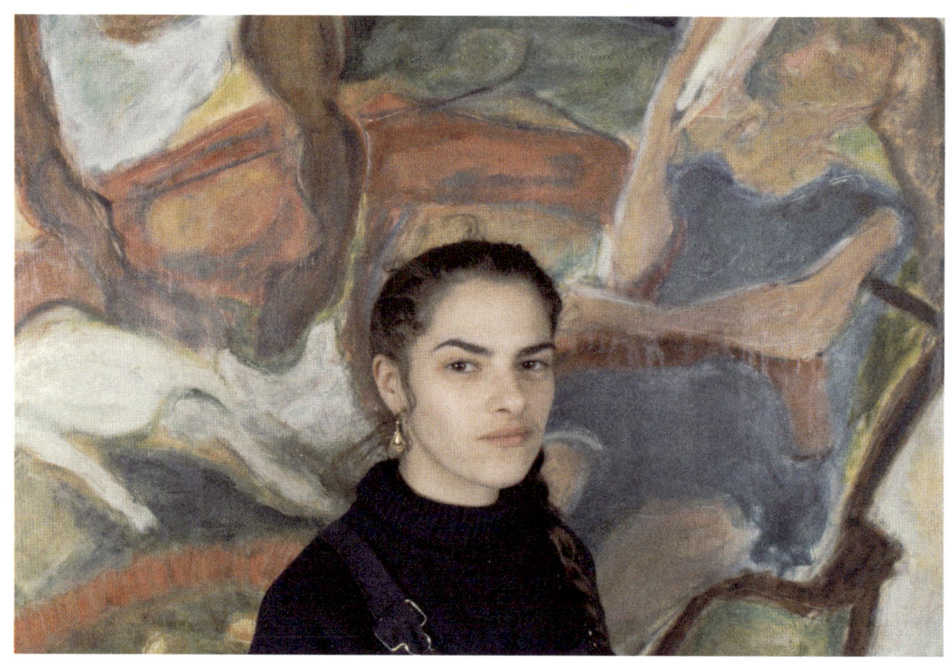

Tracey Emin at the Royal College of Art, 1989

I want to spend two years doing just that.' They said that it was one of the best answers they'd ever heard. Adrian Berg – 'Bergy baby' – told me later that it was a unanimous decision to let me in, even though they had never seen anyone come to an interview with such bad paintings. 'Then how come I got a place?', I wondered. He said, 'Because when we asked you why you wanted to come here, you said you wanted to learn how to paint. It was so refreshing.'

One advantage of the Royal College, she suspected, was that she could find a mentor and guide there – not a ghostly figure from the past such as Edvard Munch, but a living, functioning contemporary painter.



*Learning how to paint*

 At the interview, I mentioned that I wanted to go
to the Royal College because Ken Kiff was there.
They asked if I knew him, and I said, 'No, but I really
like his work. It would be very good to do an MA in a
place where there is someone's work you can relate to.
It might be a good connection.'

Emin later told the *Brooklyn Rail* how she had investigated Kiff and his work and decided that he would make a suitable teacher for her. 'I could see that Ken liked Expressionism. I could see that Ken liked Carl Jung – and I read about Ken, you know, and read reviews of his work and stuff. And for me, it really mattered that I'd be working with a tutor, that it would be someone who I responded to and liked. And who I could talk to about things that I enjoyed.'

It was a revealingly adroit move for a prospective student to make. Emin had selected a suitable teacher for herself in advance – and she was right. Kiff was the ideal instructor for a young painter who was interested in dreams, feelings, and myths. At a different institution, such as Goldsmiths, she would have encountered other approaches and attitudes, which were inspiring for artists with very dissimilar sensibilities to hers, such as Gary Hume, Ian Davenport, and Fiona Rae. But Kiff was perfect for her. She had a high opinion of him and – as it turned out – he was similarly impressed by her. As I mentioned before, almost the first thing I ever heard about Tracey Emin, from Norbert Lynton, was that the people teaching her at the Royal College thought that she was potentially a brilliant painter. That would have been information supplied by Kiff, since Lynton was a friend and major supporter of his.

Like Emin, Kiff (1935–2001) came from the kind of background that did not usually produce artists. He was born in Dagenham, Essex. His father worked in a woodyard and was killed early in the Second World War, when Ken was still a small child. He subsequently had two stepfathers. He did not talk about his mother. His work was both personal and psychological. Lynton wrote that, 'Many of Ken's pictures suggest journeys or adventures, with himself as protagonist.' In 1970, he began a series entitled *The Sequence* that finally ran to almost two hundred numbered pictures. These, Lynton noted, 'related to the artist himself openly, picturing him in various actual and imagined situations, sometimes in an almost illustrational manner, often allegorically'. Number thirteen in the series, *Talking with a Psychoanalyst: Night Sky* (1973–9), is one of those. Kiff's pictures grew slowly – as that six-year period, 1973–9, for the creation of the work suggests. Their evolution was also organic, and they ended up in ways that he had not expected or intended. Kiff described how the shapes in his paintings were:

> like amoebae, gradually becoming more and more
> specific ... If that creature/thing starts to become red,
> OK, then it is starting to firm up a little bit. If it starts
> to shoot out four legs, then it is probably going to
> become a dog. If it starts to elongate itself, it is going
> to become a giraffe. It might split up and become other
> things still.

Presumably that is how the camel appeared in the picture of the artist talking with a psychoanalyst. Kiff spent twenty years in therapy with an analyst whose approach was broadly Jungian. His wife Jane, originally an artist, became a psychotherapist. He was interested in Jung's ideas, without being a committed follower. Emin remembers that:

> What Ken and I had in common was how we interpreted
> the world through our own experience. He would talk



*Learning how to paint*

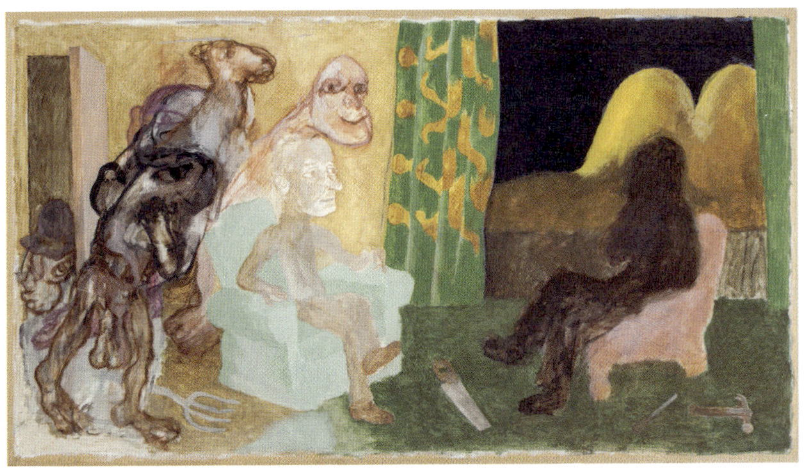

Ken Kiff, *Talking with a Psychoanalyst: Night Sky*, 1973–9

about Jung a lot. I wasn't talking about Gerhard
Richter's paint-marks with Ken; we talked about the
psychological stuff, which is what I was interested in.
And which I'm even more interested in now than then.

One lesson that Kiff imparted was that the contemporary
art that is fashionable at any given moment is not necessarily
what is truly important. With the passage of time, our viewpoint shifts and the view changes. Edward Hopper worked in
Paris for extended periods between 1906 and 1910 without
apparently noting that Fauvism and Cubism were happening in
the same town. That was not a grave oversight; it was entirely
understandable. It is only in retrospect that Matisse, Picasso,
and Braque seem so obviously, overwhelmingly important.

TE  One day, Ken walked into college and said, 'Look at this.'
It was a book of artists from the 1960s and 1970s. I said,
'I don't know hardly any of them.' He said, 'Exactly. It
takes time for people to understand what is really going
on, to get perspective on it.'

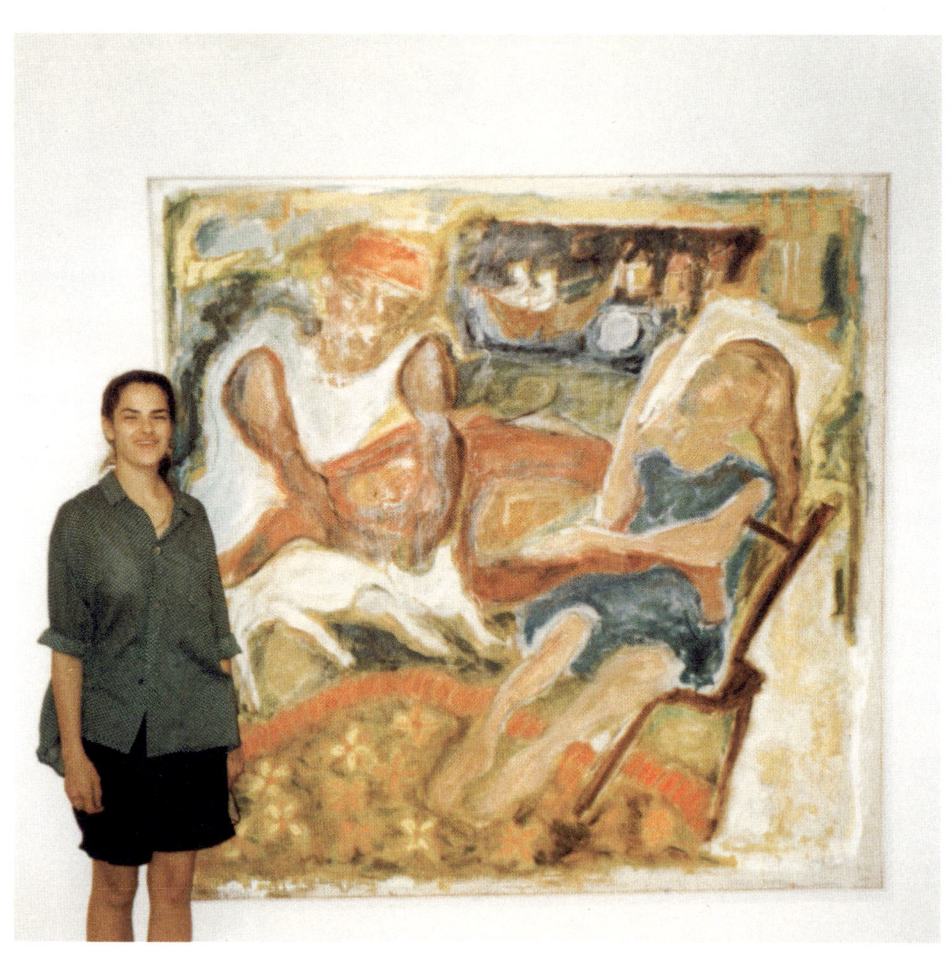

Tracey Emin at the Royal College of Art,
with *Untitled* (woman and dog painting), 1988

In the 1980s, Ken Kiff stood out as an eccentric loner in the London painting scene – but an interesting and prominent one. He was living proof that there was not just one way to paint. He became Emin's personal tutor for the two years that she was at the Royal College of Art. During that time, she accomplished her aim of finding out in technical detail exactly how painting was done.

**TE** At the end of my first year, I won a massive travel grant, the Ritblat Family Foundation travel scholarship. It was a lot of money. But there was one snag: I could have the scholarship as long as I didn't travel. Instead, I had to come into the college every day and learn how to stretch and prime canvases and how to work with oil paint. So instead of some holidays, I got a summer's tuition in painting. I was allowed to have as much canvas and as much paint from any series that I wanted. Ken and Alan Miller [(1941–2009) painter, teacher, and senior tutor in painting at the Royal College from 1989] came in once a week. Ken taught me everything about colour and compositions. He spent ages showing me what different brushes do and different colours. And Alan taught me about priming, painting, linseed oil, this oil, that oil, everything. The school technician, Peter Allen, taught me how to make stretchers and stretch the canvas. Alan then taught me how to prime them with gesso and make them really tight. I remember when I did my first big oil painting and stretched it up, he came in and said, 'You've done it! You've done it!' It was this big six-foot-by-six-foot painting. It was like, I was off!

So that was my summer holiday. Looking back on it, it was one of the best things that ever happened to me. It was really good.

Learning how to paint apart – which was in retrospect a major benefit of her time there – Emin remembers being disappointed by the Royal College and feeling she did not fit in.

TE  The Royal College of Art was so hard for me. When I was at Maidstone, there was a class thing – a lot of people had accents – but to me it was exciting and wonderful in lots of ways. You could argue, you could debate, you could discuss things. When I went to the Royal College, I thought this is going to be amazing. It wasn't. I did not feel part of it all. I remember going into the office and saying, 'I'm going back to Margate. Where are the black people, where are the fat people, where are the thick people? Where are the real people? There are none of them here.' And I walked out. They called my mum and said, 'She's got to come back, otherwise she'll be expelled' or something.

How we feel and how we appear to others, however, are quite different matters. To David Dawson, who shared a studio with Emin at the Royal College and became a lifelong friend, she seemed a powerful, self-assured presence.

Her personality filled the room and it was great fun. There were three of us in this one big studio, so we each had quite a lot of space. Tracey laid carpets on the floor. She made cups of tea; she had a little tea ceremony. She made these little watercolours and monoprints, which she hung up to dry with pegs on a sort of washing line. She created a really strong personal environment in which to create work.

We hit it off immediately and had really good conversations. We still have those same flows of

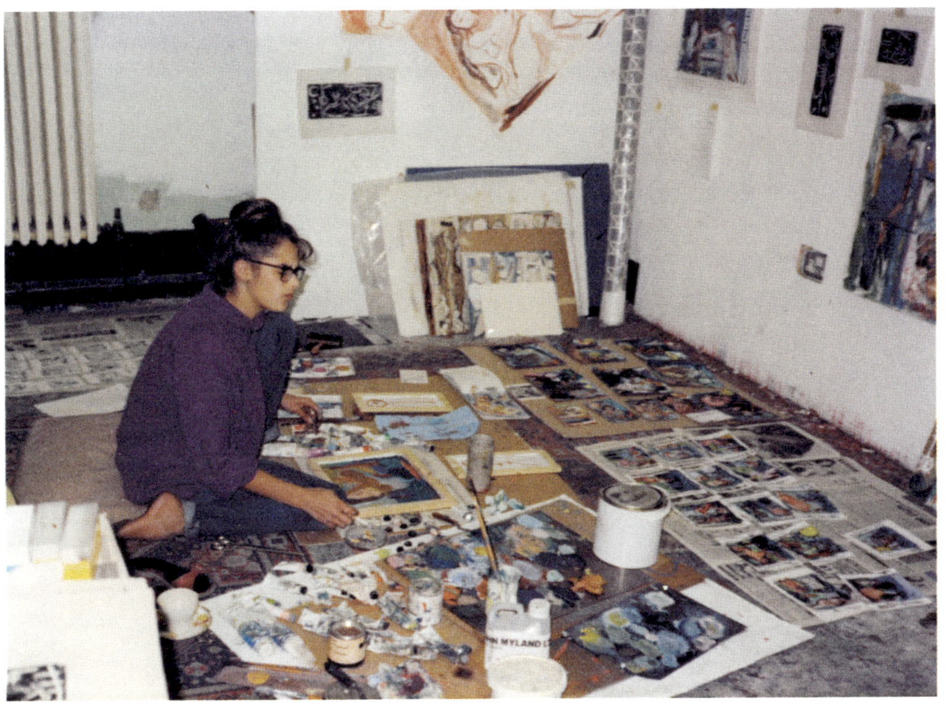

Tracey Emin in her studio at the Royal College of Art, 1989

conversation about what painting is that we had when we were students. She was very much in the centre of things; she wanted to be part of everything. But students are always competitive and divisive. There was a certain amount of arguing going on amongst us all. Sometimes it felt it was getting a bit tense. But Tracey and I were always sympathetic to each other's paintings. That was what we had in common right from the start.

*

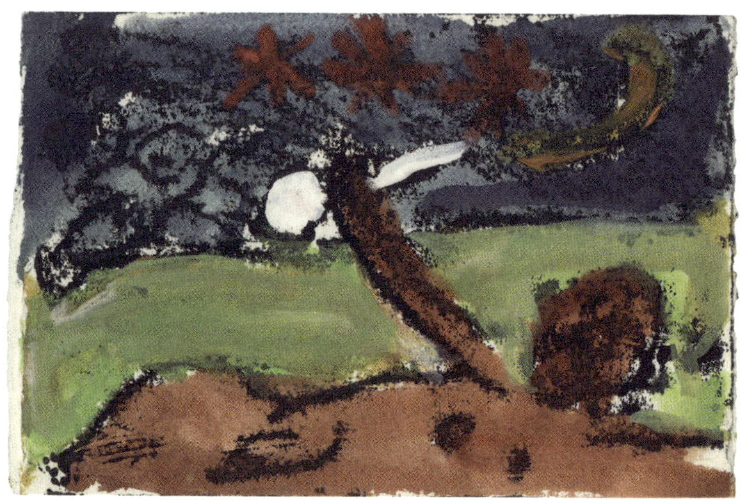

*Untitled* (naked man), *c.* 1987

There are some intriguing points of comparison between Kiff's work and Emin's. Lynton noted that often his pictures contained a 'little man', often naked, who might stand for the artist himself. Kiff's work, the critic wrote, was 'dream-like, neither a description of reality nor accounts of dreams and daydreams, but drawing on both as raw materials' – which could stand as a description of some of Emin's pictures too. Lastly, Lynton noted, 'Art lovers have sometimes been offended by the cruel or coarse actions he included, up-front and without apology.' That certainly goes for her work as well.

Even more than in the work of Carl Jung, Kiff was interested in the writings of one of his followers, Marie-Louise von Franz, author of the books *Problems of the Feminine in Fairy Tales* and *The Shadow and Evil in Fairy Tales* (titles that suggest a distinct flavour of Kiff's works and some of Emin's too). But even so, Kiff firmly resisted the idea that he was painting illustrations to psychoanalysis. 'I think I have been labelled by one or two people as a psychological painter, and that misses the point very badly.' The point was that a painting was an indivisible and fundamentally visual thing. 'You can't say this is just conscious, this just unconscious, this just form, this just content', he argued.

When Kiff talked about art, Lynton wrote in the painter's obituary, he talked about aspects that are often labelled 'formalist'. Among the qualities that he was 'eager to talk about' were 'the character and disposition of forms, the spaces between them, their firm or broken outlines, the dynamics of rising or sinking forms' – and above all colour. These were no doubt subjects that he discussed with Emin, but in a tribute after his death she recalled him often not saying much at all. 'He was a smallish man with huge eyes – he was very intense and sometimes while talking stayed silent for ages occasionally umming and ahhring.' She went on:

> We got on well … he was generous with his
> knowledge … For a dreamer and a thinker, Ken was
> practical when it came to the art of painting – he
> was a very good teacher. [He] pushed and pushed me,
> giving me confidence.… I have a lot to thank him for.
> The brilliant mad conversations we used to have about
> Chagall, Munch, Picasso, and, strangely enough, the
> downside of artists' fame. The best advice Ken ever
> gave me was 'There are no shortcuts.' He was right.

She remembers a particular exercise that he set for her, a journey into the infinite variety of colour: 'One day he said, "Why don't you do a watercolour and see how many colours you can put in it?" We counted thirty-two – he made me mix and make up colours I never knew existed.'

**TE**  I remember he said to me once, 'What's up?' I explained that I had been into someone's studio and they had this amazing pink colour, this fantastic cerise. 'I've been trying to get it, and I just can't.' I must have had about eighty different pinks that I'd mixed up. Ken said, 'You are never going to get it.' 'Why not?', I asked. 'Because it is Series F', he replied. I went to the materials shop to look for this series of paints and it was £16 a tube – this was in 1988. I was really good friends with Rachel, the girl in the shop. I had this big furry hat, which I put on the side of the counter while I looked around the shop. Then when I picked up my hat and put it on, tubes of Series F fell out. She'd put them in my hat.

Another important teacher of Emin's at the Royal College was her external tutor Paula Rego. It is hard to think of another more suitable painter to instruct her, as she acknowledged:

**TE**  When you think about it, Ken Kiff and Paula Rego, I was really lucky. Because in the 1980s, everybody was just moving into some kind of neo-conceptual, postmodernist ideas. And we really weren't. [*laughter*]

When Emin and Rego exhibited together at the Foundling Museum, London, in 2010, Gill Hedley noted that they recalled only 'discussing men, not art'. But then relationships with men – and along with them love, loss, sex, and sexual violence – were preoccupations of both as painters and as people. There is nothing neo-conceptual or postmodernist about those topics. Looking back from decades later, it seems obvious that Rego (1935–2022) was one of the most brilliant painters working in Britain in the 1980s and 1990s. But it did not necessarily seem like that at the time. When she was teaching Emin at the

   *Learning how to paint*

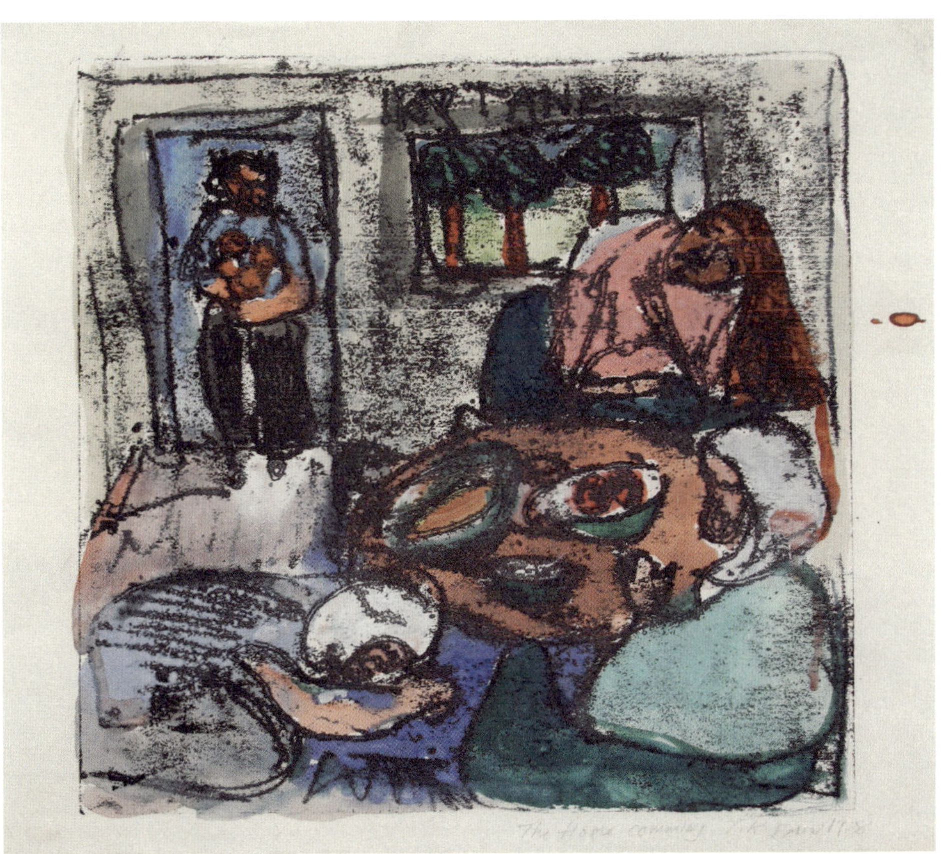

*The Homecoming,* 1988

Royal College, Rego was in her mid-fifties and only just beginning to achieve fame and success. Late in her life, a number of
fellow artists, all women, jointly interviewed Rego, and Emin
asked her whether she had ever felt unappreciated. She replied,
'I've felt frustrated and broke. It was an enormous relief whenever I sold a picture.' Emin herself was to feel much the same
in the early 1990s, after she left art school.

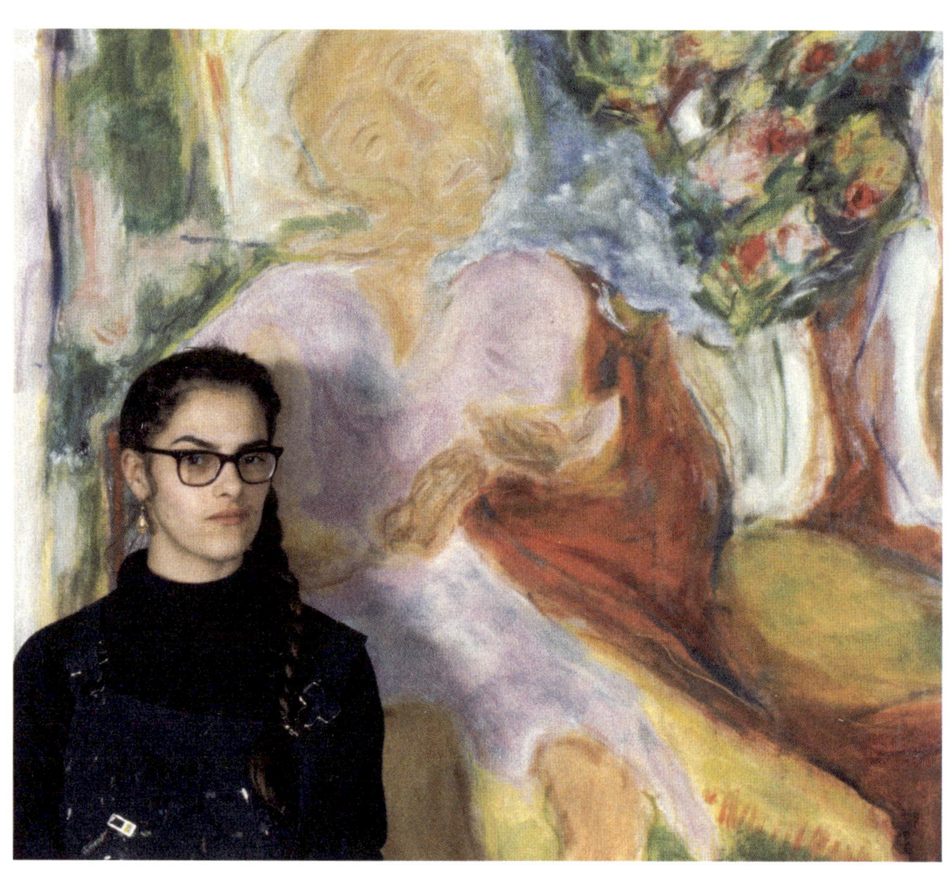

Tracey Emin at the Royal College of Art, with *Me & My Nan*, 1988

# 12

## *Destruction*

**TE** Because I had got a grant from the hardship fund at the
Royal College of Art, as well as the big travel scholarship
and a bursary, it meant that they could choose any painting
of mine to go into the college collection. And they picked
a picture that I had done of my two grandmothers, my
English nan and my Turkish one, who died when she was
thirty-six of typhoid. I put them together at a table and
thought this was really interesting. I had put me in the
painting at first, but then I took myself out and put a vase
of flowers there instead.

So the college chose that painting. But it was my
favourite one of all. One day, I waited until Stan, who was
the gatekeeper, was on his tea break. Then I took his keys
and went upstairs to where all the paintings were stored.
I swapped the painting of my grandmothers with a really
bad painting. In fact, this painting was so bad that I'd
thrown it away. I took it out of the bin, and restretched it
so that I could substitute it, because it was the same size.
It's got a line down the middle where it had been folded
in half. On the back I wrote, 'Really sorry. But I love my
nan too much to part with her. (I could have sold this one.)
It's a good picture too. Thank you Tracey.'

**MG** Why did you do that?

**TE** At the Royal College, I was nobody. I was never going to be missed; I was never going to be remembered; nobody gave a fuck about my work. Actually, I was treated a bit regressively, because they felt sorry for me. They thought I didn't get it, didn't understand what was happening in art. What I was doing was what was happening in my head. My degree show was hung in the basement, underneath a shelf, basically, so nobody saw it. I was not one of the 'wow kids'. So they had taken this painting because I'd had a bursary, but they didn't really care about it. It would probably just disappear into obscurity. I thought it was better that *I* had the painting that I wanted. So I swapped it over.

**MG** So you kept it because you wanted to protect it. Then what happened to it?

**TE** Two years later when I was pregnant, broke, had no studio, nowhere live, at the end of my tether, having to leave my studio at Elephant and Castle, I was so distraught that I threw all my paintings away. Because I couldn't look after them. It was like, if I can't have them, no one will.

Then, lo and behold, I got a bit of a name for myself. There was an event at the Serpentine Gallery that we all went to, and the dinner afterwards was in the senior common room at the Royal College of Art. It was full of all these people sitting at this big table. Then the person next to me said, 'I'm going to ask to change places.' I asked why and he said, 'I just can't stand the painting I'm looking at. It's so awful!' Then the person next to him said, 'Yes, it's really bad! How could anyone do something that bad?'

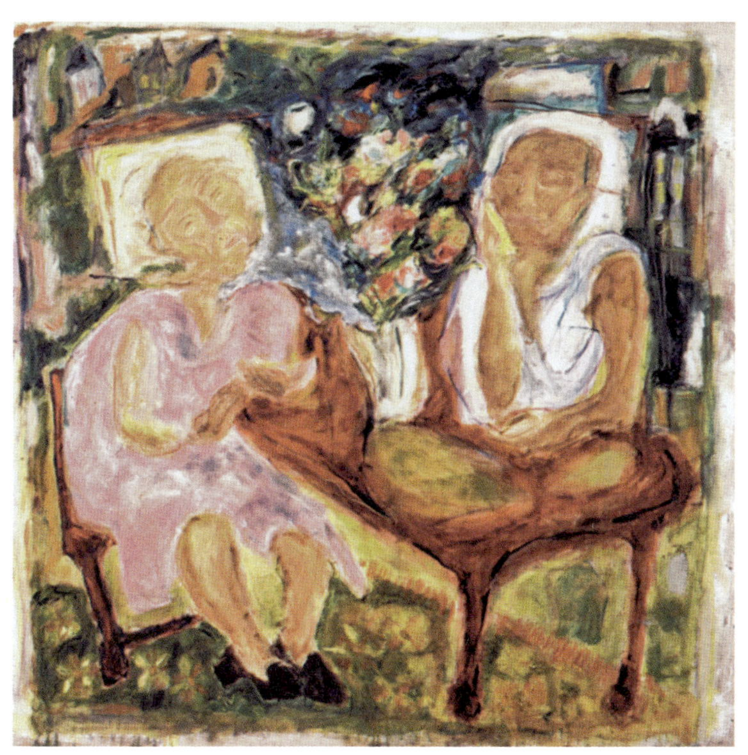

*Me & My Nan*, 1988

I said, 'Maybe the person knew it was bad when
they did it.' I was with Matt [Collishaw] at the time,
and afterwards I told him that it was my painting.
'I know it's really bad. That's why I gave it to them!'
The Royal College said later that they would probably
hang it the other way round in the future, showing
the writing on the back. I said, 'Yes please!' The moral
of the story is that, when you are eternally grateful to
someone and they ask you for something, give them
the best that you have, not the worst. Otherwise, it will
come back and bite you, like it did in that situation. I
couldn't even defend the painting, because it was so awful.

Even if one were to include that picture, which obviously no
curator would wish to do, there are not enough of Emin's early
paintings in existence to put together an exhibition, or at least
perhaps only a small one. The reason is that they were destroyed,
not by accident or neglect but deliberately by the artist who
had made them. There are just a few survivors.

**TE**  There's a small *Mother and Child* somewhere, and
there's possibly a *Marriage at Cana* and a *Last Supper*,
but who knows? There was something I really liked
about them, but they were pretty morose. They were
not happy-go-lucky paintings; they were really sombre.
*I* was really sombre, really sad, at the time.

It is not unusual for artists to destroy works they decide are
not good enough to survive. Chaïm Soutine was known to burn
rejected pictures, so was Francis Bacon. Freud put his boot
through dozens. But this was not the case with Emin. 'It wasn't
because I didn't care about them', she has explained. 'It was
because I cared about them too much.'

She had been working her way through art college by doing various part-time jobs, including cutting up vegetables for a catering firm and working as a cloakroom attendant at a Soho nightspot, Gaz's Rockin' Blues. Even so, there were limits to what she could afford.

**TE**  There were always these things that for me were hard to endure. Because I was wondering how the fuck I was going to live. For me, everything was in reverse. *I* was having to send *my mum* money; she and my nan had none. When I got the hardship fund grant, it was £2000, which was a lot. The most important thing for me was to get a new pair of glasses, because mine were broken and done up with tape. I had to get loads of stuff like that. I didn't have anything. Someone else got the hardship fund and they went and bought a Nicole Farhi suede jacket from Paris. There was a big disparity. I'd never come across stuff like that in my life. Throughout my time in college, nearly everybody had a fucking mum and dad's garage where they could store all their work. Or they worked at their uncle the solicitor's, filing or something, before they went on holiday to Mustique or somewhere. I didn't have a garage where I could put my paintings, and no one wanted them. They had no position in the world. I had to give them some dignity. So I smashed them all up.

The paintings were on wood, and she took them to the college courtyard and battered them with a sledgehammer. 'I went ballistic slashing the sledgehammer around, and no one could get near me.' It must have been a dramatic spectacle.

**TE**  I would have liked to have made a giant bonfire. People could hear me screaming. Paul Huxley [RCA professor of painting between 1986 and 1998⌉ says they wish they had filmed it because it would have been so amazing to see.

**MG**  It sounds like a piece of performance art.

**TE**  But it wasn't. I was screaming because I was so angry over everything. It was the same when I had my abortions ⌈in 1990 and 1992⌉. I was angry because I knew that if I wanted to be an artist, there was no way I could have a child. It was never going to happen. So that was another really big shift.

In the early 1990s, Emin was at a very low point. In her written *Tracey Emin Curriculum Vitae Part I: November 1962 to December 1995*, she records her first abortion in 1990, concluding that she 'cried and cried'. There is no entry for 1991. The one for 1992, after recording a second abortion, ends:

Middle of 1992 – committed emotional suicide. Emotional suicide is killing yourself without dying. Destroying each friendship and relationship, one by one, till I was alone. Destroyed all my art, left my studio, threw away my curtains, my carpet, my cushions, my comfort. Made my home into a cell and waited.

From then on, her career as an artist slowly began to gain momentum. Late in 1992, she noted, Emin 'asked people to invest in her creative potential'. This involved her writing and sending a series of letters to each subscriber for £10. One person who took up this offer was Jay Jopling, who was about to open the first, tiny White Cube gallery on Duke Street, St James's. In the same year, she became friends with Sarah Lucas, part of the Goldsmiths crowd. A few months later, in

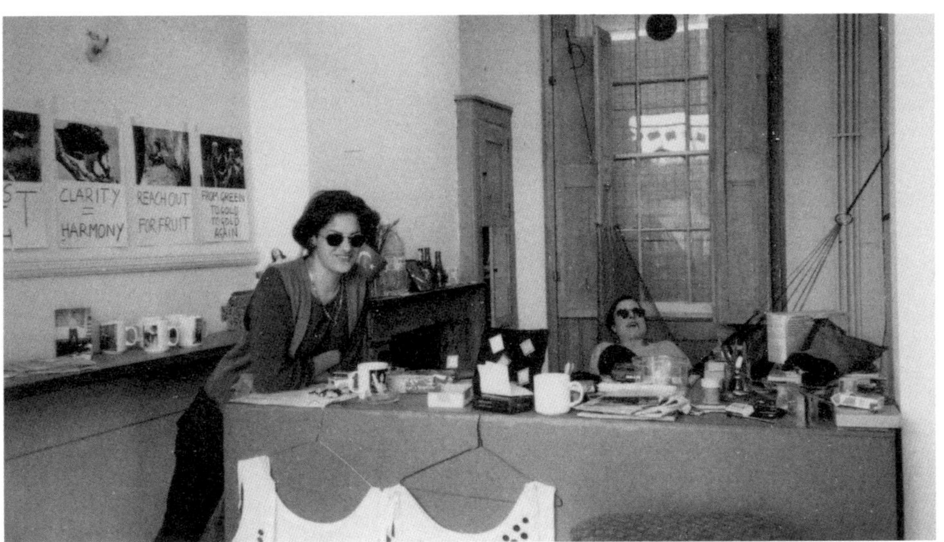


Tracey Emin with Sarah Lucas inside The Shop, 1993

January 1993, they opened a shop together at 103 Bethnal Green Road, off the end of Brick Lane. Named simply 'The Shop', it became a short-lived but celebrated YBA institution. The lease ran for six months, after which it closed. In the meantime, it sold items such as T-shirts proclaiming 'Fucking Useless' and 'You're so Sucky'; ashtrays with Damien Hirst's face on the inside bottom, so you could stub your cigarette out on it; and other items. Emin recalled in an article for *Frieze* magazine:

> I used to make rabbits out of cigarette packets.
> We would chain smoke and, when we'd finished
> smoking a packet of fags, I'd make a rabbit and we'd
> sign it, put it in the window, and sell it for the price
> of a packet of cigarettes. On Brick Lane, you could
> buy loads of fabric for £2, orange plastic sheets for
> 10p each – you could buy all of these odd, fucked-up
> materials. We'd buy whatever we saw and just make
> things out of it, anything we could think of.

The enterprise, the originality, and the effrontery of this temporary pop-up business were all quintessentially YBA.

One of the first exhibitions in Jopling's new enterprise – which was literally a white cube, since it consisted of a single small square room – was by Emin. It ran from 19 November 1993 to 8 January 1994 and was called *My Major Retrospective 1963–1993*. This was a retrospective in a double sense. It was a look back over her life up to this point, containing relics of real events, such as a crumpled cigarette packet that her Uncle Colin was holding at the moment of his death and a hospital wristband and blood-stained tissue included in a work entitled *My Abortion*. But it was also a retrospective in a more conventional sense, since it included many of the works that Emin had made up to this point, but, for the most part, in miniature. An exception was the textile elephant that she had sewn together in primary school (page 105), visible in photographs of the installation. But most of her paintings, as we have just seen, no longer existed except here as ghostly images of themselves.

**TE** In *My Major Retrospective* were tiny little images of all those paintings, sewn onto pieces of the last bit of canvas I had and put onto shelves. There was work from 1983 to 1993. Only ten years, but then it seemed like such a long time. Then there was a list of all the artists who had influenced me. People thought it was a conceptual joke. But it wasn't. I was being serious. Those were all my paintings. When I was at Maidstone College of Art, you had to do the photographic course for a month. You learnt how to use the 35-mm camera, the large-format camera, learn the history of photography, learn how to make a pinhole camera and how to print up your own photos and collage photos. After you'd passed that, you could then use any equipment in the photography department, borrow any camera. I said 'Can you really use anything in the department?' They said yes, so I said, 'Right! I'd like to use the technicians.' So whenever I'd done a batch of work, every six weeks or so, I'd get them to photograph it for me.' So I had photographs of all the work from Maidstone. It was clever. It's nice to have a record of your first degree work. Otherwise, who has that, unless their mum and dad have kept it?

At this point, Emin was suffering from physical and psychological blockages that prevented her from painting.

**TE**  For a few years after I left the Royal College of Art in 1989, I didn't paint. I got pregnant just after I graduated. The whole thing was a disaster. Because the smell of turps, oil paint, and linseed oil made me feel sick, I stopped painting. That was it. I couldn't bring myself to paint again for a number of years. I was mostly writing all the time instead. That's when I started the blankets. I've always been able to sew, and I just started sewing words and making films, with words, and neon works, and writing. But no painting.

Then, in 1996, Emin decided to force herself to paint again by putting herself in a position in which she would just *have* to. Just as the destruction of her paintings in the Royal College courtyard looked like a piece of performance art but was in reality an act of genuine desperation, so this decision to paint seemed like a conceptual conceit. In fact, it was completely for real, but this time the effect was not obliteration but creation.

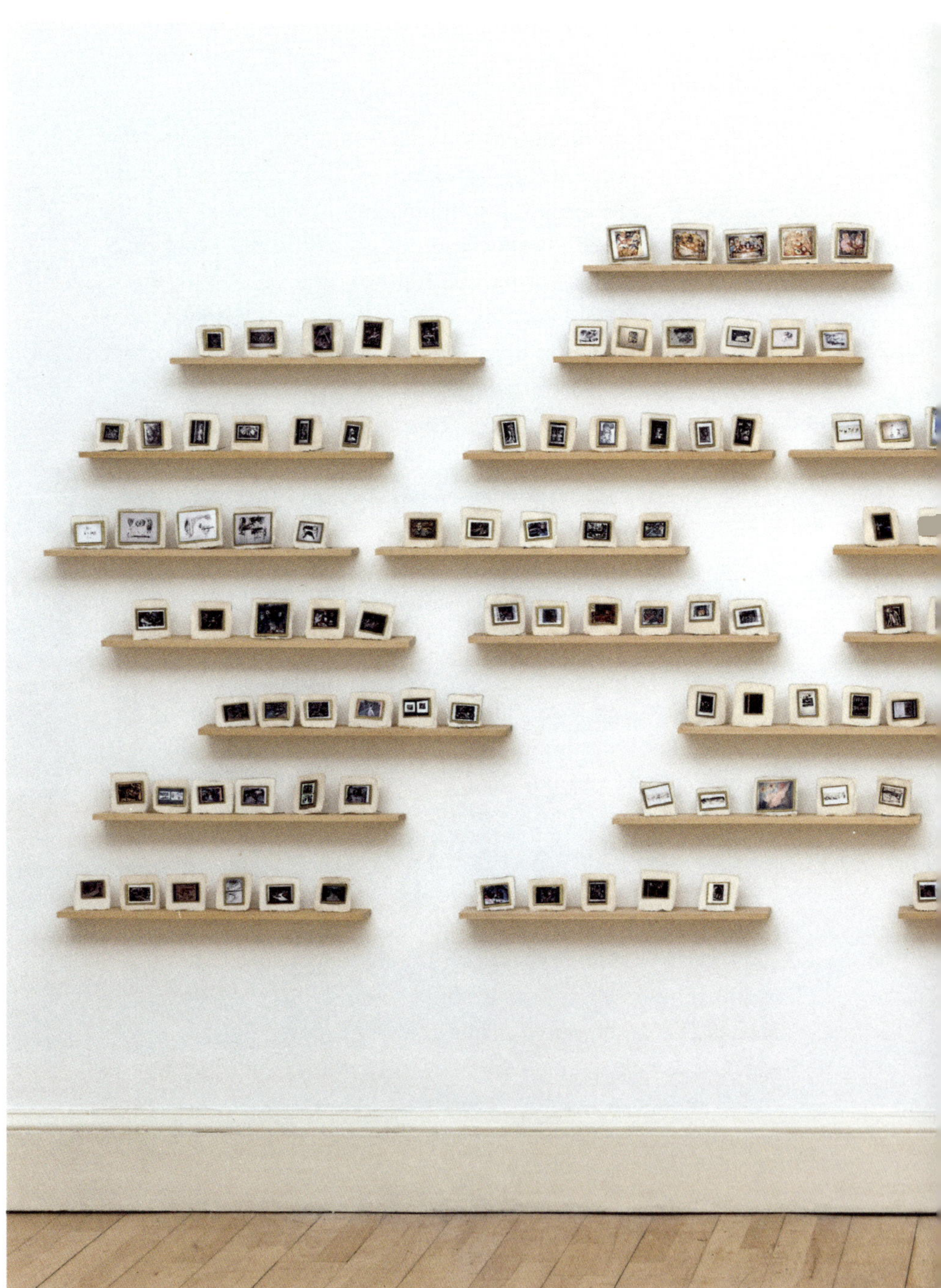

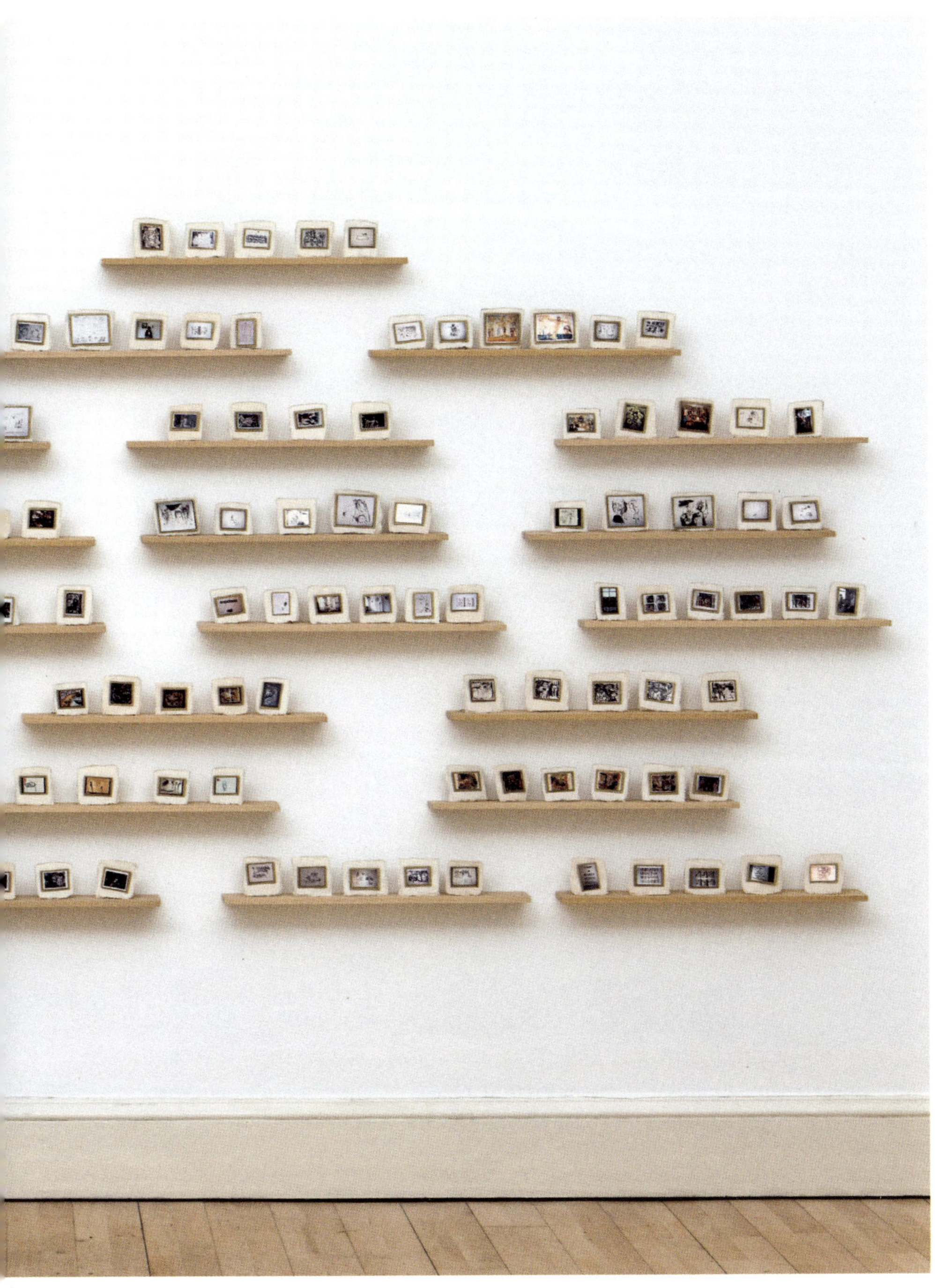

*My Major Retrospective 1963–1993*, reinstalled at the
Scottish National Gallery of Modern Art, Edinburgh, in 2008

13

*Exorcism*

**TE** The next lot of painting I did after the Royal College was
for *The Exorcism of the Last Painting I Ever Made* in 1996.
This work shouldn't really exist, as I planned to burn it in
the snow straight after its execution.

Early in 1996, Emin spent three and a half weeks inside a
specially constructed room in an art gallery in Stockholm. The
dimensions of the space in which she worked, ate, and slept were
roughly four metres by four. She was naked the whole time and
could be observed through fish-eye windows in the walls.

**TE** I did it in Sweden because I thought everyone is
naked there, in saunas and things. No one will care.
It won't be an issue, it won't be the main thing at all.
Which was right in a way. Nobody cared about the
project until now.

What she did inside that wooden room looked like a performance, and it was, of sorts. But it was a performance that was
unscripted, and for real. The exorcism of the title was an
attempt to get rid of – or exorcize – a number of genuine
phobias, which she listed when the work was re-exhibited in
New York in early 2024: 'I absolutely hated my body, hated
to look at it.' And 'I was afraid of the dark.' 'My grandmother
had just died, I was really grieving for her.' In addition, Emin
was 'scared of being asleep'.

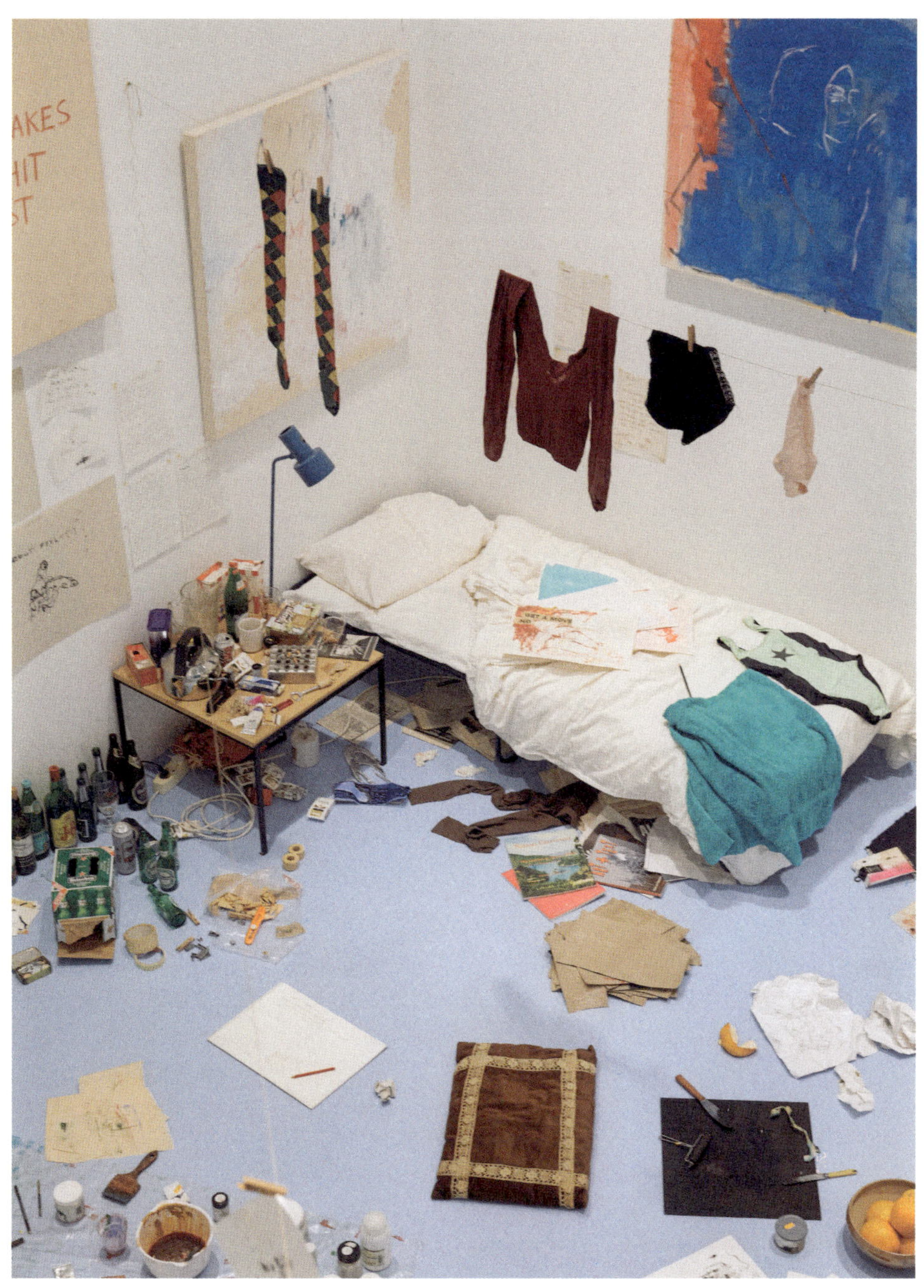

*The Exorcism of the Last Painting I Ever Made*, 1996, recreated in 2023

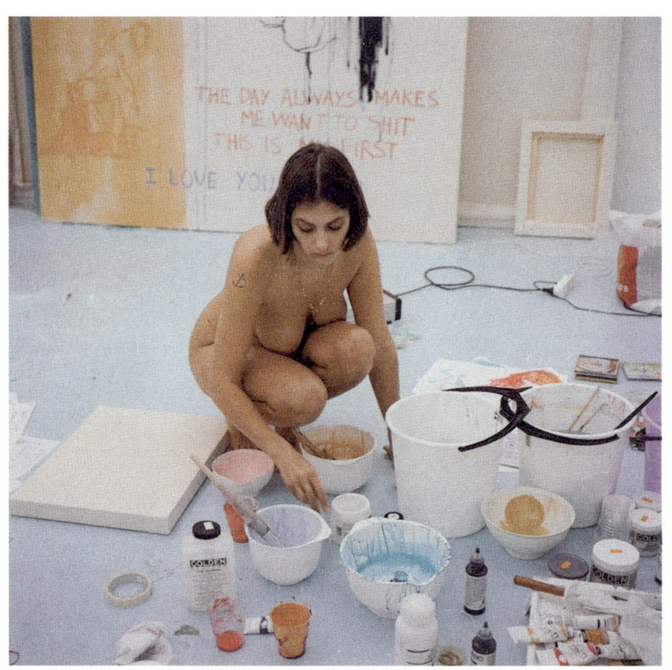


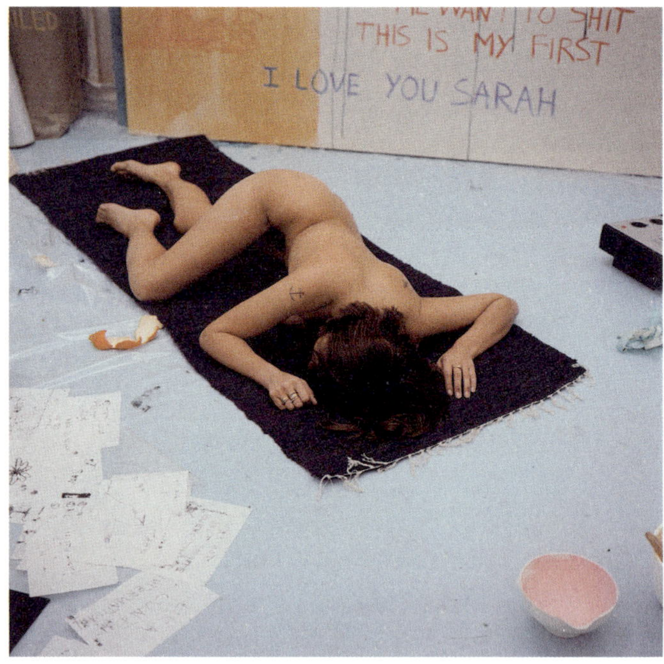


*Life Model Gose Mad I* (top) and *Life Model Gose Mad II*, 1996,
from *The Exorcism of the Last Painting I Ever Made*

I was suffering from guilt and punishing myself,
so I threw myself in a box and gave myself three
and a half weeks to sort it out. And I did.

The most important aim for her was to start painting again.
At that point, she had not done so for five years. So this was self-
administered therapy: an attempt to begin again as a painter.
She said, 'Painting for me was completely moribund: it was
completely bound up with failure. Failure = painting, painting =
failure: two things joined together which I wanted to separate.'
Surprisingly, it worked. The result was a triumph, not least over
herself. Perhaps every painter has to undergo a process of breaking through inner blocks and inhibitions if they are to find true
originality – though not always so publicly and dramatically.

It was about being stripped and it could have been about
being vulnerable but actually it wasn't, it became about
the ego and about the strength of the ego. The strength
of my failures are all amalgamated together.

In retrospect, Emin feels amazed by the whole affair – that
she felt she needed to do it, and that she did it at all:

It was the kind of project you would never do.
It would be incredible if I did it now with my body
at sixty! But if I look back on it, at how my body
was, what *was* my problem, what *was* I feeling, how
demented was I? The whole thing was really strange.

For weeks, she was more exposed than perhaps any painter
has ever been, before or since. Not only was she stripped bare,
literally, the public could also watch her at work through those
fish-eye holes in the walls. Most artists, even extroverts such as

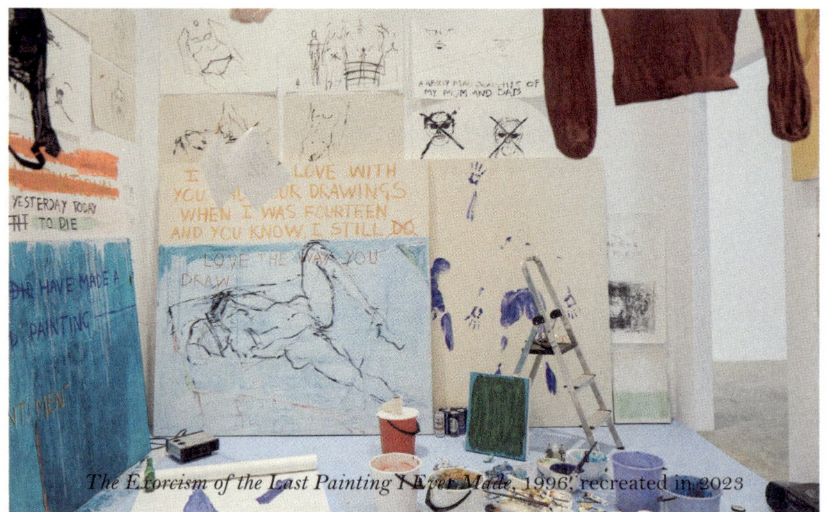



*The Exorcism of the Last Painting I Ever Made*, 1996, recreated in 2023

Robert Rauschenberg, hate to be scrutinized at work, even by a film crew. Those who accept it, as Picasso did for the documentary *Le Mystère Picasso* directed by Henri-Georges Clouzot, tend to put on a contrived performance. But although the photographs of the naked Emin (page 152) *were* a kind of performance – 'I set them up; they're posed' – the paintings were done in earnest.

At the time, this might also have seemed like a conceptual piece, a sort of live version of a Damien Hirst sculpture: an old-style painter in a tank. But for Emin it was absolutely real: it was high-stakes shock therapy. *The Exorcism* was designed to force her to overcome inner resistance and begin painting again. It was an immensely risky endeavour, and at the start it looked as though it was going to fail.

> What happened when I first got there in Sweden was that I couldn't paint. I'd never used acrylic paint before, I'd always used oil paint. Suddenly I had all this acrylic paint and I didn't know how to paint with it. I realised I'd really set myself up. The whole thing was really quite nutty. When I got there, my first reaction was, 'Actually this isn't a very good idea. I want to go home.'



*Exorcism*

Then she was struck by an idea.

I thought, 'I know, I'll go through my idea of art
history.' So then I started going 'Egon Schiele, Pablo
Picasso, Käthe Kollwitz', all my own versions of these
artists. And I just started painting.

During those twenty-five days, she produced, among other
works, twelve paintings, seven body paintings, seventy-nine
works on paper, and seven letters. By doing so in that room,
Emin found her place in the ever-unfolding story of painting.

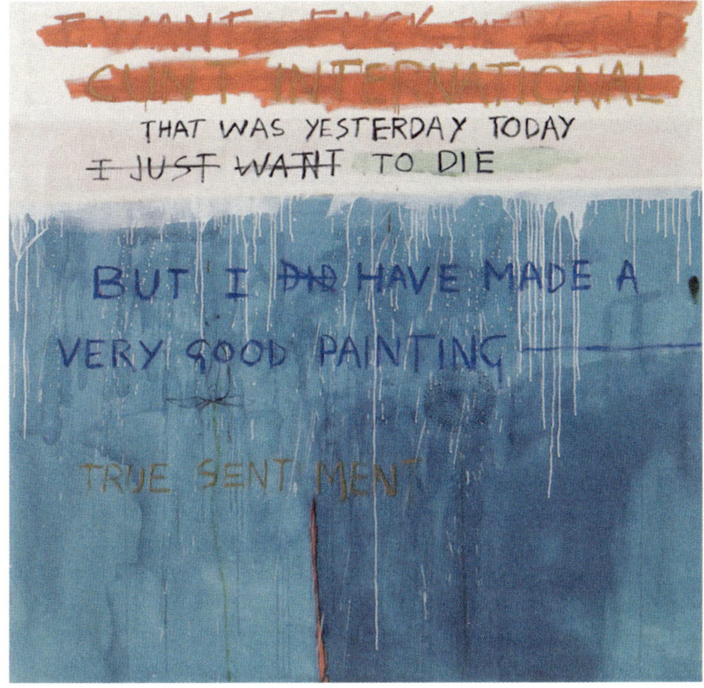


Untitled painting from *The Exorcism of the Last Painting I Ever Made*, 1996

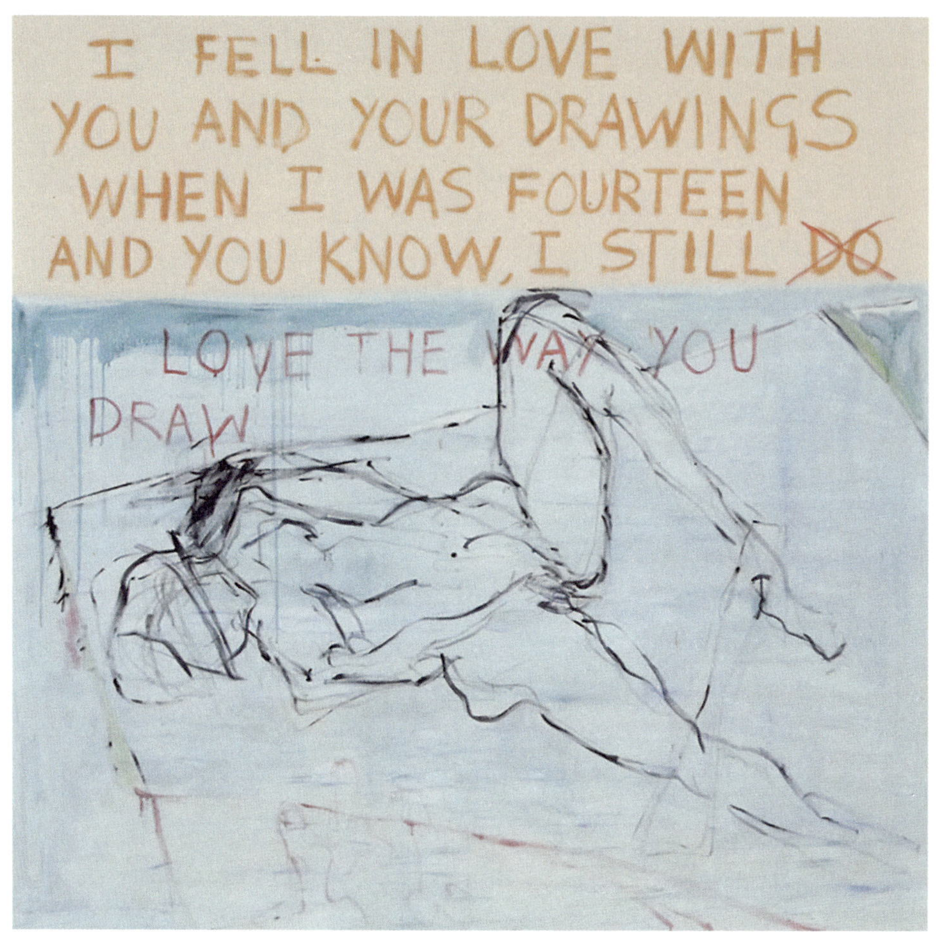


Untitled painting from *The Exorcism of the Last Painting I Ever Made*, 1996

As noted before, most major artists develop their own personalized account of what went on in the past, leading up to what they themselves are doing right now. And she did it in public, with no hiding place in less than a month, by channelling the predecessors she most admired. Above a reclining nude, for example, she wrote a paean to Egon Schiele: 'I fell in love with you and your drawings when I was fourteen and you know, I still do love the way you draw.'



*Exorcism*

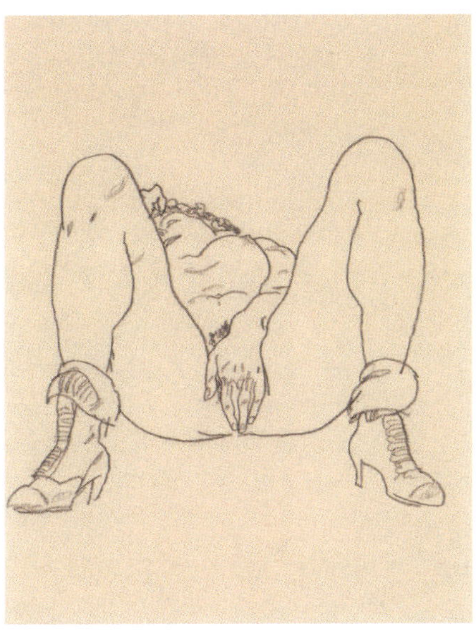

Egon Schiele, *Reclining Nude with Boots*, 1918

One of the more unexpected forerunners whose work she re-enacted inside that box in Stockholm was Yves Klein. The work that interested her was not his abstract monochrome paintings but what he called his *'Anthropometries'*, measures or indexes of humanity. For these, Klein used naked female models as 'human brushes'. Their bodies were coated with International Klein Blue, the intense azure that he had patented. They then followed his instructions to make direct prints of their anatomy on large sheets of paper. These events, like Tracey's *Exorcism*, took place in front of an audience. They dramatized the truth that painting is simultaneously a physical act and a mental process. Michelangelo once wrote that you paint with your mind, not with your hand, which is half true. Of course, in reality you need both (and, David Hockney would add, echoing an old Chinese saying, also the heart). In the *Anthropometries*, Klein himself directed operations while immaculately clad in a suit, representing the controlling intelligence. 'I stayed clean', he explained. 'I no longer dirtied myself with colour, not even

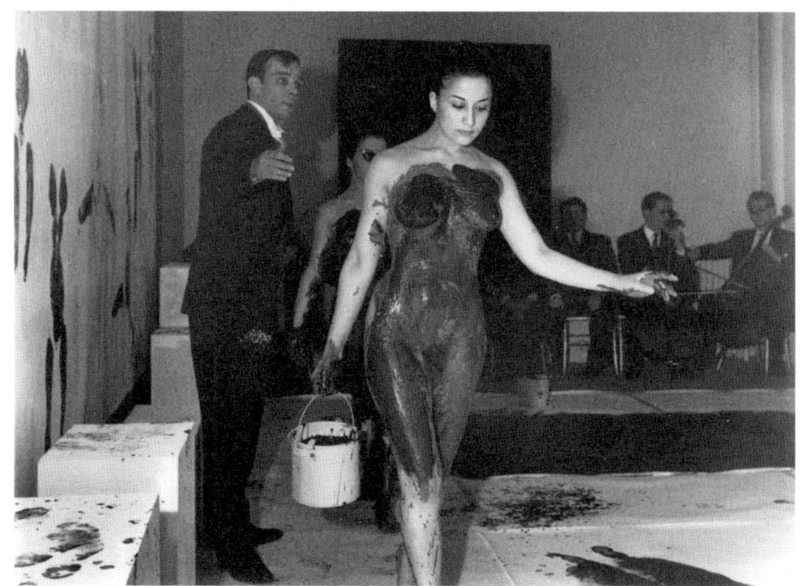

Yves Klein and a model during an *Anthropometrie* performance at the
Galerie internationale d'art contemporain, Paris, 9 March 1960

the tips of my fingers.' Meanwhile, musicians performed his
*Monotone Symphony*, which consisted of a single, high-pitch note
played and then followed by an interval of silence.

In contrast, his models made art in the most direct way possible with no tool except their bodies, which became coloured
a deep blue. It echoed some of the earliest images created by
prehistoric people, who sprayed powdered pigment from their
mouths to make prints of their hands on the walls of caves. But
making those handprints required precision and skill. So did
the movements of Klein's 'living brushes', as Emin pointed out:

> You might think Klein was being sexist by using
> those models like that, but actually it was something
> remarkable. Those women were not 'muses', they
> were dancers, and he was like a choreographer, and
> there was a fantastic skill involved.

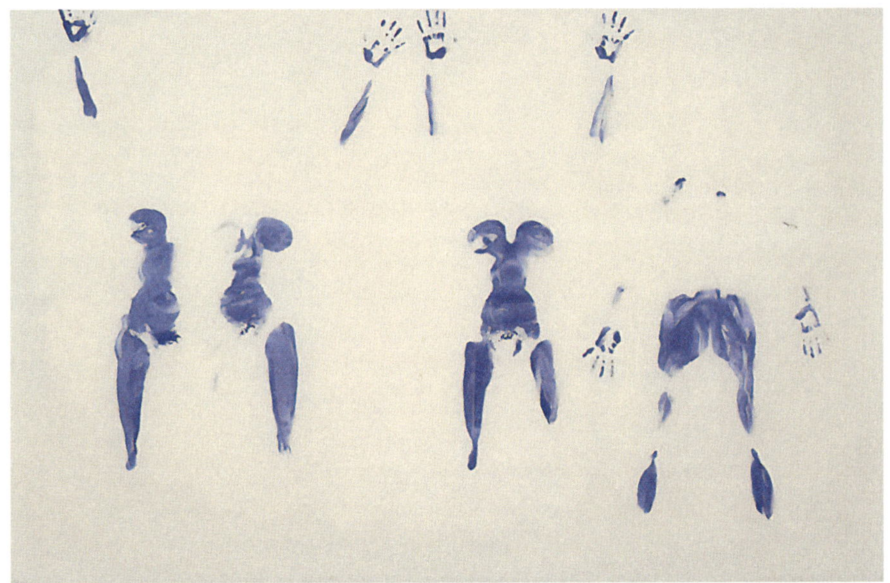

Untitled painting from *The Exorcism of the Last Painting I Ever Made*, 1996

Of course, the process of painting, just like playing the violin or hitting a winning shot at tennis, requires extraordinary levels of muscular control and coordination. A brilliant brush-stroke involves concentration, intuition, decision. What Klein's models were doing – and what every good painter does all the time – is summarized in the line in John Donne's poem *The Progres of the Soule*: 'one might almost say, her body thought'.

One day in that small Swedish box, Emin reenacted Klein's *Anthropometries*. It was a moment that really caught the attention of the spectators, she remembers:

> When I was doing the Yves Klein, and they [the people outside watching through the fish-eye windows] didn't know I was going to do it, I heard a stampede across the gallery and 'She's doing an Yves Klein!' – all these people fighting to get at the portholes.

Emin was not just imitating Klein's works; she was moving the idea forward a stage by combining the roles of Klein himself and his models. She became both controlling artist and 'living brush'. In this, she set the pattern for her painting in the future. In making her *Anthropometries*, and in the other works that she produced in that little cell, she used her body, intelligence, and emotions (Hockney's 'hand, mind, and heart'). That is one reason why, looking back, she sees *The Exorcism* as:

> somehow an important step in my development as
> a painter. What's really clear about this room is that
> you can see how I think as a painter. You don't just
> see the paintings; you see how my mind works. I can
> see my sincerity of how hard I was pushing things.
> And my idea of learning and pushing myself. In three
> and a half weeks, I did all that work. I was thinking
> about the process of painting and being alone. And
> being fragile and being vulnerable and being naked and
> what it meant to lay yourself bare like that as an artist.
> What does it mean? And the mental process of doing
> that. I came out of it a different person.

The most extraordinary aspect of *The Exorcism* is that it succeeded. This was the point at which Emin the painter was reborn. What she is doing now is visibly related to what she did then.

TE I like the paintings in that project. If you saw the paintings on their own, they are like these in the studio now. You'd ask, 'When did you do these?', and I'd say 'Ah, 1996'. They can never be sold separately; *The Exorcism* has to stay as one thing; that's how it's managed to survive really. I was supposed to burn them, but the gallerist didn't let me.

The immolation of the paintings was part of the emotional extremity of the whole project. It was not essential to it, however, and the gallerist was wise and far-sighted enough to prevent the artist from torching all those pictures. In 2024, she posted on Instagram her reflections on what she had done.

The truth was that it was my stupid, pent-up emotional guilt. I punished myself by sacrificing what I loved. Well, twenty-seven years later, I'm painting like a banshee. There's no stopping me. I will paint till I die. My only regret about this project was that I didn't carry on painting from that moment. It took me another five years before I started painting again.

# 14

## *Battling it out*

TE  I remember Nick Serota saying something to me.
There was this timeline thing of artists at the Tate,
and I was placed in the 1990s with the YBAs. There
was a discussion about it, and Nick said, 'I didn't want
you there.' 'Where did you want me?', I asked him.
He said, 'Over here, in the future.'

That was a perceptive remark, although the then director
of Tate would probably have been surprised to be told that in
the 2020s, Emin would be hailed as a masterly painter. But of
course, the past changes as the future unfolds because we are
seeing it from a different place. In 2024, Emin described to an
interviewer how she then saw her career.

> You know how you have these different phases in
> your life? It's only after that you see them clearly.
> Well, when I was young, I was eager and hungry
> and excited and learning at art school. And then
> there was this middle bit. If you're reading this
> really good novel, there's always a bit where they go
> into the cave and it's really dark. My cave was like a
> giant fucking pothole that went underneath the earth.

This is how she now considers the years in which she became
a celebrity and – in the eyes of the media and the public – she
vied with Damien Hirst for the status of the most famous

Young British Artist of them all. Today she considers this to have been a diversion from her proper course.

**TE** I know what kind of artist I am. I did when I was at the Royal College of Art really. That's why I was resistant to a lot of things, I think. But it's easy to be swayed, be moved by things, and if there's enough of that, you just get taken the other way. Now I think things have gone full circle. I'm just doing what I want to do, and that's turning full circle with me as well. That's why it's working. Because it's so sincere and so genuine and so me. I've caught up with myself, and my painting's caught up with me.

As we have just seen, *The Exorcism of the Last Painting I Ever Made* was an exercise intended to jump-start her painting. It was necessary for various reasons, inner and outer, but a crucial factor was that the kind of picture she wanted to create was deeply unfashionable.

**TE** When I stopped painting, I wrote all the time because my painting wasn't accepted. Baselitz, Kiefer, those Expressionist-type people – their work wasn't going anywhere in the late 1980s and 1990s. It wasn't going in museums; it wasn't being hung on walls; it wasn't being taken seriously. Because there was a new trend of what I would call 'highly polished Perspex'. You could polish a piece of Perspex, put it on the wall, give the dimensions, and write a whole thesis about it, saying why it was art. Whereas if you were me and said, 'I'm painting this because this is how I feel', it wouldn't necessarily have been accepted.

After *The Exorcism* in 1996, as Emin recalled at the beginning of this book, she 'sort of painted, but never showed anyone' her paintings. She 'started painting again properly in about 1999, then just carried on painting and painting and painting'. Even so, it was years before she became known as a painter. When I first talked to her in 2005, we chatted for an hour or so without mentioning painting, partly because I had never actually seen one of her pictures. At that date, few people had. A large, heavily illustrated book, *Tracey Emin Works 1963–2006*, which was published the following year, contained no easel paintings at all – though there were numerous drawings and watercolours from the series *After My Abortion*, which she had done in 1990.

One thing that we did discuss was Emin's future ambitions. I asked whether she would like to be the artist representing Britain at the Venice Biennale. The answer was emphatic.

**TE**  A lot of artists would. It's a fantastic thing! When we were there last time, I said to my friends: 'Look, given the choice between being in Venice out of season in a beautiful hotel making love to someone you're mad about or representing Britain at the Biennale, which would you rather have?' They looked at me and said, 'What? Why have you got to make a choice?' And I said, 'Because life's like that.'

Two years later, it came to pass. And as Andrea Rose, the then head of visual arts at the British Council and commissioner of the British Pavilion, explained at the time, it was one of Emin's small paintings in the Royal Academy Summer Show of 2006 that drew her attention. Rose had been a long-term proponent of painting and painters, three of whom had represented Britain in recent Venice Biennales (Leon Kossoff in 1995, Gary Hume in 1999, and Chris Ofili in 2003). She hoped that Emin would produce some canvases for the 2007 edition, and the artist was excited about the idea. Emin rented a new

     *Battling it out*

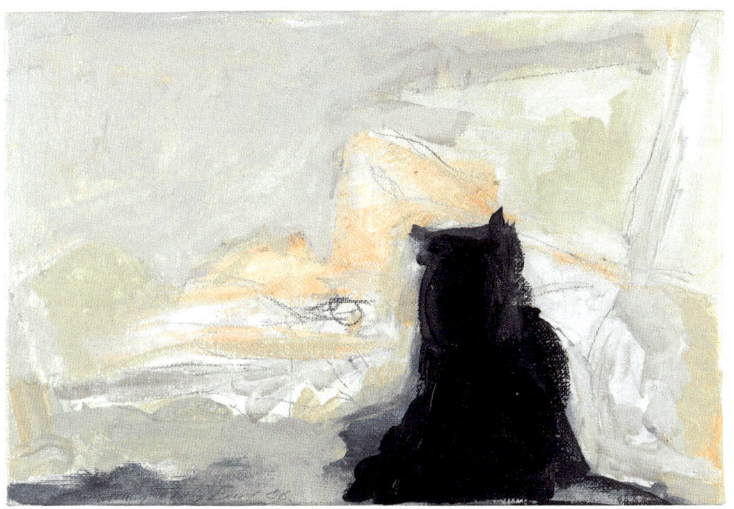

*Cat Watching*, 2006

studio space in which to paint and bought lots of canvas. Then there was a pause. Rose started to worry. She told Lynn Barber that the paintings:

> just didn't seem to be coming. [Emin] started about six, two of which were good, but then she didn't push it – painting needs real concentration. And I was a bit perturbed that [Emin's friend the American painter and film-maker Julian] Schnabel said to her at one point, well, Tracey if you're not enjoying it, it's not you.

A national pavilion at the Venice Biennale is about as prominent – and exposed – a place in which to exhibit as can be imagined. Just about the entire international art world – curators, critics, museum directors, dealers – will be there and will form a lasting impression of an artist based on what they see. It is not surprising that, on top of the anxieties she already felt about painting, the prospect of producing pictures to hang in this particular setting caused an extra layer of inhibition.

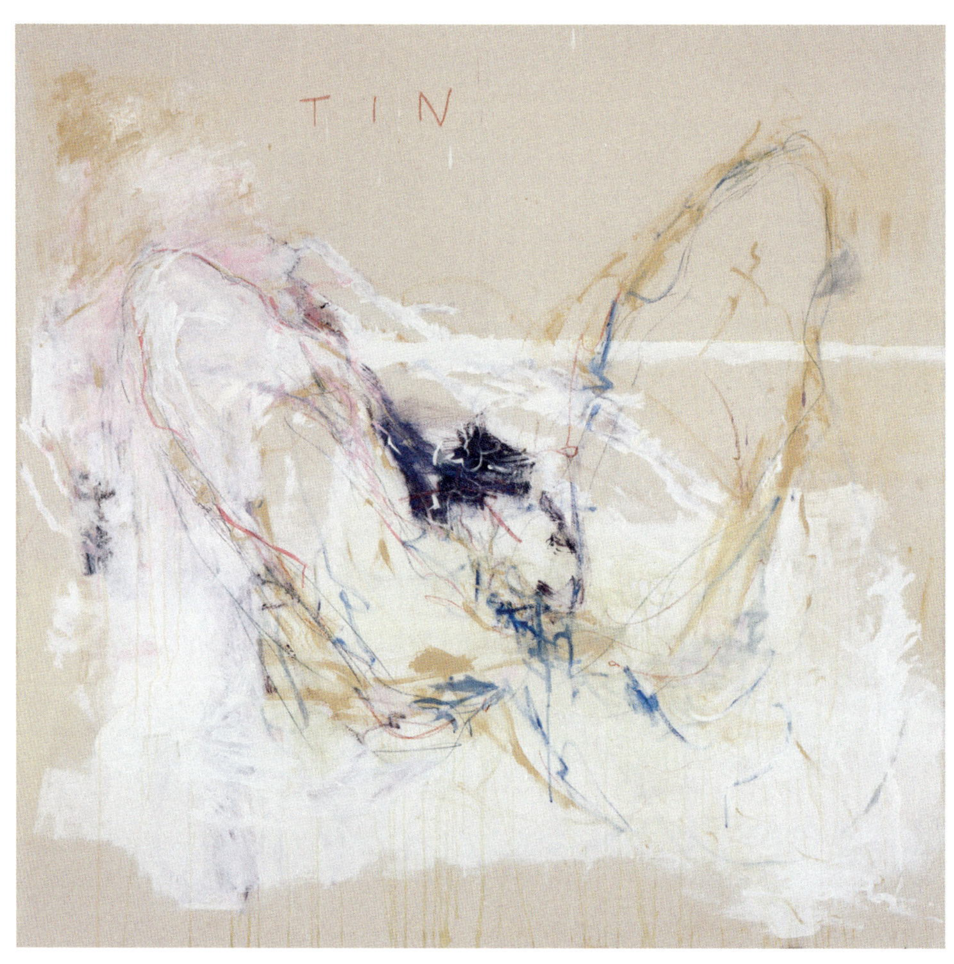


*Ruined,* 2007

Standing in the room of the British Pavilion where her new paintings were hung, the critic Waldemar Januszczak asked her whether the pictures in the exhibition were the ones that had caused her trouble. In answer, she did not just say 'Yes', but made a statement about exactly what had caused those difficulties.

Painting is a lonely, solitary pursuit. It's taken me three years to finish these paintings. I don't want to make drawings in paint; I want to make paintings that exist for themselves.

The effort of making big paintings for Venice, Emin told Rose in the catalogue interview, had been, 'tortuous, absolutely tortuous'. The reason for the difficulty, she explained in the same conversation, was partly the standard she set herself.

Loads of people can make a good painting. So what? There's got to be more to it than that. One of the main things is enthusiasm. I'd rather make something which looks insanely crap but has something for me rather than just make something which is formulaic. I have very – this sounds awful – very low regard for artists who just make formulaic things. I think, you twat, you're obviously really talented, you have all this stuff, why are you just doing the same thing again and again.

With startling honesty, Emin said in that same interview that she knew from some of the big canvases she was working on that in years to come her paintings would be 'really good'. But not, she added, in time for the Venice exhibition.

The Biennale show was a watershed in Emin's career – and a surprise for many who came to the opening. Those familiar with her public image might have expected something outrageous.

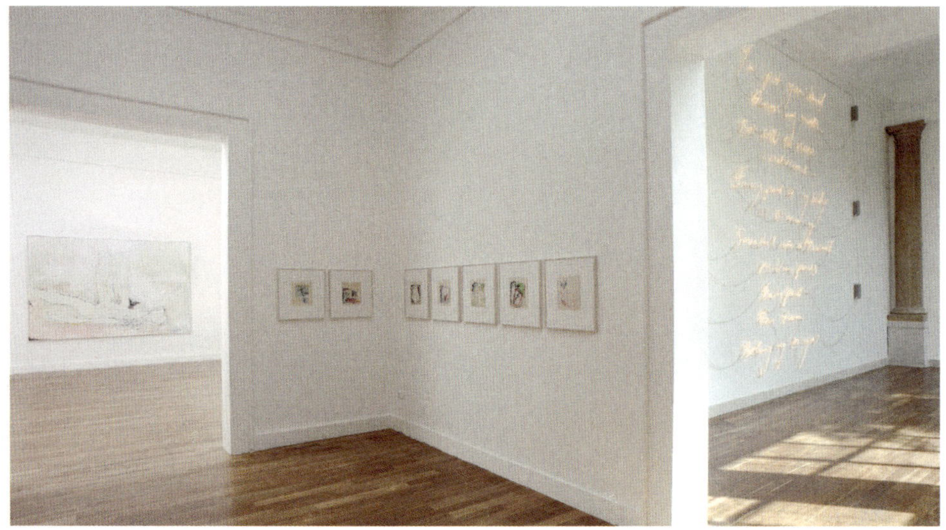

Installation view of Tracey Emin's Venice Biennale exhibition, *Borrowed Light*,
British Pavilion, Giardini della Biennale, Venice, 2007

Playing up to this, she told various people, including her friend
Lynn Barber, interviewing her for the *Guardian*, that she
intended to transform the pavilion into a swimming pool. 'It's
costing £150,000 for the concrete alone, but I'm getting Speedo
to sponsor it and they're paying a million', she fantasized.
'Everyone will be given towels saying "Tracey by Speedo"'.

In reality, she treated the British Pavilion, an Edwardian-era
tearoom in the classical style, with the reverent care with which,
John Ruskin argued, Venice's medieval churches and palaces
should be restored (but generally were not). Rose, who presided
over the British exhibition at many Venice Biennales, felt that
no other artist had been as sensitive to the character of the
pavilion. The interiors were elegantly minimalist in the manner
of the buildings that Emin would later restore in Margate.
The exhibition concentrated on wooden sculptures, drawings,
and watercolours from the *After My Abortion* series and a room
of paintings. However, she was correct in her prediction that it



*Battling it out*

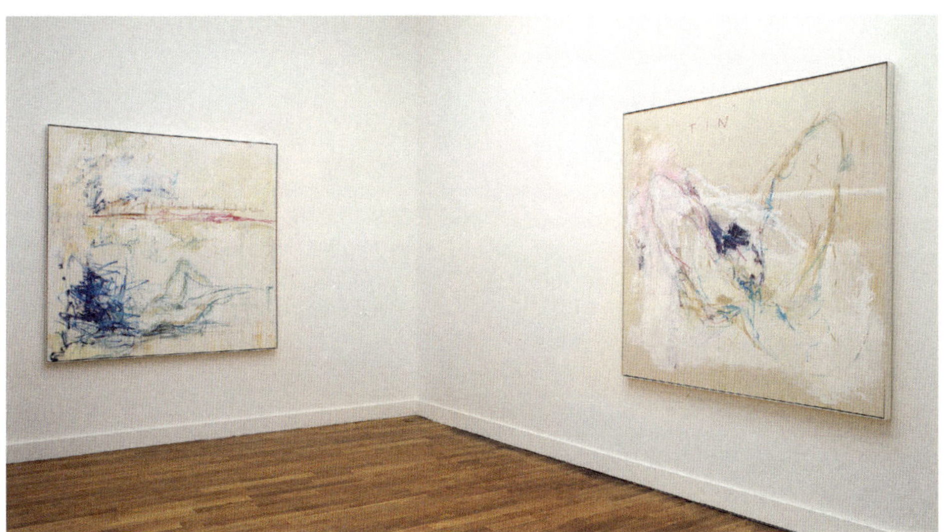

Installation view of *Borrowed Light*

took a while before she fully conquered those big canvases. In fact, it took longer than the three years that she estimated.

**TE**  This sounds really conceited, but David Dawson will back me up, I don't think I wanted any success with my painting until I had conquered it. Until I was able to go into battle with it and *win* on a certain level. Painting for me was over there; it would be something I was scared of. It would intimidate me. Now it doesn't intimidate me. You can see by the way I paint – it's really physical. I just go in there, and the painting doesn't know what's going to happen to it. And it's tchooow! Battle it out!

As I mentioned before, Harry Weller once showed me a film that he had taken on his mobile phone. It documented Emin shouting with rage while attacking one of her canvases with violent, slashing strokes, as if she were taking an axe to a tree.

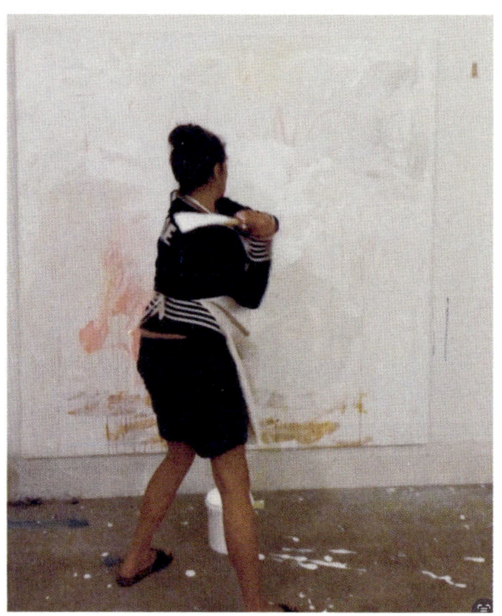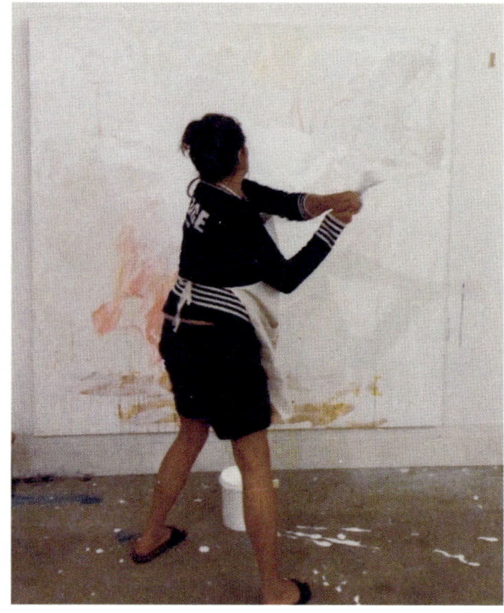

Tracey Emin working on *I Said No*, 2005–15

It concerned a work that she had begun in 2005, before the Venice Biennale, and which reached its final completed stage a decade later. I asked her what had happened.

TE  I had this canvas with a beautiful ground. I'd had it for so-o-o long – but that was when I was still scared of painting. I was really scared of this canvas. What if …? But in the end I thought fuck it! I just got rid of it.

Weller had caught the moment at which she obliterated what had been there before (although some words still show through). But eventually the signs of struggle disappeared. The final work displays none of the frustration that went into making it.

TE  It's a really beautiful painting. It doesn't look aggressive at all. The figure in it is so lovely and gentle and beautiful, and the colours are so dreamy, you would never believe that I was painting it so aggressively.

 *Battling it out*

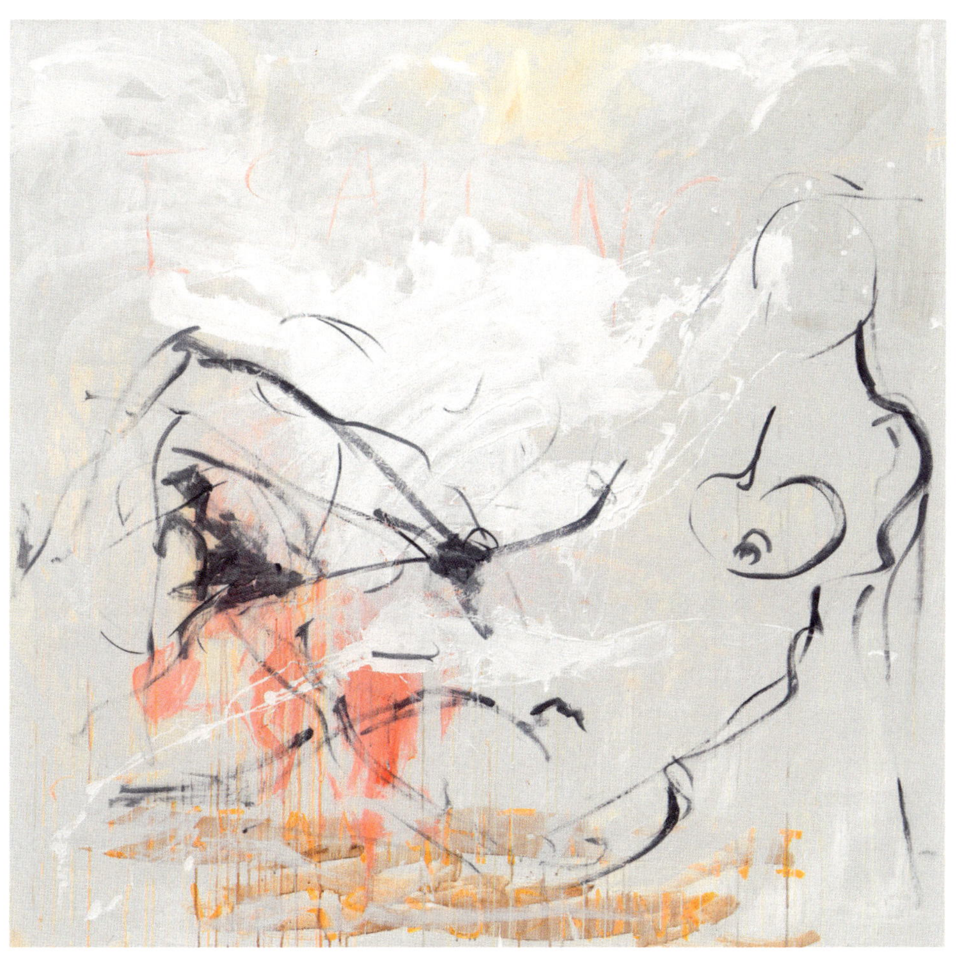

*I Said No, 2005–15*

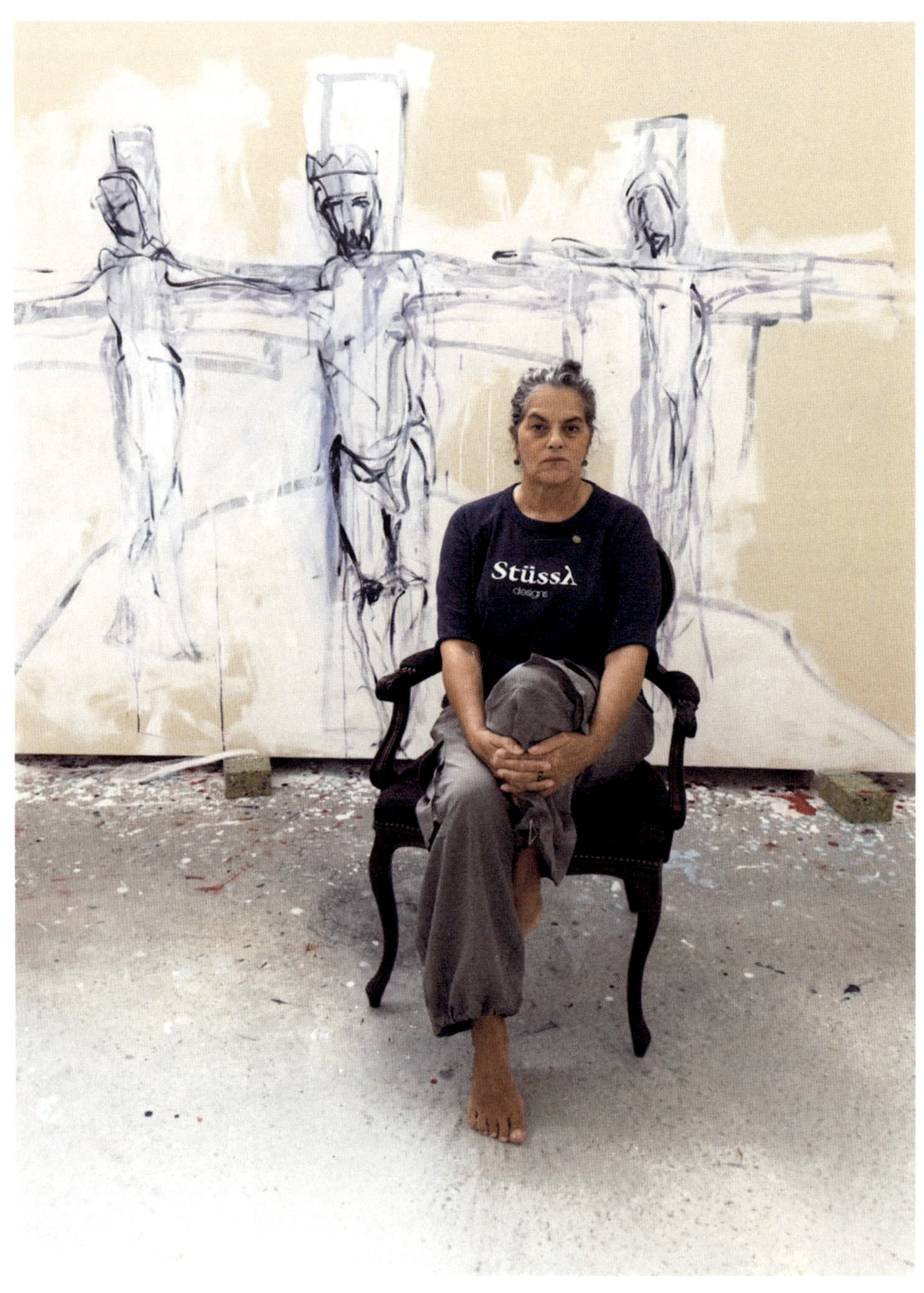

Tracey Emin in her Margate studio, 2025

# 15

## *Painting is like a seance*



**MG** One of my favourite quotations from Vincent van Gogh's letters is about the difficulty of making a good painting, which is no easier than it is 'to find a diamond or a pearl'. It is terribly hard and 'you stake your life' on it. Do you find the same thing?

**TE** Years ago, for me, painting was difficult, difficult, difficult. Then in 2016, when my mum died, I decided that I was going to stop it from being so difficult. I was going make it as easy as possible. So I made a rule that I couldn't repeat an image twice. I could do the same drawing again and again and again, and every drawing would be different. But what I couldn't do was take a drawing and blow it up onto a canvas or make a big drawing and try to produce the same emotion of that moment again. I had to have a brand new moment. At the beginning, I thought, 'I'm going to paint a picture of my mum, or I'm going to do this or I'm going to do that.' Then, after I short while, I never knew what I was doing.

**MG** Robert Rauschenberg said something like that to me once: 'I want to be the first one to not know what I am going to do next. For my own excitement, I would also like to be the first one to be confused and bewildered by what it was I did do next, after I've done it.' Then he added, 'You can't have that with a plan.'

So you're not thinking your paintings out in advance as some artists do – as even Van Gogh did, spontaneous as his pictures look.

TE    I'm not thinking out *anything*. The giant crucifixion in
      the studio at the moment didn't start as a crucifixion at
      all. I did a really bad figure drawing, then drew the hill
      I think, then drew the other figures. To be free in what
      you do, and to have your own language marked out for
      you by what you do, is the greatest freedom. I didn't know
      this was possible when I was younger. I knew that there
      was something there that you went towards as an artist,
      but I didn't know that it was *this*, because you don't know
      about it until you do it.

MG    When did you begin working like this?

TE    A lot of the things I was doing before the cancer were
      good and definitely on their way. I think I *was* doing it,
      but I was frightened that I was doing it. Then after the
      cancer, I stopped being frightened and understood what
      I was doing.
          Painting can be like a seance. You ask, 'Is anybody
      there? Are you friendly? If you are, knock three times.'
      Everybody's really scared. 'Do you know any of us?
      If you do, knock twice.' Then everybody wonders who it
      is. 'Is it my mum? Is it my dad?' 'Are related to anybody
      in the room?' Yes, they are. 'Are you Enver?' No. 'Are you
      Pam?' 'It's my mum! It's my mum!' The paintings are like
      that. First of all, you say 'What have I done? What have
      I done?' Then it gets warmer and warmer and warmer.
      I was talking to a yoga person, and they were claiming
      that the level of meditation in yoga is very different from
      painting. I asked why and they replied, 'In painting you
      have something at the end of it, whereas meditation is
      just being free.' I said, nicely, 'What do you know about
      painting?' He asked me, 'How do you paint?' 'It sometimes

                    *Painting is like a seance*

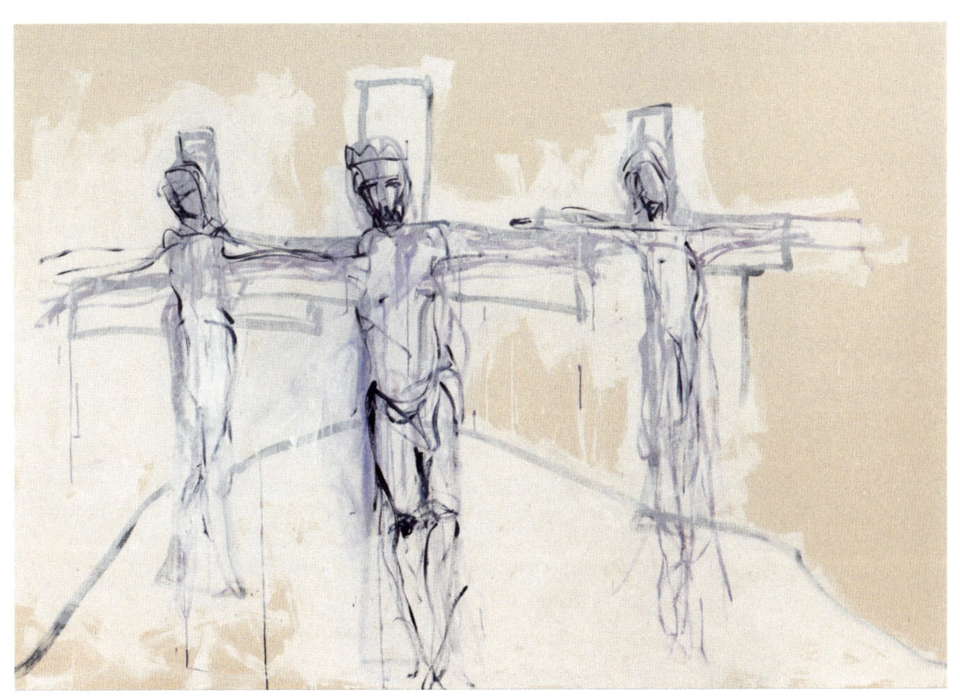

*The Crucifixion, 2025*

comes from behind you and goes *through* you', I answered.
'And as it goes through you – bamm! – you catch it all
on the canvas, there. It can come back again, and it fills
you with this amazing strength of feeling. Or if it doesn't,
it's there on the canvas for everybody to feel. It can
emanate out.' This guy just looked at me; he really wasn't
expecting that. I said, 'It's not about making a *picture*.'

MG I suppose if you want to surprise yourself, you can't do
something you already know. So you've got to find a way
of making something that you *don't* know.

TE Yes. I want a painting to tell me something that I didn't
know before, not something I already knew. The more
surprises I give myself, the more I learn and the more
excited I am by it. Some of my paintings look like things
that we might have seen before, because we know what they
are: two lovers in a bed, blah blah blah. They are classic
images that we know. It's like the words in my neons: you
think you've heard them in a song or read them in a poem
or seen them in a quote from someone. But they're not that;
they are, more or less, a universal thought that goes around
in people's heads, which I put it into words.

But often I manage to make a painting where I've never
seen anything like it before in my life and it just totally
freaks me out. Usually, when I've done that, I want to paint
over it or change it; I find it really unsettling. We have to
hide the painting. But then I will look at it later. Often it
is the breakthrough for something else. On its own, it tells
me something that I never knew before – something big.
It's like going to a soothsayer or tarot reader. You walk
away thinking that that was a load of rubbish. But then
later on, it all comes into fruition. Similarly, you have this



*Painting is like a seance*

painting and you think, 'God, that's really mad, it's awful, it's a bit embarrassing!' Then later on you realize that the reason you feel like that is that you are suffering from being the person responsible for making it, for bringing it into the world, because you've never seen anything like it before. And you have to deal with the consequences of that. It's a hard thing, but fun. It's exciting.

**MG** So the process is a struggle?

**TE** Let me tell you something funny. These days, I can't lift up big canvases like I used to, but often Harry and I will move them across the studio together. Sometimes I think, 'Fucking hell, this one's really heavy!' Then I look and on the side of the canvas there's so much paint, five layers even, because I've painted over it again and again and again and again. Even though they are very thin layers of paint, building up five layers makes it really heavy.

The one with the text you can see is just two layers of paint. If I was to paint over that one, I might draw – I don't know – a woman lying back. Then I might think, 'That's a bit boring.' Or 'I don't like her leg.' So I get rid of the leg. But then I think, 'That's a bit odd because it looks as though her body is twisting.' Next I might paint some blue underneath and think that it looks like the sea. And then I might paint over the woman altogether. So I'd have a canvas that was just blue with the faint words 'I don't want' coming through. That changes everything, because it's like 'I don't want blue, I don't want the sea.' And my mind's working differently from before. My mind goes on a kind of journey. So my painting isn't boring for me. It isn't technical. It's not an exercise. It's just me, moving through the canvas and moving through the ideas.

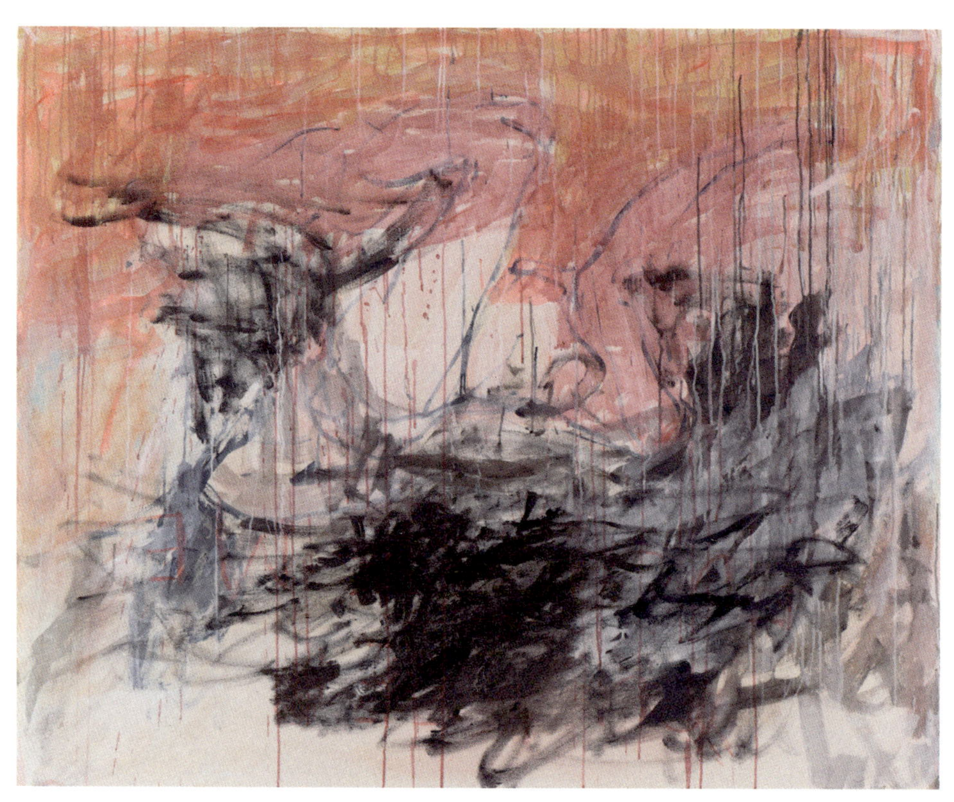

*The Ship*, 2019

**MG** Sometimes you let a ghostly form come through from underneath and that plays a part in the painting.

**TE** There was a painting of a bed with a couple, which was painted quite well, of them embracing. The man was kneeling, holding onto the woman. It was all quite Munch-like. But I didn't like the couple – not because they were too Munch-like, but because they were too real. So I rubbed them out, I thought. But they hadn't gone completely. It looked as if they were in a kind of dust swirl of embracing, like a ghost couple. I thought 'Wow! I really like that. It's exciting!' The whirlwind couple and the bed and wallpaper looked really good, and I kept it like that for about a year. But I didn't like that the man had a really long calf. You could still see it. I realized that he would be very, very tall. I've got nothing against tall men, but it's not my preference. So this long limb irritated me; I couldn't sleep.

The work was almost going off to an exhibition, but I thought, 'No, I can't stand it! I've got to get rid of the long limb! I don't want this man in my picture.' I started getting angry, so I rubbed them both out. So it ended up being this picture of me, half-child, half-woman, with all my guts spilling out with the ghost of my mum looking over me. It had started off as something completely different. It's about the journey of the painting and not being afraid to paint over it and finish it.

**MG** One of your pictures that made a big impression on me was *The Ship*. It had energy, and feeling, and force – but for me it was impossible to say exactly what it was, even whether it was abstract or figurative. When I was working on a book called *How Painting Happens* a couple of years ago, I chose this work to illustrate and write about.

**TE** That painting is the best I've ever done, and probably will ever do. It hangs in my house. It's alchemic and magical – how painting happens and how that happened. It was a shocking happening. Originally, it was a very beautiful painting, a real *Tracey* painting, just so nice. Anyone who likes my paintings would have loved it.

**MG** What was the subject of that original picture that had disappeared?

**TE** It was a painting of a couple. It was a woman being fucked up the arse from behind. She was on all fours and the male figure was behind her. It was such a brilliant painting! It was so good, the colours, everything. I took photos of it and sent them to Harry and a few friends. I was in France on my own, and it was about eleven o'clock at night and I'd had a bottle of wine and I was really happy. So happy with this painting. I sent off the photos and opened up another bottle of wine and I carried on painting. I thought, 'I'll just put a bit more red in, a bit more brown …'. And I completely destroyed this beautiful painting. It was so bad! In the morning, I woke up with a terrible hangover. I was getting messages from Harry, saying 'That painting is brilliant! It's fantastic! Don't touch it! Don't touch it!' It was seven in the morning and I thought, 'Oh my god! What have I done?!' I got up and ran down to my studio, which is down a little hill. And the painting was so-o-o bad! It wasn't there, my beautiful painting – it was horrific.

**MG** Other painters have described that 'aargh moment' when they come back to the studio after working late at night and confront what they have done.

                    *Painting is like a seance*

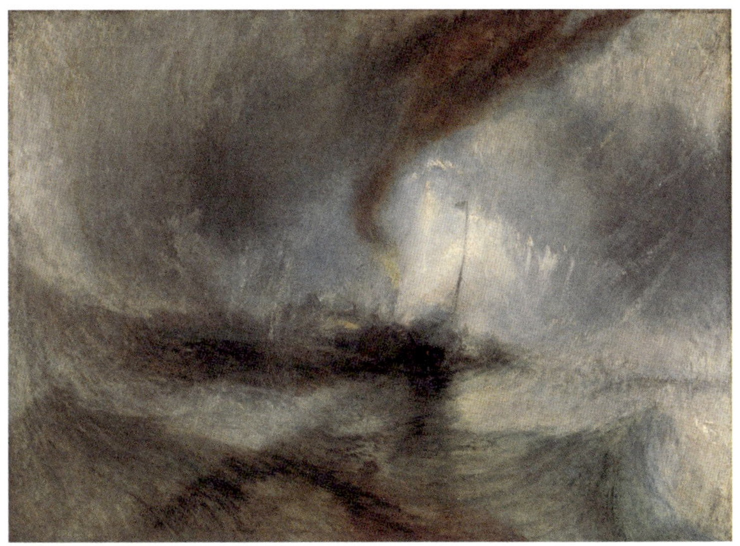

J. M. W. Turner, *Snow Storm: Steam-Boat off a Harbour's Mouth*, exhibited 1842

**TE**  I was so upset that I decided to get rid of the painting altogether and paint it out black, because sometimes if you've got a full, thick painting, you don't want to put white on top of it because it will come through. You put black, or dark, dark grey, on top of it first and then white over that. I turned it upside down because I couldn't stand it – I didn't want the image or the drawing or anything – and started painting it out with black, really aggressively. Then, suddenly, I went back to it and thought, 'Oh my God! It's a tall ship! Oh my God, I love this painting!' It was by this time, like, eight o'clock in the morning. I now have it in my house in London.

**MG**  It's a bit like a Turner, *Snow Storm: Steam-Boat off a Harbour's Mouth*, for example, or *The Fighting Temeraire*.

**TE**  But it's not only a tall ship. It's a ship going through some terrible storm. Or sometimes it's a *giant* cup and saucer.

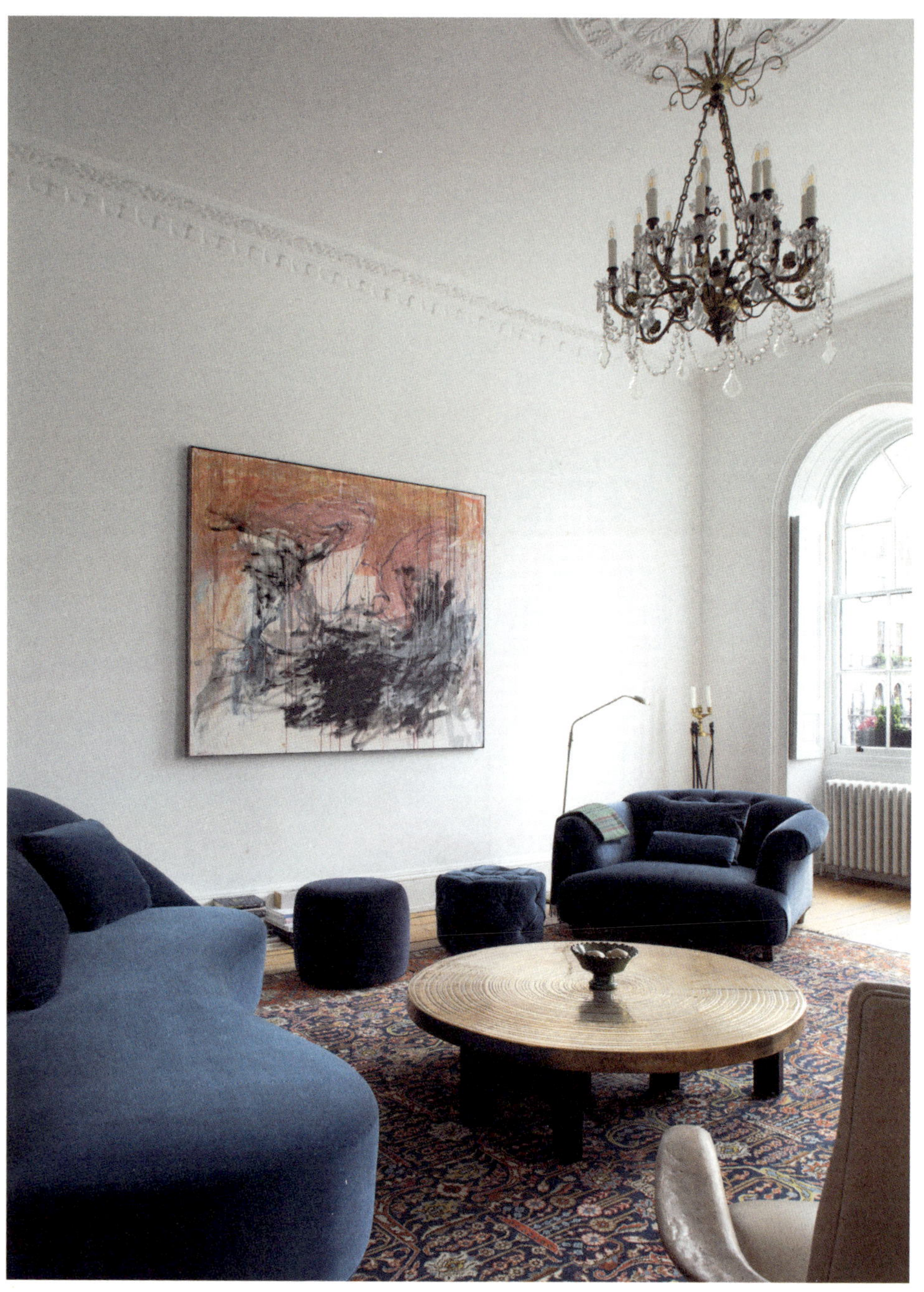

*The Ship*, hanging in Tracey Emin's London home

And also an elk or bull-like creature charging through
the picture. There's something magical and mystical
about it, and so unexpected and so unplanned and so
genuine. It's just about paint. But it's also about a journey,
about a ship going through a storm, which is a great
metaphor for life. I love it because I see all these different
things in it. It's definitely my favourite painting I've done
in the last ten or fifteen years. I know it's good because
when collectors come to my house, they always want to
buy it or museums want to show it – everyone loves it.
I think it's because it's hanging in my house and it's not
available.

**MG** So it's a picture you live with, one of the few, because your
living spaces seem very coolly minimalist.

**TE** There are hardly any paintings hanging in my house.
I find living with art quite difficult. Because my brain
makes lots of images all the time, I see everything in
images. For me, reading a novel is like watching a film.
But I need to be calm all the time, so it's hard for me
to have things everywhere around me. The paintings
in my house I have to more or less 'buy', otherwise
I won't have them. Once I've bought one, and it's in
my head, hanging on my walls, no one else can have it.
Then I will always be responsible for it.

# 16

## *Twilight is the best time*

TE We were going to paint last night. But I didn't know
what I was painting until four o'clock in the morning.
I said to Harry that if I'd started then, I would have
carried on. He said, 'Yes, and we would probably have
been dead by this morning.'

MG There are quite a few painters who prefer to work
by night. Philip Guston was one. He once described
how he crept into his studio the following day with
a feeling of 'My God, did I do that?'

TE I think it's not about the night-time. It's about the
twilight hours, the magic hours when day goes into night,
night goes into day – no man's land, unreal time, dream
time. That's probably the best time to paint. Evening or
very early in the morning would be amazing. I would love,
if I had a choice, to get up at six in the morning, get up
with the day, and paint, spend the afternoon with the cats,
swimming, then go to bed at around seven in the evening.
That would be something to aim for.

So Emin is not exactly a night painter or a day painter as
much as a crepuscular painter. This makes sense because her
paintings are not so much figurative or abstract, which anyway
are categories so clumsy and arbitrary as to be almost useless,
as pictures of emotional and psychological metamorphosis.

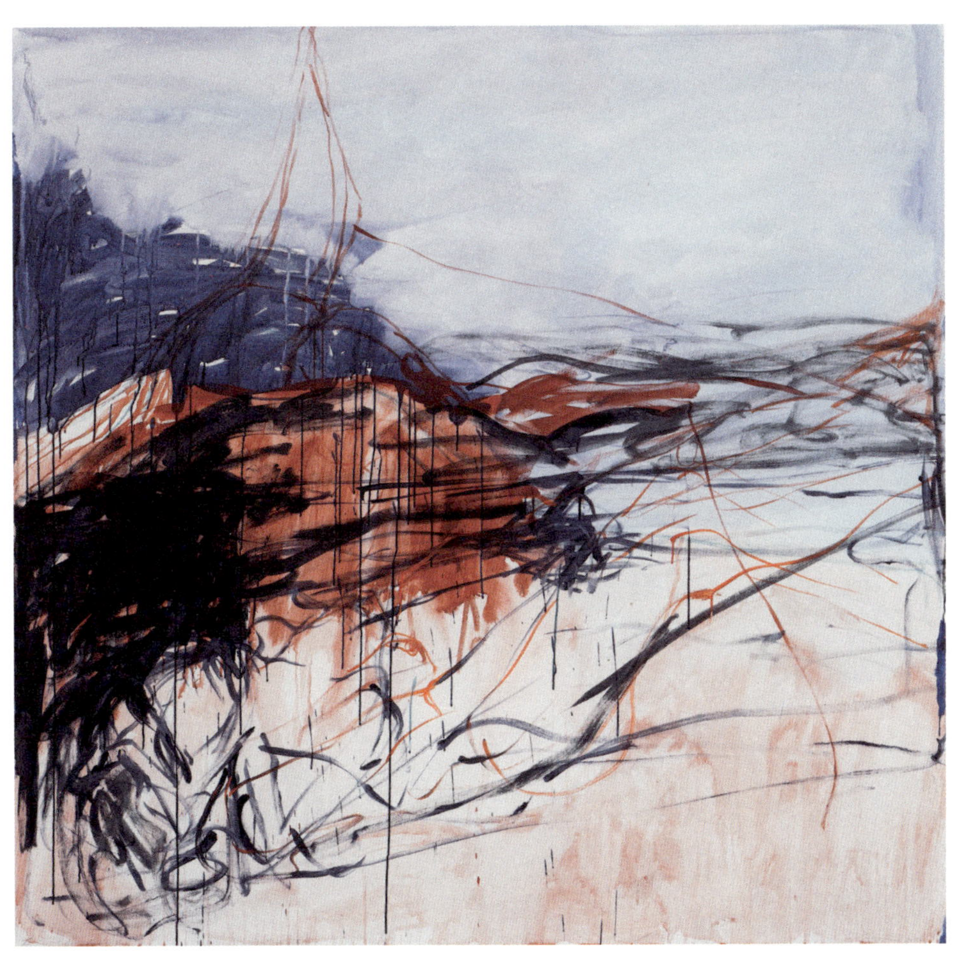

*I Sailed Away from You*, 2024

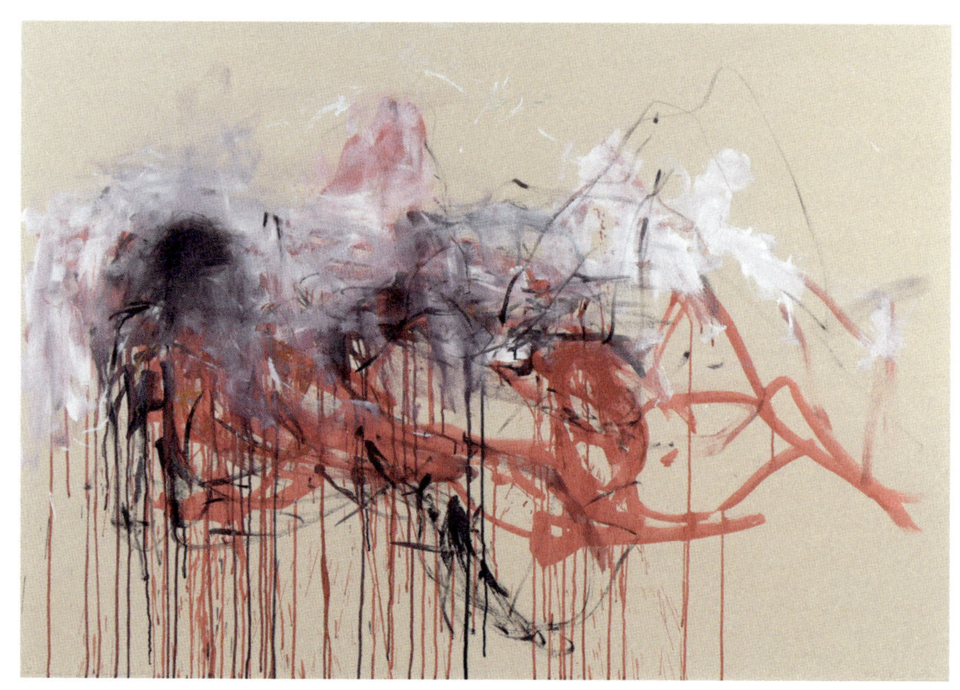

*I will look for you in every sleeping hour*, 2017

You can usually find a human figure or figures – though sometimes, as with *The Ship*, it is not easy – and often other items: a chest of drawers, a carpet, the sea. But also you can frequently make out erasures and half-obliterated forms that dimly come through the paint that has been brushed over them – and that is entirely intentional.

Occasionally, a painting seems to be all about erasures. The title of *I will look for you in every sleeping hour* tells us that it is about dreaming, and there is a slumbering nude somewhere in the mêlée. But it is almost disintegrated into a trio of humps like distant mountains, a tangle of vehement red brushstrokes and a torrent of drips. As Emin says, the painting is about a process of discovery: 'It's just me, moving through the canvas and moving through the ideas.'

She used a Hammer Horror metaphor when she was explaining her creative process to Geordie Greig:

> If it's a full moon and I'm dying to work and it's
> all inside me, it's like a werewolf situation. I've got
> to paint, I'm going mad, and then I go into the studio
> and release myself, and I go crazy, and it's fantastic.
> So it didn't matter that I didn't paint for four or five
> days. Everything stacks up into this amazing force,
> and it comes out!

A great deal of painting has been, partly or completely, the result of a process of discovery. This involves taking advantage of unexpected marks that have appeared on the canvas. Francis Bacon wrote about how 'painting today is pure intuition and luck and taking advantage of what happens when you splash the stuff down'. Bacon, too, spoke of painting as a kind of seance. 'I always think of myself not so much as a painter but as a medium for accident and chance.' But there was a difference.

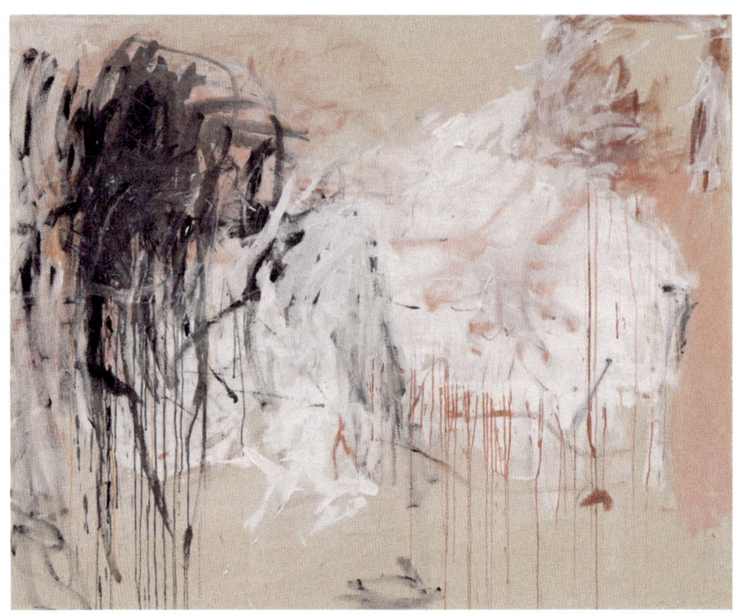

*The Memory of your Birth*, 2018

He was searching – or perhaps 'waiting' is a better word – for a chance configuration of brushstrokes, smear, or splatter that would transmit a more vivid sense of reality than a conventional figurative painting could convey. Emin is after something different. She is not attempting to create a more violent – Bacon's chosen word – sense of experience, but trying to discover how she truly feels. And to do that by finding a form of painting that's never been seen before.

TE  I really believe that it's like all the bad things, tears,
    shit, that fester inside us – they have to come out.
    There's stuff like that with the creative process.
    It's also life affirming; it has this double thing.
    When you completely empty yourself out, it means
    something else has come out – your soul or something
    – and you've got to wait for it to come back again.

   *Twilight is the best time*

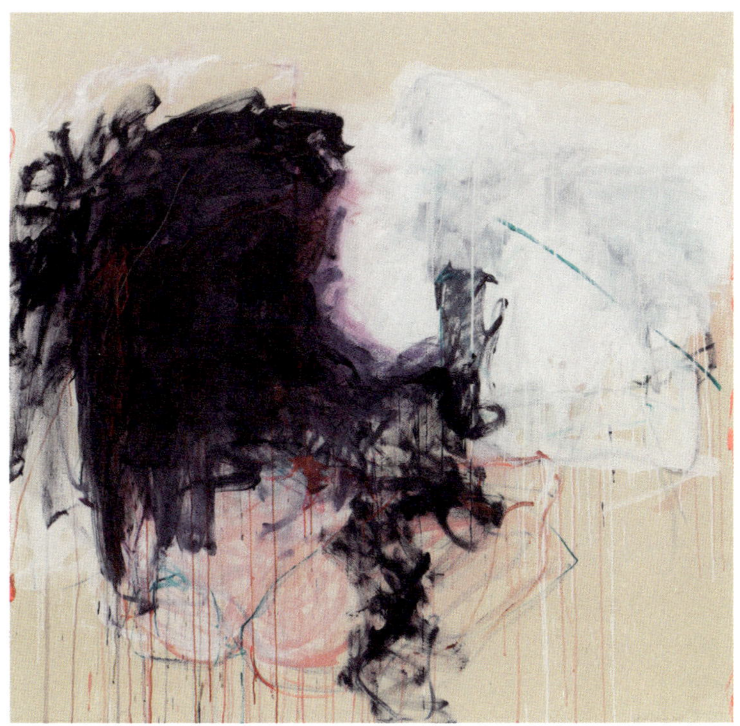

*For one year I wrote to you everyday*, 2018

It would not be wrong to call Emin's approach to painting 'therapeutic', because her work has actually been propelled by one type of treatment. 'Art therapy' is offered to patients with cancer and other physical and mental ailments. According to the website of Cancer Research UK, it can provide emotional support and 'helps people communicate difficult thoughts and feelings'. The website reassuringly adds that 'you don't need to be able to draw or paint'.

At the point Emin started doing this, she had been painting and drawing for many decades. Nonetheless, she found the therapy unblocked something. You might say it helped her move from depicting what she knew to making a picture of what she did not know.

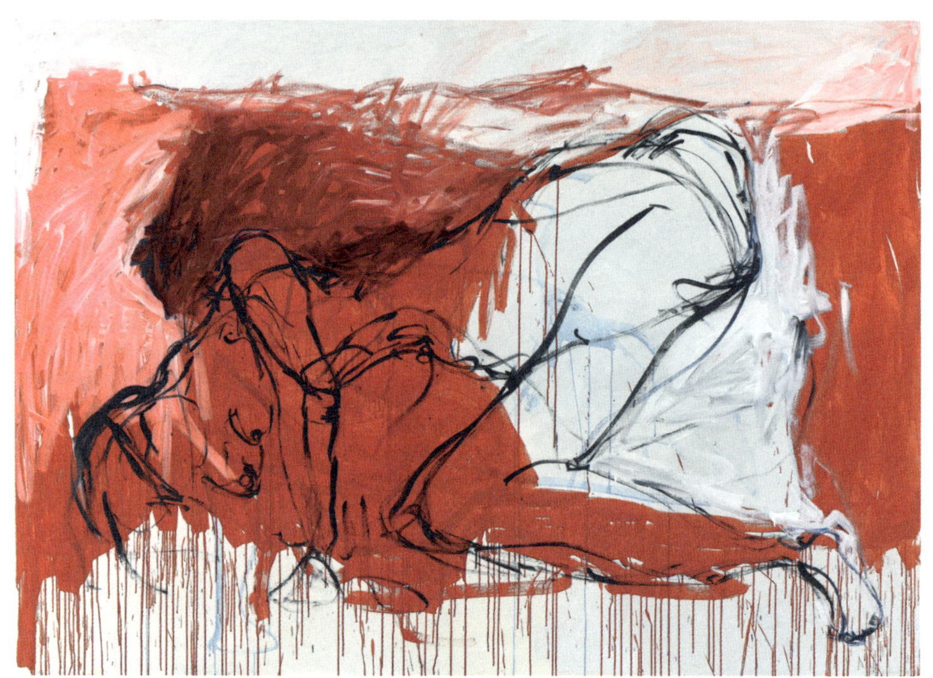

*Yes I miss You, 2023*

**TE** Something that informs my paintings is that I go to a clinic and do basic art therapy. You have three colours: blue, yellow, and red, children's paints with simple brushes on wet paper. When I first started doing it, it was hard for me not to paint what was in my head – a Tracey thing. But I had to open it up because I wanted to see what was going on, psychologically.

When you've done it, you turn the paper upside down or sideways and see what you can see in it. I've done hundreds of them now. It really helped me with my painting. I first started doing it when I hadn't done any work for a while, because I didn't do any for a year with the cancer. When I went to the clinic to try to get better and I did this art therapy, it was so brilliant. It was the first work that I'd done for ages.

I was really enthusiastic. You are only supposed to go
for one session, but I went to every single session I could
and came back with all these things. It's been brilliant for
helping me open up with the big, giant paintings, because
that is about using these swathes of colour and being really
expressive about how I feel – then finding what's inside
the picture and pulling it through.

Trying to paint what you do not know is not such an unusual
ambition. Philip Guston confessed that his pictures baffled him.
'That's all I'm painting for.' Frank Auerbach observed that it
seemed to him that, 'One of the differences between interesting
and uninteresting painters is that interesting painters start
anew every time they paint a picture.' Of course, Emin's pictures aren't much like Bacon's, Guston's, or Auerbach's. Echoing
Tolstoy, one might say that every uninteresting painter tends
to be uninteresting in the same way (because they are just
making pictures like other pictures), but every interesting
painter is interesting in a different way. That, indeed, is part of
what makes them interesting.

It follows that, even if their appearance comes as a surprise
to her, Emin's pictures look the way they are because she is the
person she is. But that, of course, is an extremely complicated
matter and is not made simpler by the fact that she has lived a
good deal of her life in public, has been the subject of uncount-
able interviews, blogs, television programmes, and newspaper
columns. Even in the case of such an individual, precisely what
makes them their own unique person remains difficult, perhaps
impossible, to disentangle. There are many onion skins to separate when it comes to identity. It involves biology, biography,
education, and geography (to mention only a few ingredients),
and all of those may affect how a painting looks. In considering
Emin's art, we could start with her DNA.

# 17

## *Ancestry*

Emin is not alone in being fascinated by her own heredity. Tracing one's family tree is a widespread pastime. But is it any more than that? She believes it is.

**TE** Does it matter where we come from? Yes, it does! Because it's our imprint, our body memory. We carry that with us and it's part of what we do. Once, I would not have looked back; it would have seemed a bit embarrassing. But now it's not embarrassing – it's brilliant, it's fun, it's exciting, it's another dimension to me in my life. This is the difference now. I don't care if people think it's stupid. I enjoy it, I love it. I think that that is about having confidence in your own personal knowledge and journey. If I've come back to Margate to open up myself to all these things about myself, I think that's a nice thing. It's not something to be ashamed of – it's to celebrate, really.

To an artist whose work is so intimately concerned with her own feelings, memories, and experiences, obviously who she is, physically, matters (so does who she *thinks* she is). Emin's genetic identity, like everyone's – but perhaps a bit more than most people's – is a palimpsest. That is, it is like a document in which text after text has been written each on top of the one beneath. Or, to change the metaphor, like a canvas on which image has been painted over image, but thinly, so the ghosts of the earlier shapes still can be seen. Recently, she had her DNA analysed.

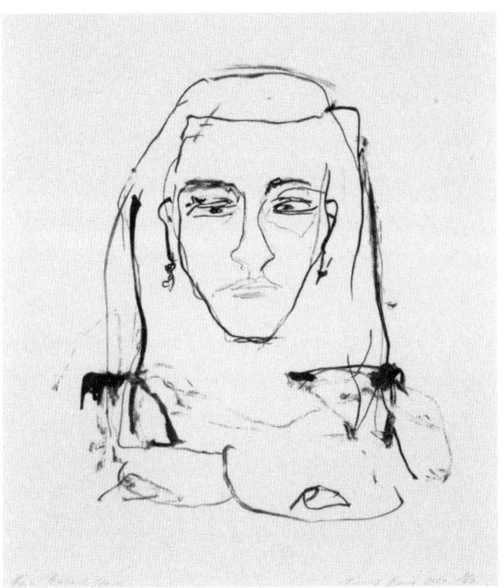

*Four Thousand Years, 2020*

**TE** It was 39% English, 33% Cypriot, and 17% Nilotic, from the Nile valley. Then 3% Welsh, 7% Scottish, and 1% from the Arab peninsula. So I'm a nearly a fifth Nubian from my great-grandfather. The 33% from Cyprus really surprised me. My dad is from Cyprus, but my great-grandfather was from Nubia – he was kidnapped by the Ottoman empire when he was thirteen or something, and was a slave until he was given some sheep and his freedom around 1900.

Nubia, roughly speaking, occupied the territory of modern Sudan and part of southern Egypt. It was the location of the ancient Kingdom of Kush and was also ruled by Egypt, Hellenistic Greek rulers, and Rome. The Egyptian link seems important to Emin. Harry Weller told me that, 'For at least fifteen years, she's had a bust of Nefertiti on the chest of drawers beside her bed.' When asked which person from the ancient world she would like to meet, Emin replied, 'Definitely somebody ancient Egyptian. Either Nefertiti or one of the Cleopatras.'

She told Waldemar Januszczak that one of the faces on the bronze doors of the National Portrait Gallery was based on her Nubian ancestor. But, as she explained, each face began as herself, but then – as Januszczak put it – 'she let her imagination drift and flow' and 'they turned into other beings and became themselves'. So the faces incised on those doors both are and are not self-portraits; indeed, they not really any sort of portrait. Or rather, they represent Emin's novel take on the question of what a portrait might be, as she said at the time.

There are so many different ways to experience somebody's, let's say, soul. It doesn't just have to be what they look like. It could be a portrait of the soul, for example. It could be lots of different things. So I think [the National Portrait Gallery] wanted it to move away from the idea of classic portraiture. To stretch it.

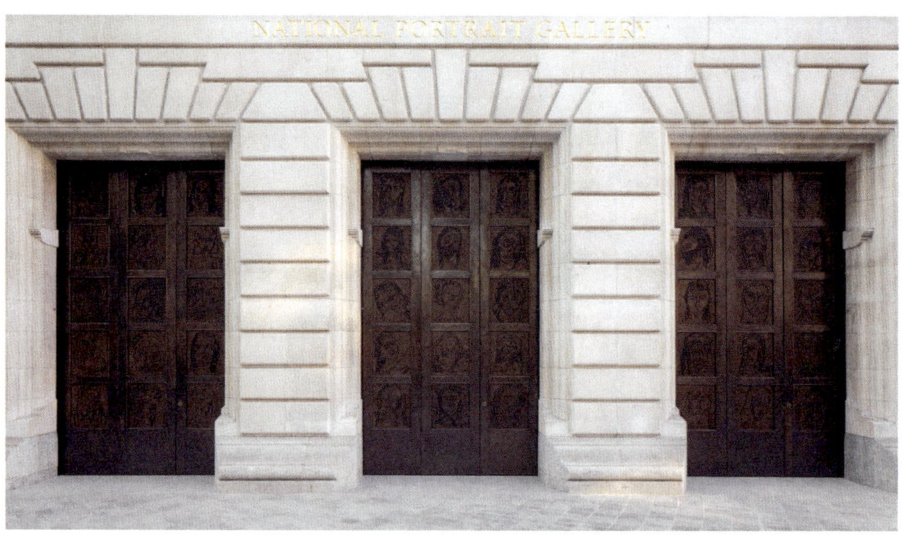

*The Doors*, National Portrait Gallery, London, 2023

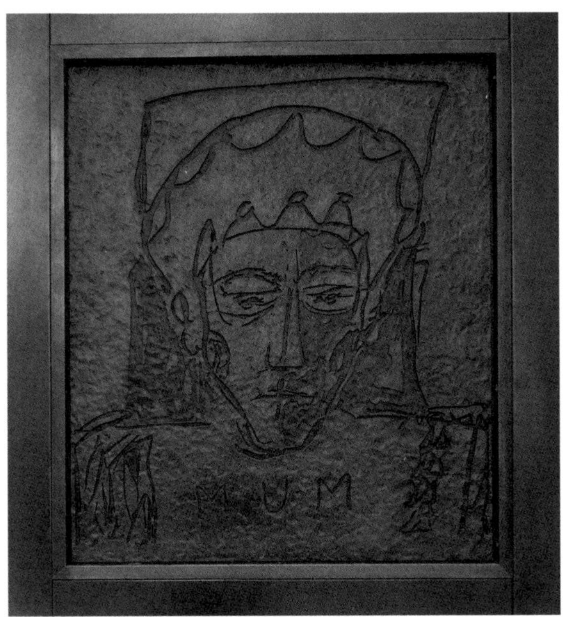

Detail of *The Doors*, 2023

You could think of the faces on those panels as being an anthology of all the different aspects that the personality of one person might have. The multitude of ingredients in Emin's genetic make-up is at the least a metaphor for that complexity.

TE  That 17% means that my dad's grandfather's wife was also Nubian, and my grandfather was Nubian but brought up in Cyprus. But whomever they married on the other side must have had old Cypriot blood. In Cyprus, there were Venetians, Normans, a mixture! It is such a strategic island.

In addition, Cyprus is also the island of Venus, the 'Cyprian goddess', who emerged, the ancient Greeks believed, from the sea nearby and was carried to its shores. The tragic drama of Othello and Desdemona, with its blend of fatal passion, jealousy, and love, was set on the island. It was also one of

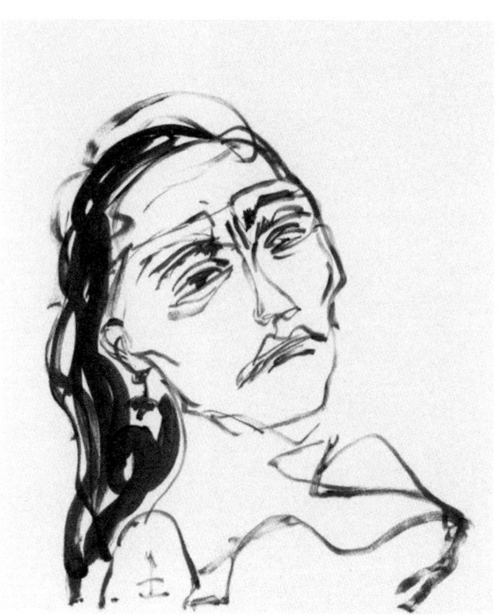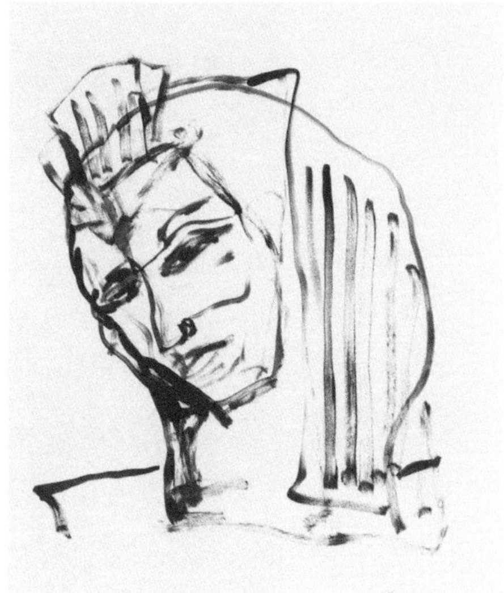

Original drawings for *The Doors*, 2023

first destinations of mass sun-and-Mediterranean-sea tourism, booming in the 1960s and 1970s. Indeed, it was one of the places that reduced Margate to a semi-derelict ghost of its former self in the years that followed. Cyprus has been where the Greek world meets Turkey, the Levant, and North Africa. It was ruled by French Crusaders and the Emperor of Byzantium. It has been a colony of Venice and part of the Ottoman empire. If you wanted to find a place that best represented the patchwork of Mediterranean culture, Cyprus would be a good choice.

Of course, the Cypriot and Nubian portion of Emin's DNA represents only a part of her genetic make-up. To be precise, exactly fifty per cent, but the other half, which was derived from the British Isles, also contained a surprise. When she participated in the BBC programme *Who Do You Think You Are?*, Emin was delighted to discover that her mother's side of the family were Travellers. 'I'm gypsy, I'm beautiful, proper gypsy! They were tent-dwelling, travelling, broom-making, creative people. Brilliant, brilliant, brilliant!' Her great-grandfather on



*Ancestry*

her mother's side, Henry Hodgkins, was sent to reform school for stealing as a teenager. That was in the East End of London, but *his* father Joseph, Emin's great-great-grandfather, was born in rural Warwickshire, where his family made brooms for a living. She declared herself 'thrilled' to discover that her forebears were skilled in a craft and delighted by this lineage. Earlier she had muttered, 'If I discover I'm from a simple, ordinary family from suburbia, I'll slit my wrists.'

Does this cellular coding really have any effect on whom we are? The truth is that no one can say with any confidence. But it seems plausible that we are the product of a complex interaction between our physical make-up and the world around us, each affecting the other, setting up feedback loops, with an element of random accident thrown in.

Emin's Nubian ancestry certainly had a decisive effect on her life in one respect: without it, she would not exist at all. Her father, Enver, was in the process of emigrating from Cyprus to Australia when he stopped in London in 1948 to change ships. At that point, she wrote, 'he received an urgent telegram from his cousins who had already settled in Melbourne saying "ENVER DONT COME, YOU WON'T GET IN YOUR SKIN IS TOO DARK".' So he stayed in Britain instead. That same year, he met Emin's mother, Pamela Cashin, at Heathrow airport. 'They were both married but they started an insane affair', she wrote, 'Totally out of control'. The result, some years later, was Tracey and her twin brother Paul.

Now, after surviving cancer, she told Greig, 'Like all great Egyptians, Nubians, I am set to make my own tomb.' Her monument is not to be a pyramid, looming over Margate, but the TKE Studios and other projects by which she is transforming and embellishing the town in which she grew up and where she had formative, often traumatic experiences. 'Love of art is number one for me', she has said. 'Number two is love of Margate.'

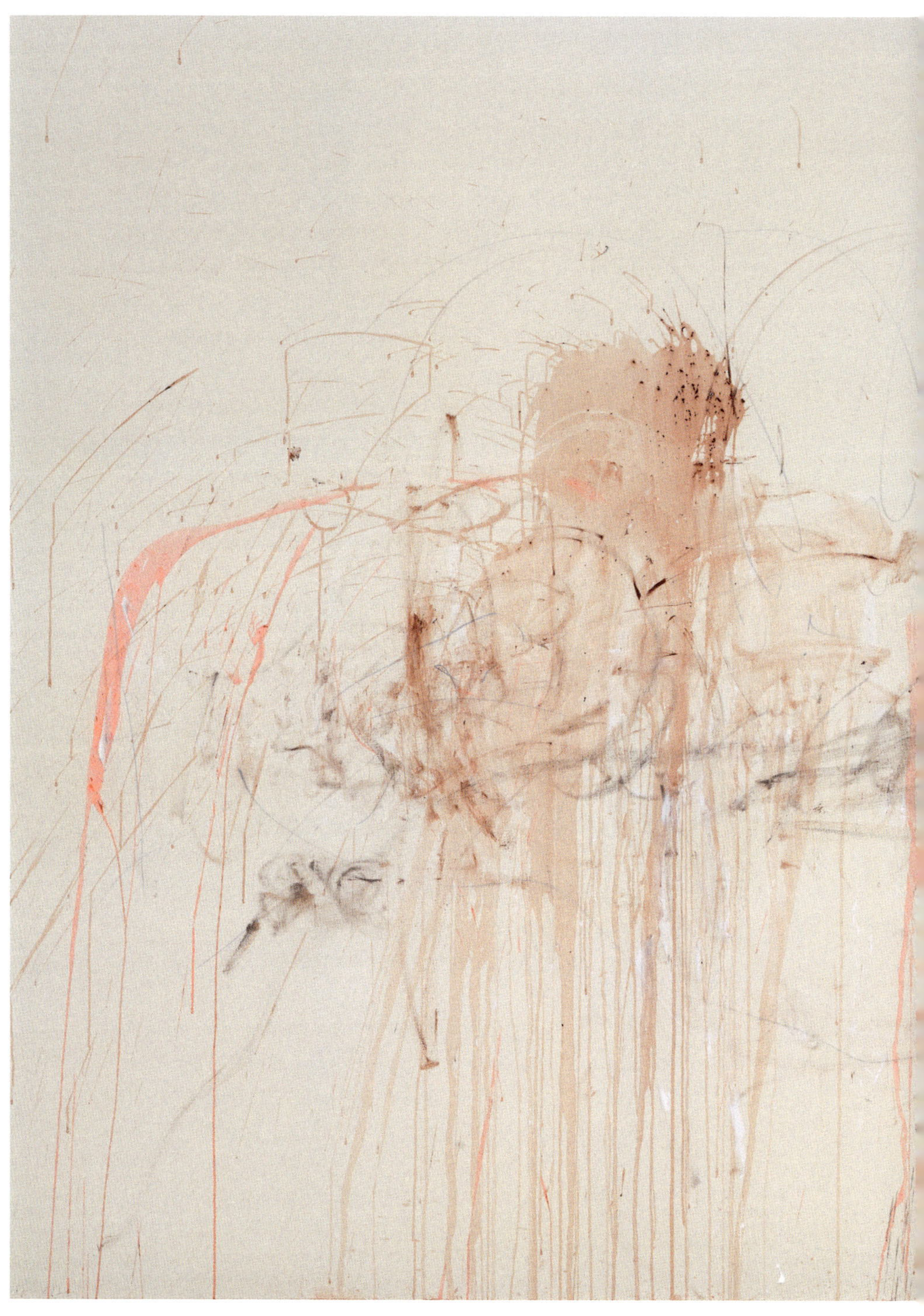

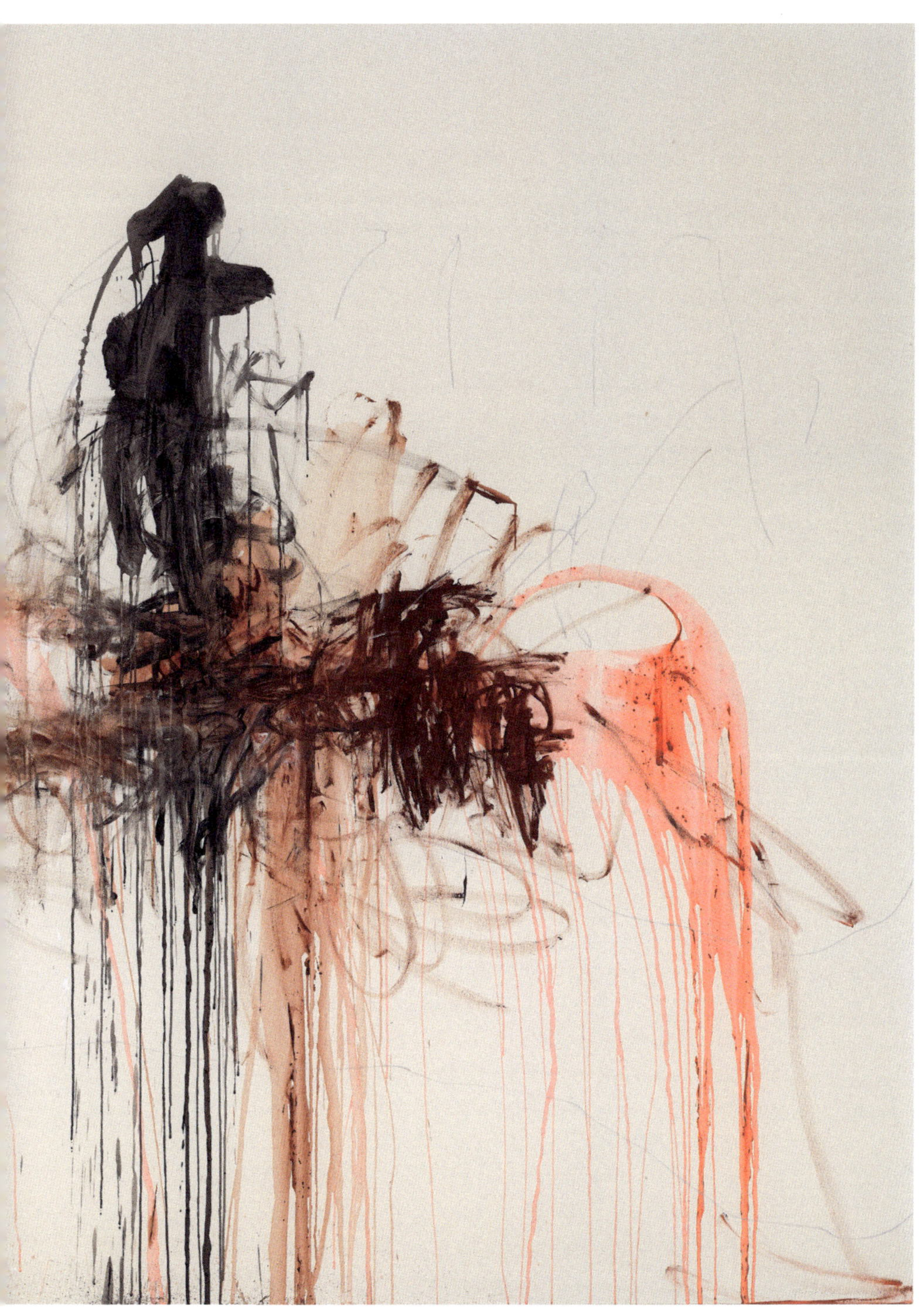

*Mum & Dad*, 2017

# 18

## *Byzantium, Turkey, and Islamic patterns*

'Everyone focuses on the sexuality of my work', Emin once complained. 'Why doesn't anyone ask me about my thoughts on God?' Eventually someone did – and the answer was illuminating. In 2006, Tate invited young artists to ask Emin questions. One sixteen-year-old named Hannah asked, 'Do you think religion is still relevant to modern art?' To which, perhaps surprisingly, since not much contemporary art could be described as 'religious', Emin answered, 'Yes'. Then she qualified that response: 'Not necessarily religion but faith. When I was younger I was very, very influenced by Byzantine frescos and early Renaissance religious painting.'

She explained more when talking with me in her studio on Maundy Thursday, the day before Good Friday, in 2025.

**TE** I wanted to paint this weekend because it's crucifix time. Normally, it takes me into the studio for the whole of Easter. I painted one in January and then started another, so I don't need to paint one this Easter. But perhaps I will.

I'm not religious at all, but Easter to me is the most important time. I really love Easter Sunday. I love everything it represents, *everything*. It's a really good metaphor for life. Like the phoenix rising from the flames, taking your own power, rising from the dead, nothing is the end, there is always hope, there is always more. This isn't *it*. All of that is really my philosophy of life. It's what keeps me going.

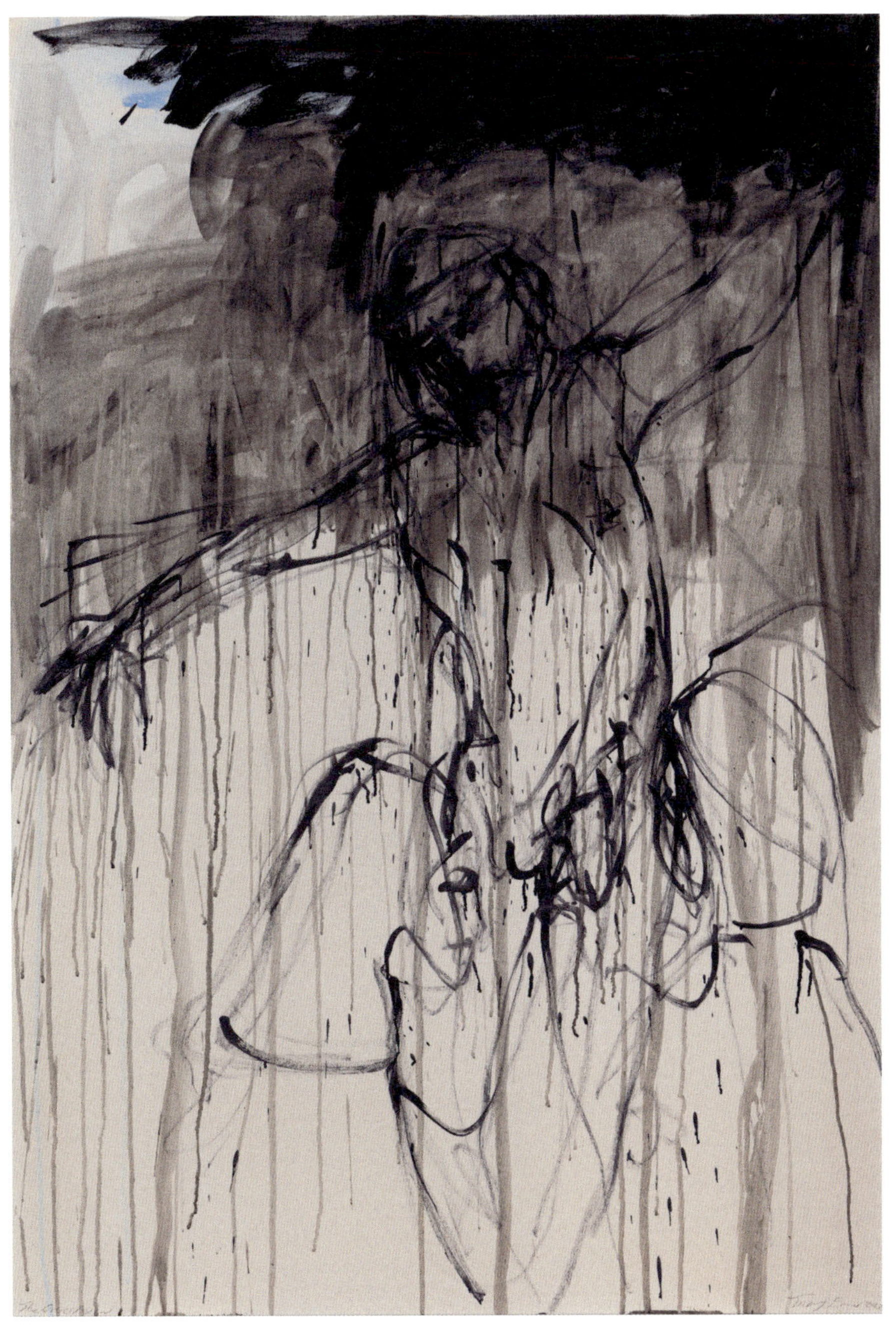

*The Crucifixion, 2022*

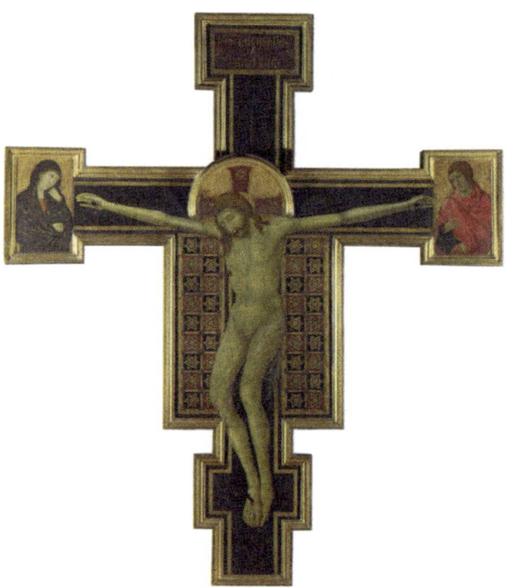

Segna di Bonaventura, *Crucifix, c.* 1310–15

I also love the idea of the sacrifice that's not a loss, that it becomes something greater. It's like when something bad happens to you and then you spin it around – like my cancer. It's one of the best things that ever happened to me. Not in terms of my body, but me in general.

David Dawson always says to people, 'The reason why Tracey can paint and draw is that she used to hang out at the National Gallery.' When I was at the Royal College, I lived at Elephant & Castle, so I got the bus to Westminster then the tube to South Ken, because the college was next to the V&A. Sometimes I would just stay on the bus and get off at Trafalgar Square and go to the National Gallery. It opened at nine in the morning, and all the medieval and early Renaissance paintings were in the basement. I used to go there and look at these Giotto-period paintings, then I turned round and went out through the doors and I would imagine my own paintings next. I would go, 'Urrm, urrm, the day I can imagine my paintings there is the day I'll know I'm OK.'



*Byzantium, Turkey, and Islamic patterns*

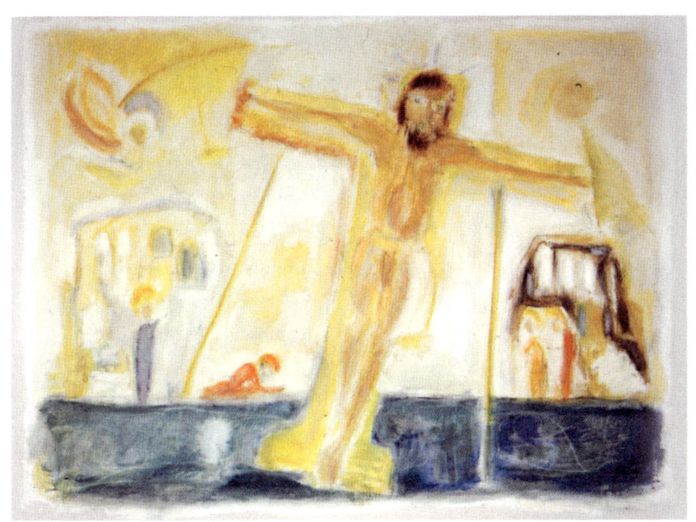

*Disposition of Christ*, 1990

I used to go round the museum doing lots of drawings of the paintings, but in my own style, my own weird way. By the time I left the Royal College, I was doing very, very big oil paintings that were like a cross between Byzantine frescoes and Edvard Munchs. Before that, I was really influenced by Turkish miniature painting. Nearly all the works I did in the first year were like miniature paintings. All the works I did in the second year were large oil paintings that went from a semi-Expressionist style to this Byzantine-Munch-y-fresco thing.

One quality shared by fourteenth-century Italian paintings and the work of Munch is that they are both concerned with the intense expression of feeling. 'Naturalism' and 'realism' do not come into it (and, as Hockney has pointed out, 'reality is a slippery concept'; it is impossible to describe, let alone define, just what it is). The images that Emin found on the lower floor of the National Gallery were not intended to be placed in a museum, an institution that did not exist when they were made.

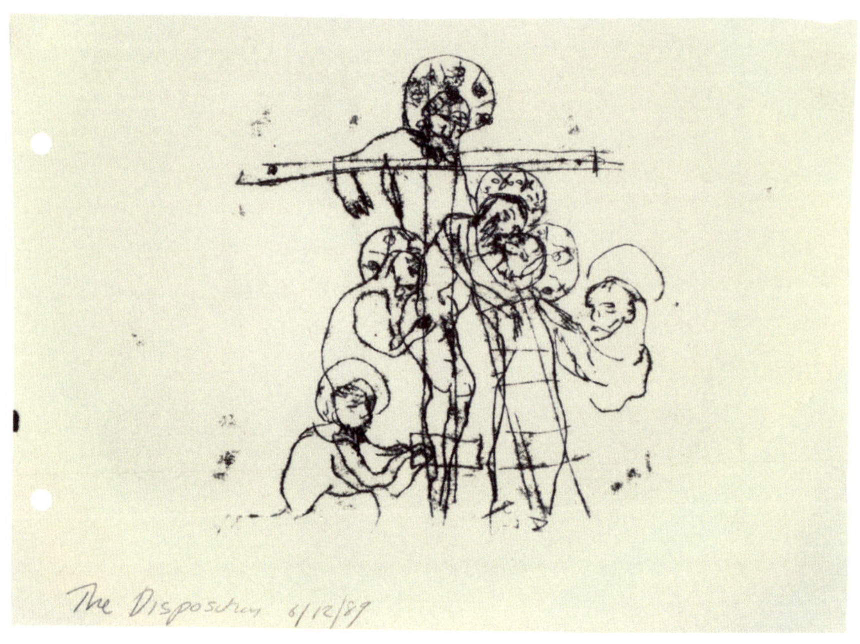


*The Disposition,* 1989

The idea of 'art' would have been barely comprehensible to Cimabue or Duccio. Their religious pictures – and a large majority of surviving paintings from medieval Italy are concerned with religion – were intended as a focus for deep beliefs about life and faith. They were to be placed on altars, hung in churches, set on private shrines. People prayed, wept, and confessed before them; mass was said, the dead were buried, marriages took place, sermons were given about sin, hope, love, death, resurrection, and charity in front of them.

The same is true of most fifteenth-century Flemish art, about which Emin has also talked. One of her 'touchstones' among old master paintings, Jonathan Jones pointed out, is Rogier van der Weyden's *Deposition from the Cross* (*c.* 1435), which must be among the most moving expressions of sorrow ever created. Talking in 2020 to Alison Cole about this work,



*Byzantium, Turkey, and Islamic patterns*

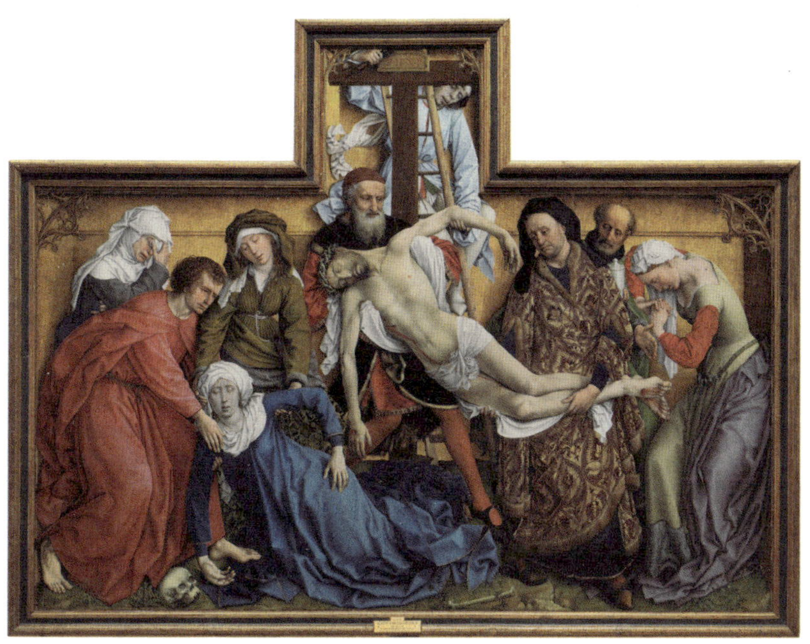

Rogier van der Weyden, *Deposition from the Cross*, *c.* 1435

Emin explained that she loved it for reasons to do with its deep emotion. And it was when she herself was in an emotional crisis that she first 'really paid attention' to this masterpiece. 'I was in Hong Kong alone in my hotel room … crying…. I couldn't stop crying…. I find it passionate … sensual … erotic … the way they are all connected, all touching, all touched by the death of Christ.' She also noted 'the colours, the clothes and textures', all of which added up to a sort of visual oxymoron: 'there is an opulence through death'. Most of all, she loved 'the way Mary's body emulates that of Christ', the way 'they are together' in posture, her body rhyming with his. Of course, her own painting is given its charge by the emotional force of shapes, colours, and textures.

*

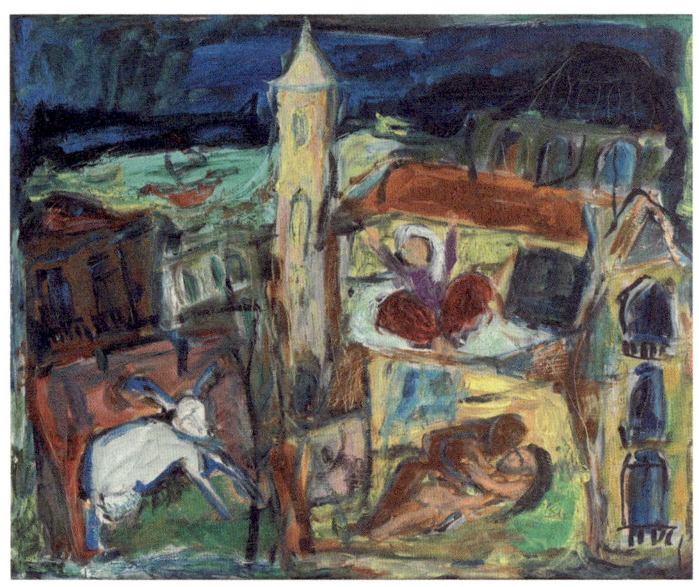

*Istanbul*, 1988

In 1986–7, between her time at Maidstone College of Art and beginning to study at the Royal College, Emin went to Turkey for 'quite a few months', during which she had her tempestuous affair with a married fisherman eighteen years her senior. On her return, she published her first book, *Six Turkish Tales*, a sequence of stories about her journey to see her father. It begins with a quotation from Munch: 'I shouldn't like to be without suffering. How much of my art I owe to suffering.'

Around this time, she made some watercolours of Turkish interiors and a vivacious Paul Klee-like townscape entitled *Istanbul*. Possibly this visit was the origin of her interest in Byzantine painting and Turkish miniatures. Istanbul, previously Constantinople, contains many of the greatest works of Byzantine art (which was the point of departure for those gold-ground Renaissance paintings in the National Gallery). Ottoman miniature painting, an unexpected ingredient in Emin's artistic mix, would have been a source for an element that has returned

     *Byzantium, Turkey, and Islamic patterns*

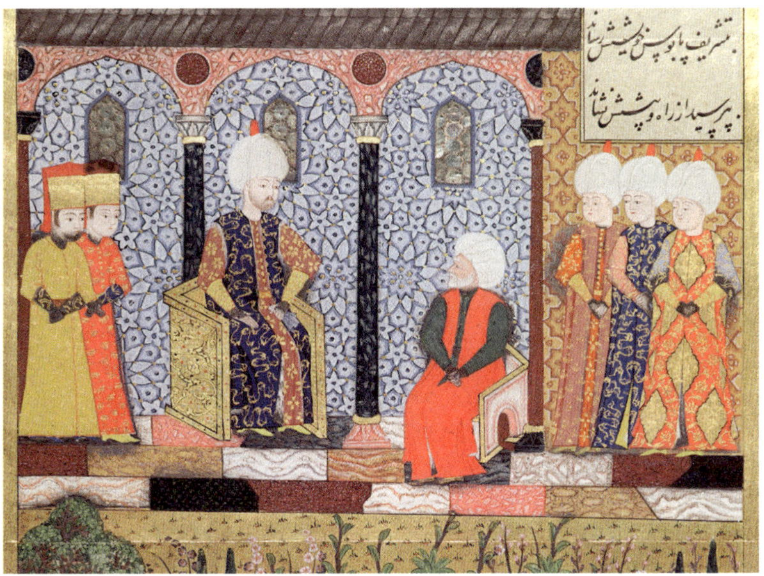

*The presentation of gifts to Suleyman I in 1530*, from the *Suleymanname*, 1558

to her work in the last few years: Islamic pattern. Fifteenth- and sixteenth-century Turkish paintings contain figures and tell stories. But these are set against blocks of flat patterning that stands for tiling, carpets, and carved woodwork. Pictures of hers such as *I watched Myself die and come alive* (page 12) are made up of just this combination.

TE  When I was at the Royal College of Art, my second subject was sacred geometry, because I really loved Sufism and Eastern esoterica, miniature painting, and a lot of Turkish painting, Cypriot pots, the whirling dervishes, all that kind of thing.

By a lucky chance, fate made it easy for her to follow up her interest in Islamic patterns. The world's greatest expert in the subject had his office right next door to her studio. His name was Keith Critchlow.

Critchlow (1933–2020) was a remarkable figure in his own right: an artist, theorist, renowned expert on the subject of sacred geometry, and professor of architecture. But one of his achievements was the effect he had on two leading contemporary painters. The first was Frank Bowling (b. 1934), who arrived in Britain in 1953 on a boat from Guyana and promptly joined the Royal Air Force, realizing that he would have to do national service in Britain at some point. In the RAF, he met Critchlow, who introduced him not only to painting, but also to artists including Frank Auerbach and Leon Kossoff. Bowling has acknowledged the effect his friend had on him: 'Keith Critchlow really invented me as an artist.'

Subsequently, Critchlow reinvented himself as an architect, and an authority on the subject of sacred geometry. In the 1960s, he encountered the American engineer-architect Buckminster Fuller, who paid him a remarkable tribute: 'He is one of the most inspiring scholar-teachers I have had the privilege to know.' For many years, Critchlow was also professor of Islamic Art at the Royal College of Art. It was a chance discovery of Critchlow's book *Islamic Patterns* that enabled the architect and engineer Minwer el-Meheid to understand how to reconstruct the *minbar* – or pulpit – of the al-Aqsa mosque in Jerusalem. This great twelfth-century work had been destroyed by fire in 1969, and both the craft skills and the theoretical knowledge necessary to recreate it seemed no longer to exist – except, as it turned out, in Critchlow's book. In one of her columns for the *Independent*, Emin described the society that he cofounded, the Research into Lost Knowledge Organisation (RILKO).

For those of you out there who don't know what that is, it's a group of people who are interested in the things that we used to know that we don't know any more, in terms of our collective knowledge. For example, how far

away mountains are, the shape of the Milky Way
— just general things that we ought to know, such as
sacred geometry and a natural awareness of space.

The latter two were subjects that Emin had probably always known about. Middle Eastern textiles were part of her environment as a young child – and have been ever since. 'A lot of my paintings have carpets in them', she told *Cultured* magazine, 'because I was brought up with them and I have a lot in my house – Persian rugs and Turkish rugs.'

TE  When I was at the Royal College, as a device in my
     paintings, I painted all these intricate carpets – and
     then quite Expressionist figures.

As David Dawson recalled, she had these carpets in their shared studio at the college. The critic David Sylvester, a passionate advocate of Islamic carpets, used to say that some of the greatest abstract art came in the form of these ancient textiles from Turkey, Iran, and Egypt. But also, for biographical reasons, Emin probably saw more in them than simply 'abstraction'. 'When I was a little girl, I used to meditate and I'd see these amazing patterns, these brilliant geometric crystal shapes.'

With this background, she was open to Critchlow's reading of the patterns in such things as Islamic tile-work and carpentry as at once mathematical, cosmological, and spiritual. Despite her disappointment with aspects of the Royal College, she 'really enjoyed' her secondary courses: Esoteric Mysticism and Sacred Geometry.

Emin's rediscovery of these patterns came after her recovery from her illness. She began painting again, but her energy sometimes gave out. When that happened, Harry brought her a chair and she worked in a different way on another scale.

**TE** Last year, when I wasn't at all well physically, I couldn't paint, but I really, really wanted to. So Harry pulled up my highchair and we placed the painting up high. I had a tiny brush and I just sat there painting all these carpet patterns across my giant canvases. I love it. It's like what I was doing thirty-five years ago – I'm back to doing it. It's like clearing all my mind out. It's just such a fantastic thing to do. I had a show recently in Brussels that had a lot of my carpet paintings in it. I'm so happy doing it.

The result was a sequence of pictures that have exactly the dual quality – human figures juxtaposed with areas of complex design – that you see in Ottoman miniatures. It is also there in a Byzantine-influenced painting such as Segna di Bonaventura's *Crucifix* (page 202) – and in that case the human body is charged with passion and drama. That is true in Emin's paintings too.

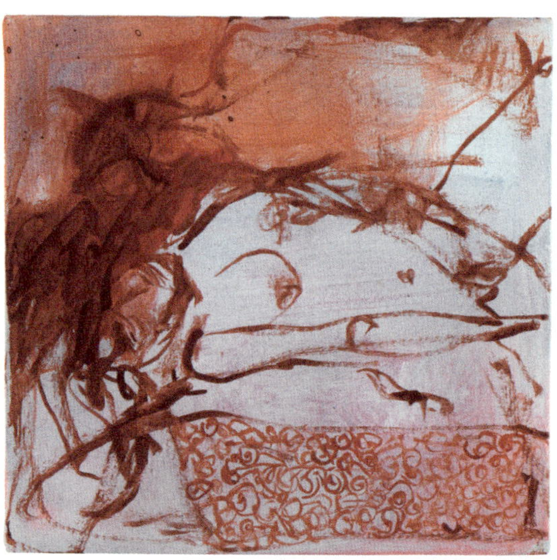

*Lust, 2023*

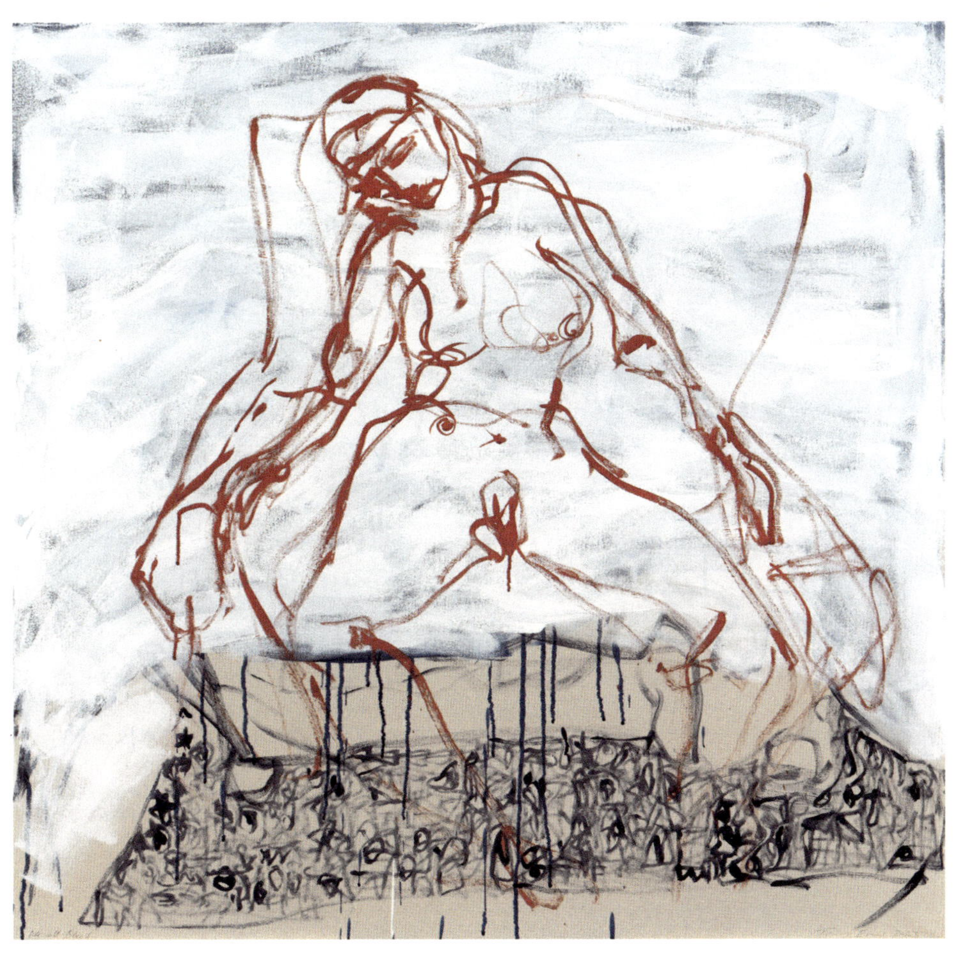

*We all Bleed, 2023*

19

## *Writing and painting*

While we were chatting one day, Emin told me a story about an epiphany, or a moment of sudden realization, that had come to her a few years ago.

**TE**  I was in my kitchen in the south of France, and I had these yellow wild roses in a vase and the light was coming in on them and it looked so lovely. I thought, 'Oh, I'll take a photo of that.' So I took one and it looked shit. I changed the setting on my phone, took another, and it still looked shit. Changed it again and it still looked crap. I thought why doesn't it look the way I can see it, with this dappled light? And I suddenly realized what Impressionism was about. I'd never given that any thought, only how it looked, not what it was *about*. I thought, 'Oh my God, what a breakthrough in painting. They decided to paint how that light *felt*, not just how it *looked.'*

**MG**  David Hockney asks whether the world looks like a photograph, and answers that it doesn't, not quite.

**TE**  No, it doesn't! It's something else. How we see light and how it transfers through things is changing, constantly, constantly, constantly. Our perception of the world never stands still, light never stands still, nothing does. A pure moment in time is all we have – this *second* – and then it's gone. Then there's another one, and another one, and

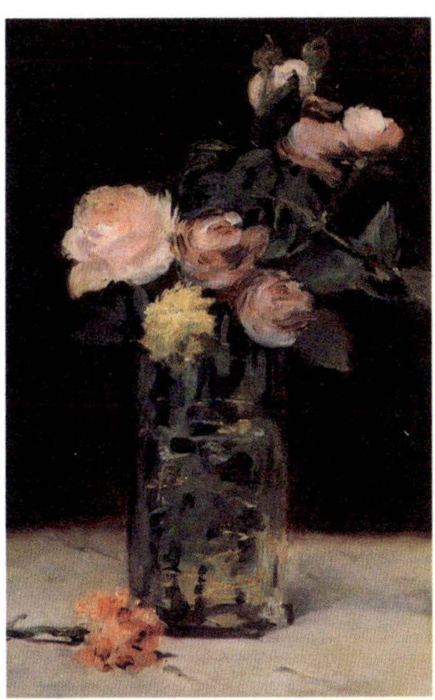

Édouard Manet, *Roses in a Glass Vase*, 1883

another one. I understood this by looking at these fucking flowers in a vase in my kitchen. It could have been the 1890s and I could have been having a conversation about that very subject as we got out our Box Brownie cameras.

With art, people can tell you things a thousand times, but you don't know until you *know*. You have to experience it. I'm sure people might think what I've just said was really thick. This is so obvious. But it's not. People can tell you about it, you can read about it, but if you actually *see* it for the first time, it's different.

**MG** There is a limit to how far you can get with words.

**TE** Yeah, but I like words a lot.

She certainly does. Her work is full of them. The neon pieces consist of nothing else, except perhaps for a heart or a few lines made out of glass tubing – and, of course, light. The quilts, too,

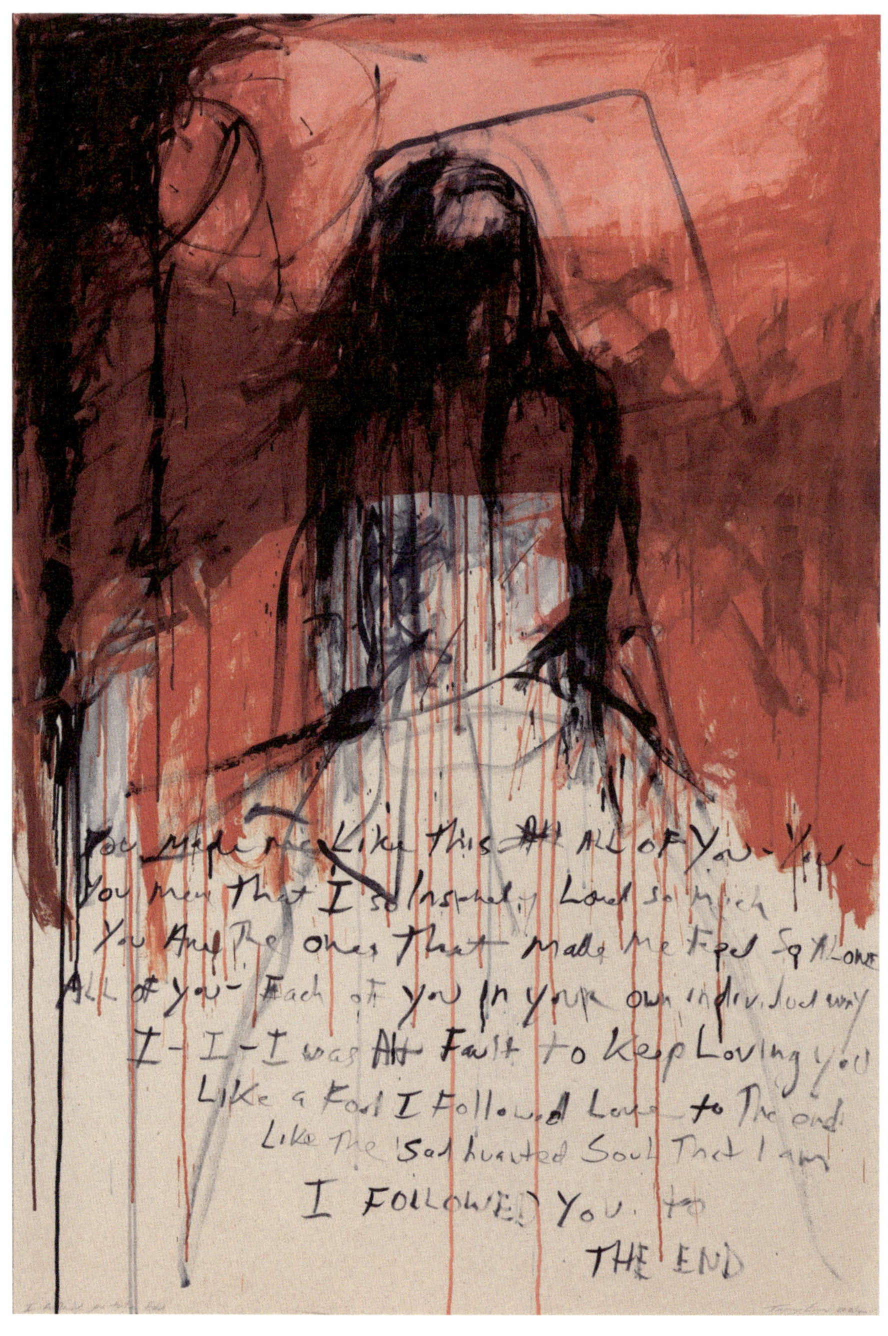


*I Followed you to the end*, 2024

214

are covered in words. Certain works, and sections of works, consist of nothing but handwritten texts. In addition to being a painterly painter and a painter-drawer, Emin also belongs to another, somewhat rarer group. She is a painter-writer, in that not only is she an artist who also happens to write (like Van Gogh or Constable), but also that she is a painter who writes on her paintings, and does so with an impulsive, premeditated freedom. Harry Weller told me about how one of the paintings in the studio had been finished:

> She loved this figure and didn't want to touch it or
> paint over but wasn't completely satisfied. I literally
> went round the corner and she just started writing
> on it. It's automatic. There's no prepared text beside
> her; it's immediate. She is genuinely surprised by it
> when the text comes out.

It was not the way I had seen Lucian Freud conclude a picture: by pondering it for a long time, then stepping forward, adding a touch with the brush and pronouncing, 'I think I'll stop now.' It was closer to an anecdote Gary Hume had told me about a certain work that he felt needed something more, but he was not sure what. Eventually, after puzzling for days, he realized what it was: a bag of sweets. He put this in and the picture felt complete. But what Emin had done was less intentional than that. It sounded more like the psychography, or automatic writing, practised by mystics and mediums and cultivated by the Surrealists.

TE  Harry loves getting it on film when I'm writing,
    but sometimes he's looking the other way when I do it.
    I don't know what I'm going to write. The title of the
    show *I Followed you to the end* [at White Cube in 2024]
    was at the end of what I wrote on the painting.

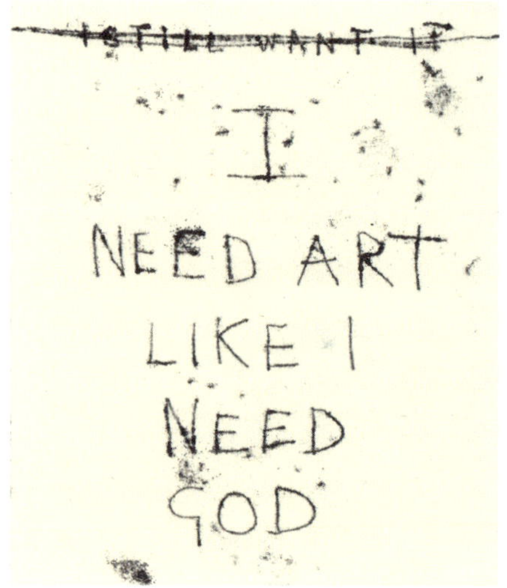

*I Need Art Like I Need God*, 1998

I don't even think about what I'm writing;
I just write it. We are always amazed how it fits
perfectly into the space. It just fits, but I'm not trying
to *make* it fit. If it didn't, I'd treat it like a painting and
paint over it. I won't rewrite it. There's a painting in
Brussels that is pretty good, in which I spelt a word
wrong. Then I crossed it out and wrote it again, not
realizing that I'd spelt it wrong again. But the painting
looked really good, so I left it like that.

**MG** If a picture looks good, it *is* good.

**TE** There's a painting that I'm working on at the moment
with 'Don't argue at my funeral' written on it, which I
think is really funny. The reason that I wrote that was
because of all these flowers I have here. It will be painted
over, but one thing is for sure: it won't be a painting that's
incongruous or wrong with those words. It will fit them
for whatever reasons.



*Writing and painting*

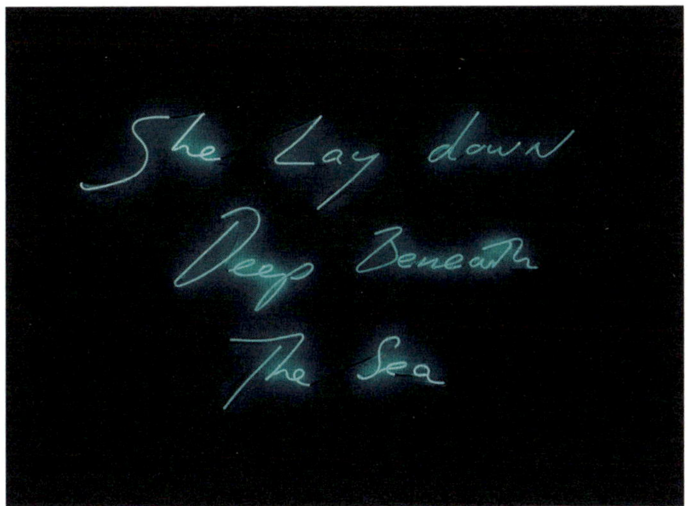

*She Lay down Deep Beneath The Sea,* 2012

So the meaning lingers even when the words themselves have gone. On the other hand, the physical appearance of a letter matters even if it's the wrong one as the dictionary has it. This gives a clue to what part the words are playing in her paintings. The meaning is important, but so too is how they look. She had told me much the same years ago, in her studio in Spitalfields:

**TE** Sometimes, when I'm doing a blanket, I put something down, and they go, 'Oh, you've spelt it wrong!', and I put it right and it looks shit. It physically doesn't look right. The pattern of it doesn't flow or something. Then I might change the whole word.

And again, that the medium was *part* of the message, or at least particular sentences and phrases fitted particular media.

**TE** Certain words would be brilliant in neon and crap on a blanket; others need ten paragraphs to spin out the meaning.

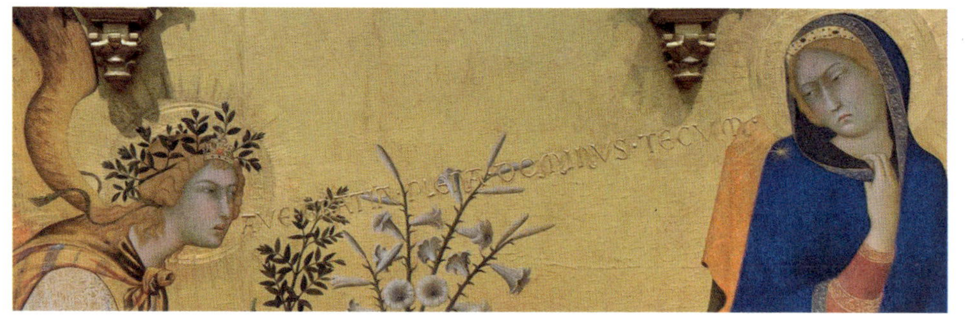

Simone Martini, *Annunciation*, 1333 (detail)

One of the powers of forceful contemporary artists is that they make the art of the past seem different. Thinking about Emin's paintings has made me more conscious of painter-writers in general. Although pictures with writing on them have not been the norm in Western art, there are actually plenty of them around. Pictures containing text were quite normal in the Middle Ages. Simone Martini's great *Annunciation* (1333) has the salutation 'AVE GRATIA PLENA DOMINVS TECVM', or 'Hail Mary, full of grace, the Lord is with you', in raised gold letters across the golden air between archangel and virgin.

William Blake was a writer-painter (or perhaps writer-drawer) *par excellence*. Some of the pages of his illustrated books have a resemblance to Emin's paintings in the balance between text and imagery and the way that the writing is an intrinsic part of the visual whole. Take this example from *The First Book of Urizen* (1794). A crucial point with both Emin and Blake is the way the artist's handwriting blends with the drawing. In fact, you might say it *was* a species of drawing. In her case, it is a skill that began in primary school.

TE  When we did scripture at school, we had to listen to the scripture and at the same time write the words of the text in this italic writing with beautiful letters. My handwriting is still very curvy. I remember doing it and taking absolute

  *Writing and painting*

pleasure in making these medieval letters. It's not the
sort of thing most tiny kids of six or seven like doing, but
I remember loving it and I enjoyed it because I was doing
something serious with my hands. I understood that.

Like Blake, and unlike other artists who put words on their
pictures – such as René Magritte, Joan Miró, and Ed Ruscha –
Emin is also an author of books and journalism, including the
column in the *Independent*. But, as she told me when her memoir
*Strangeland* was published, she has always been aware of how her
handwriting was related to her bodily and emotional condition.

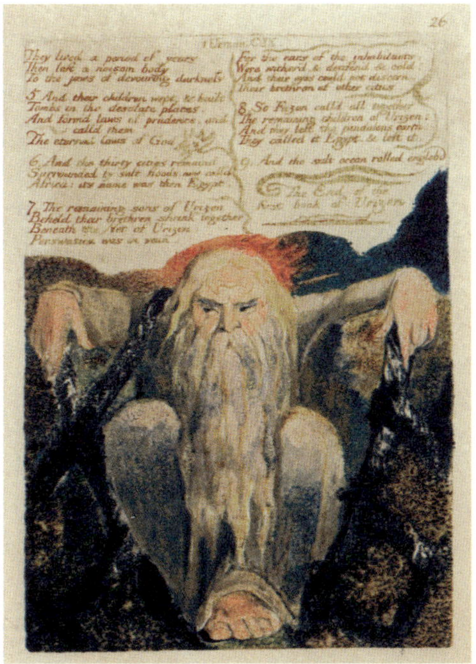

William Blake, *The First Book of Urizen*, 1794

**TE** I've been writing for longer than I've been making art. I've kept a diary since I was thirteen. I've always been a furious letter-writer. It's old fashioned, it's lovely. You can see 'Look, she was really tipsy when she wrote that, it's all over the place!' or 'She was in a really anal-retentive mood because it's so neat and tidy.'

Then there is the question of unconventional spelling. This is a tendency that Emin has in common with numerous other visual artists – Lucian Freud and David Hockney are two others. This is for various reasons, and switching language at the age of ten probably played a part in Freud's case. Other major artists such as Rauschenberg suffered from dyslexia. Hockney, like Emin, has accidentally spelled words wrongly in works of art. But there is a question about when doing something wrongly is right, because it is your way. In our first conversation, Emin confided that her friend the journalist Lynn Barber had advised her not to strive to improve her orthography.

**TE** She said, 'For God's sake, don't do that!', because she thinks my spelling's enchanting. For Lynn, a woman who can spell everything totally correctly, it's more a question of, 'Don't lose what you have; don't lose your personality; don't try to clean up the act too much. It's OK to have these bruised bits, and dishevelled bits, and bits that don't work properly, because that's part of your character.' When I send emails, I've got spellcheck, so I can actually learn how to spell a word. But apart from that, who else would teach me how to spell? I'd have had to go to evening classes, wouldn't I? I'm honest, so I'm trying to learn. If there's a spelling mistake, it's genuine.

   *Writing and painting*

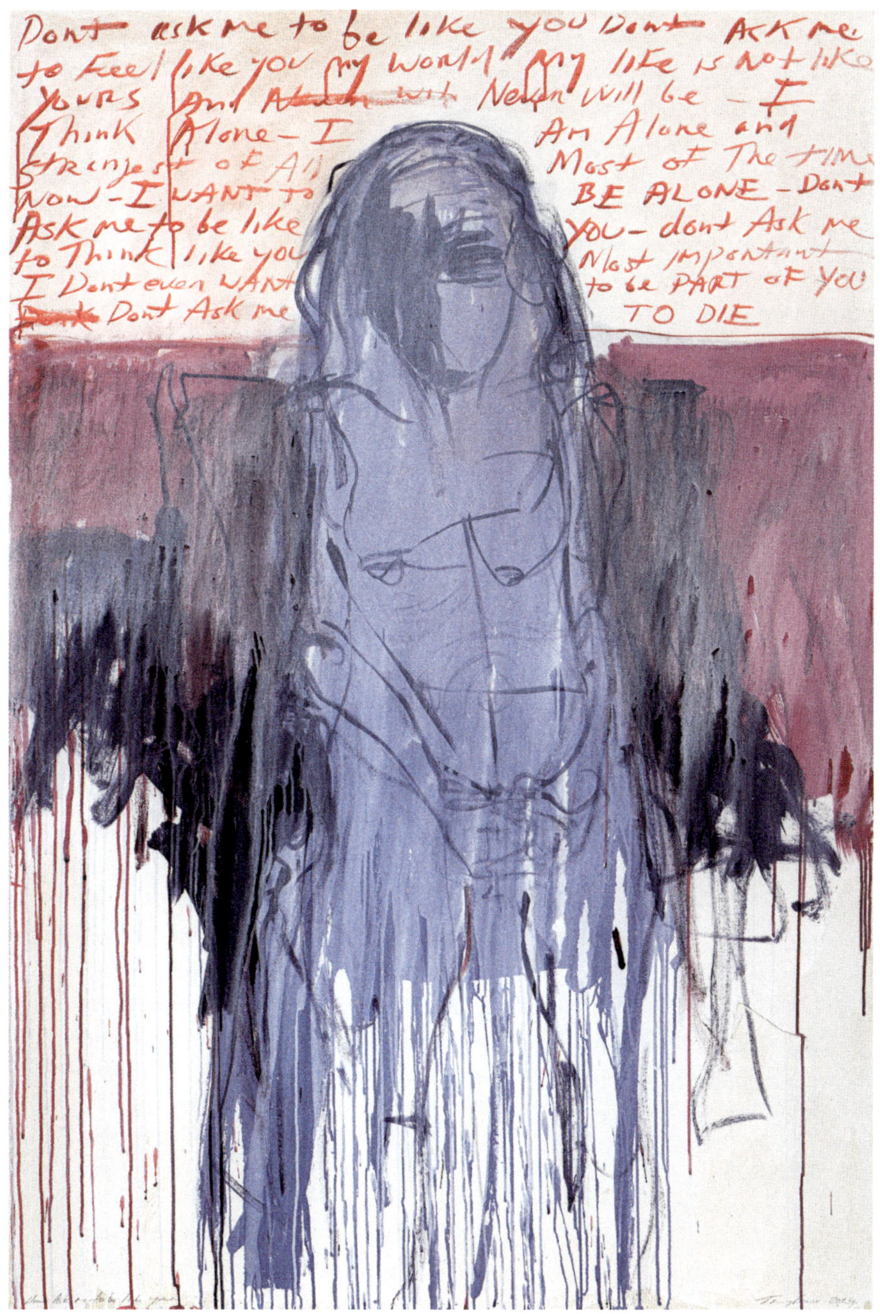


*Don't Ask me to be like you*, 2024

20

*Tracey and Louise*

TE A really quick Louise Bourgeois story for you. I was friends with Louise, and she made these giant marble sculptures. Nobody wanted them and she couldn't afford to keep them, so what she did was buy this piece of scrubland on Long Island, just a piece of sandy land by the coast. And she buried the marble sculptures in the sand. To cut up all these marble sculptures would have been difficult, and she didn't really want to get rid of them, so she just buried them in sand dunes. But those dunes were in the Hamptons, so by the time she dug up her marbles, they were worth a lot of money, but so was the piece of land, which had been worth nothing when she bought it. She had just bought it to protect her sculptures. I think this is a really great story about having some kind of faith: how it came back and helped her later on.

The context to this story was that we were talking about growing older and taking responsibility for what you do – and also believing in it.

TE As an artist, when you are younger, you think it gives you an excuse to be totally irresponsible. Then, as I've got older, as an artist, I've realized how *responsible* you have to be. Because I'm putting these things into the world. And they are probably going to stay here long after I'm gone. I'm just making them, I'm just the maker – the deliverer.

We don't know how long we're going to be around for,
or the world, or anything. But I've got to accept that my
works are going to be around a lot longer than me.

Louise Bourgeois (1911–2010) was around for longer than
most of us. When she died, she was ninety-eight and a half. As a
young woman, she knew Claude Monet and learned from
Fernand Léger. She could easily have met Munch too, if she had
travelled to Norway, but as it happened she did not. Emin knew
Bourgeois's work before she realized how old she was. She first
saw it in an exhibition called *Rites of Passage* at the Tate in 1995.
Its curator was the critic Stuart Morgan, who soon afterwards
became Emin's friend. He told her that if he had known her
work earlier, he would have put in the show beside Bourgeois's.
He predicted that she would really get on with Louise. From
then on, Bourgeois was 'just Louise, a friend of Stuart's. I'd never
read about her. It never occurred to me that she was old.' When
eventually she discovered that Bourgeois had been born in 1911,
'I couldn't believe it. I couldn't believe the physicality of her
work, the big and the small of it. I was so impressed.'

Eventually they met in 2008, became friends, and it turned
out that the feeling was mutual: Bourgeois was impressed by
Emin. 'At the time [in the USA], I was considered to be just a
bit YBA-ish. But Louise didn't think that. She understood that
I was coming from a completely different place – she took me
really seriously, and she respected me.'

Bourgeois had had to wait a long time for recognition. It was
not until after her husband, the art historian Robert Goldwater,
died in 1973 that anybody paid much attention to her. Her
breakthrough was in 1982, when the Museum of Modern Art
in New York held a retrospective of her work. At that date,
she was already more than seventy, hence the lesson Emin
drew about the importance of having faith and carrying on.

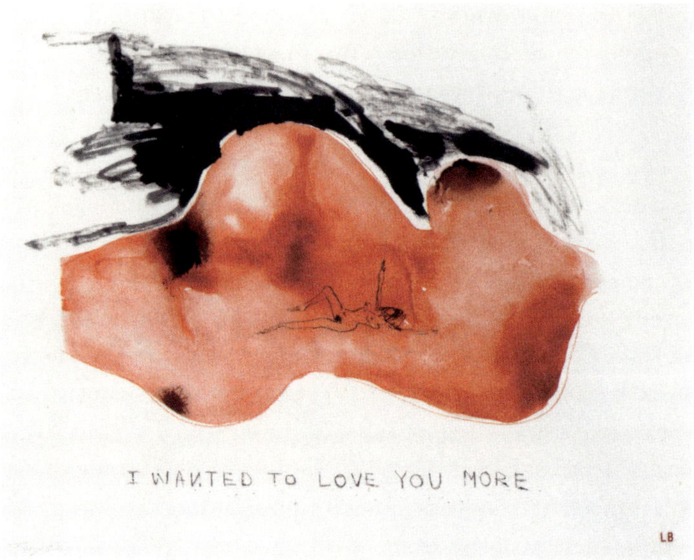

Louise Bourgeois and Tracey Emin, *I wanted to love you more*,
No. 1 of 16, from the series *Do Not Abandon Me*, 2009–10

Shortly before Bourgeois died, she and Emin collaborated
on a series of prints, *Do Not Abandon Me*. Bourgeois had always
resisted the idea of collaboration. Then towards the end of her
life, she decided to work with a writer, an architect, and an artist.
The artist was Emin, who was anxious about the project.

**TE** The collaboration took me two years to do. She made
a set of prints and sent them to me in London to work
on them directly. It took me that long because I was
so fucking nervous. Every time I looked at the prints,
I thought, 'I'll do it tomorrow.'
Then one day, I was in my studio, and I laid all the
prints out on the floor and just looked at them. And then
I inked up a piece of glass the same size and just did them,



*Tracey and Louise*

one by one. I did all those prints in a day. That was
a Sunday; on the Monday they were dry, I rolled them
all up, FedEx'd them to New York, and they arrived on
Tuesday morning. I was so nervous. So nervous. And
then Jerry [Jerry Gorovoy, Bourgeois's studio manager]
called me and he told me that he unfurled them to her
one by one as she sat up in bed, and as she saw each one,
she clapped her hands and laughed.

Emin's contribution to these works tended to be on a different scale from Bourgeois's. In one, for example, a tiny Emin
woman raises an arm and a leg inside the huge, pink pregnant
form of a female Bourgeois figure. Suitably, one of the lessons
that she learnt from the older artist was about scale. Among
Emin's favourite works by Bourgeois is *Maman*, the giant spider
that she made to be exhibited at Tate Modern in 2000.

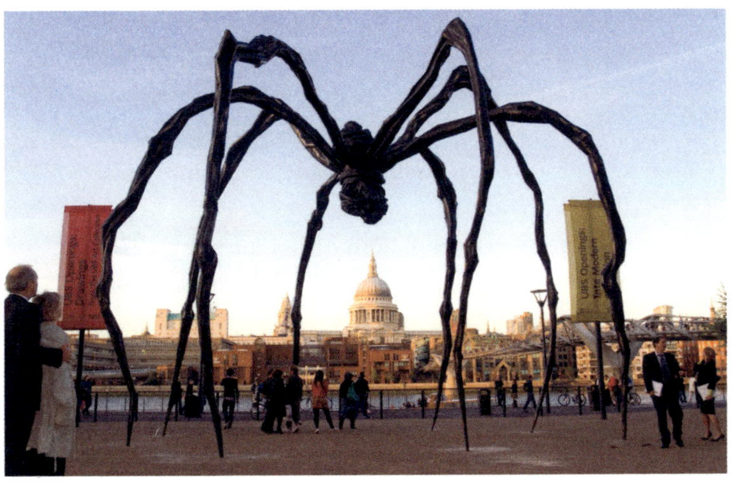

Louise Bourgeois, *Maman*, 1999, installed outside Tate Modern, London, 2007

It's one of the world's largest sculptures, more
than thirty feet high and thirty-three feet wide,
a huge spider made of bronze with a sac that
holds thirty-two marble eggs. Some people really
disliked it, but I loved it. I loved its romance. I loved
the idea that, say I had a lover, I would tell them
'Meet me underneath the spider.' And I loved the
scale of it – that's one of the big things I learnt from
her: the fact that you can go from tiny to giant.

That applies to paintings as well as sculpture. One of the striking
aspects of Emin's recent work is the way that she moves from
very small to large format, and how the two are interrelated.

**TE** I go into the studio, mix some paint up. Harry goes,
'What are you doing?' I go 'red'. So I get some red paint.
Then I walk around the studio and start on a really
big one, then I might have some little tiny canvases.
Then I paint them all that red, all of them. Then white.
Then I put some pink on big ones, then on the tiny ones.
It builds up like that. Then the little ones stop and I
just have a ground, and they might stay like that for
a year or something. Then when I'm feeling a little
bit cosy, especially in London, I sit down at my table,
my desk, with all the little canvases, and one by one
I start working on them. Out of ten, maybe four work.
Three don't, so I have to paint over them. Sometimes
the little ones get really thick; you can see all the brush
marks underneath. It's really been a battle. Some are
just white with a line on, but you can see that there
are loads of pictures underneath where I've worked
on it again and again and again. So sometimes the big
ones come much easier than the tiny ones.

                    *Tracey and Louise*

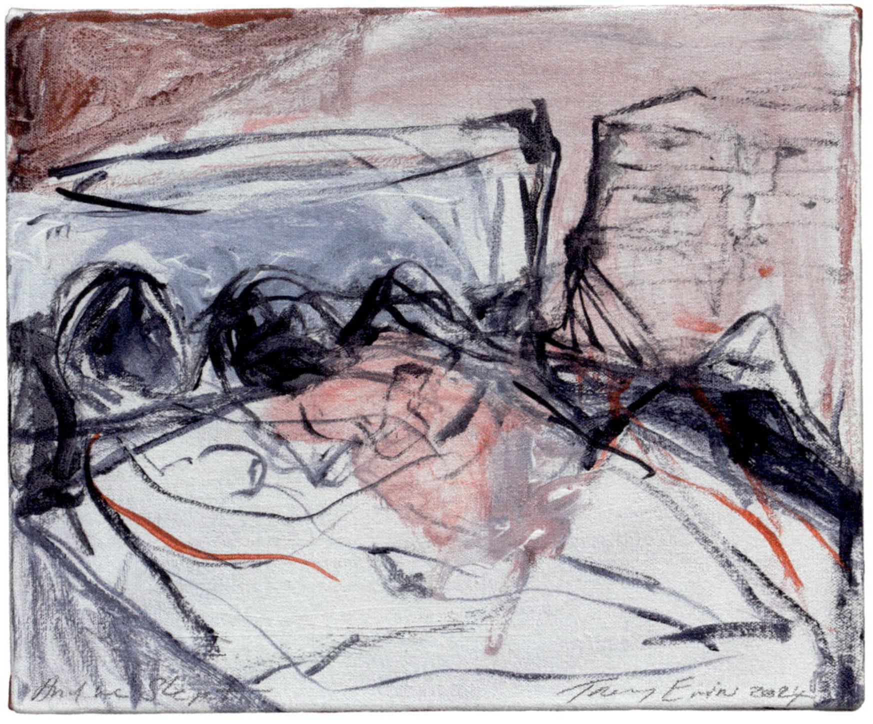

*And we Slept*, 2024

What's brilliant about the big ones is that you can really *paint* – booof! I say it's like being a conductor. You load up the paint and kerrbamm! You can really paint. Whereas with the little ones, obviously you can't because it's myopic and you are looking *into* it. I love it when I see images in a book or digital images and you can't tell if they are big or small. Some of the really big ones look like they are small watercolours, and the tiny ones look like they are really big paintings loaded up with really thick paint. But they're not.

21

# *The naked artist*

In his classic study *The Nude: A Study in Ideal Form* (1956), Kenneth Clark discussed the sculpture and painting of unclothed human bodies as an idea or set of conventions. His short answer to the question 'What is the nude?' was: 'It is an art form invented by the Greeks in the 5th century BC, just as opera is an art form invented in 17th-century Italy.' The nude in that sense exists only in Western art, or in cultures influenced by the West. Other traditions produce plenty of depictions of undressed people, but they are not 'nude' in the same way. Nor, Clark argued, are all the undressed people in European art necessarily nudes either. In one chapter, he described an 'alternative convention'. These figures resemble 'roots and bulbs, pulled up into the light … pale, defenceless, unself-supporting'. They are the ungainly resurrected souls of a gothic Last Judgment. Clark recognized their awkwardly unclassical bodies in the works of northern European artists such as Albrecht Dürer and Rembrandt.

Emin's works are full of figures who are not wearing clothes, most of them women. But the bodies that she paints, draws, and sculpts do not fit into either of Clark's categories. They are not nude or naked in the sense of Shakespeare's 'poor, bare, forked animal'. Nor, again, are they 'naked portraits', the category that Lucian Freud devised to describe his own works (and also those of some predecessors such as Edgar Degas). So what are Emin's undressed people?

Often, it turns out, they stand for the artist herself. 'Many artists have used female nudes in their work', she has

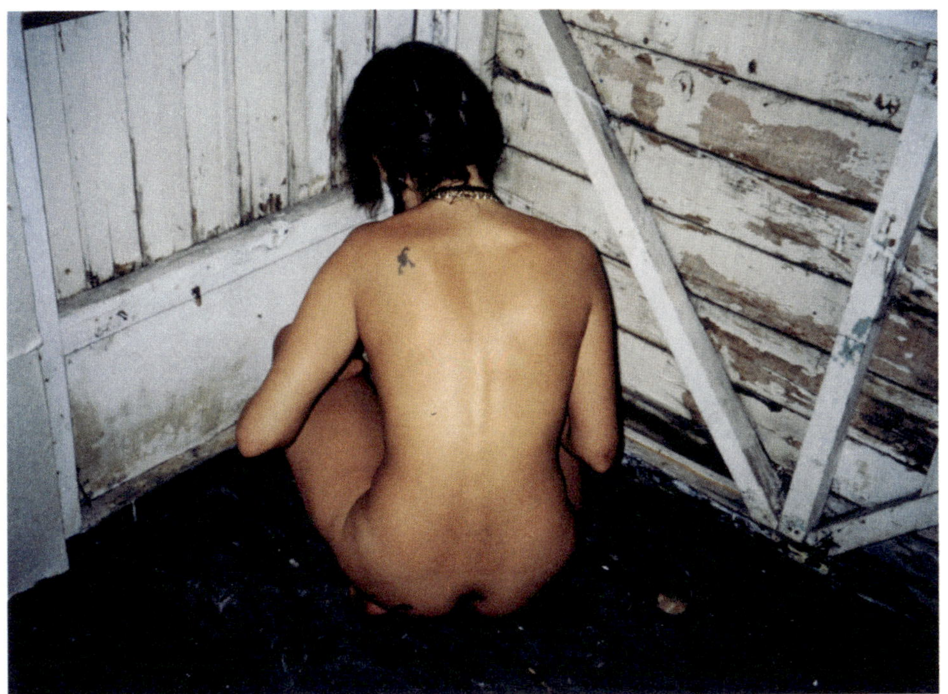

*The Last Thing I Said to You is Don't Leave me Here II*, 2000

explained. 'I've got a good female nude I can use whenever I like and its mine', so, she concluded, 'I'm my own muse.' Accordingly, she appears naked not only in drawings and paintings, but also in photographic works such as *The Last Thing I Said to You is Don't Leave me Here II* and also, as we have seen, in person and in photographs of *The Exorcism of the Last Painting I Ever Made* (page 152).

This is partly an affirmation of her belief that clothes are, as Lucian Freud put it, 'a technicality'. 'It's so liberating to be naked', Emin has said. 'You have a better sense of your own being.' But it is also an expression of her belief that our identity is not just confined to what goes on our faces and in our heads. She made that point when talking about a series of gouaches from 2014.

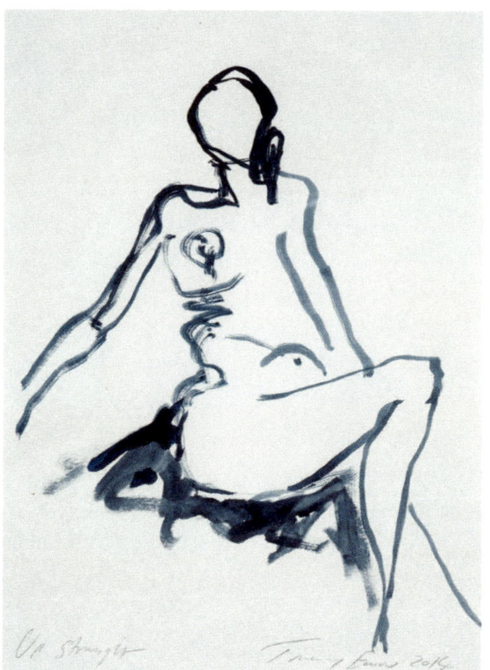

*Up Straight*, 2014

The gouaches are self-portraits of me. Not of my mind but of my body. It was about being fifty plus. I realized I was still drawing myself like I was twenty-five. I wasn't responding to who I am now or where I am going. I wasn't responding to my future. I was in some kind of denial. So I made myself look at myself, then I made myself draw myself again. Those gouaches are the result of that. I don't need to put my face in my picture. Because I know who it is.

She went on to widen the argument:

I really, really believe that the nature within a human being is reliant on so many other things and so many



*The naked artist*

different layers. If someone said me that all there was
to me was my face, I'd be really insulted. I walk with
my left foot turned in; I have really, really soft skin.
They are things you can look at and describe me by.
But on top of that, I have my mind and I have my soul,
and all that lives somewhere inside of me. That isn't to
do with my face; it's to do with all of me.

When she said that, she was talking in 2015 at the Leopold
Museum in Vienna, in a conversation about her affinity with
Egon Schiele. As we have seen, Emin's first sight of Schiele's
art was one of the experiences that impelled her to become an
artist. He painted and drew many self-portraits of himself, like
this one in which he looks warily at himself, his discarded trou-
sers still around his feet. Emin once observed that, 'Every artist
that I really adore works with the self and their own emotions.'

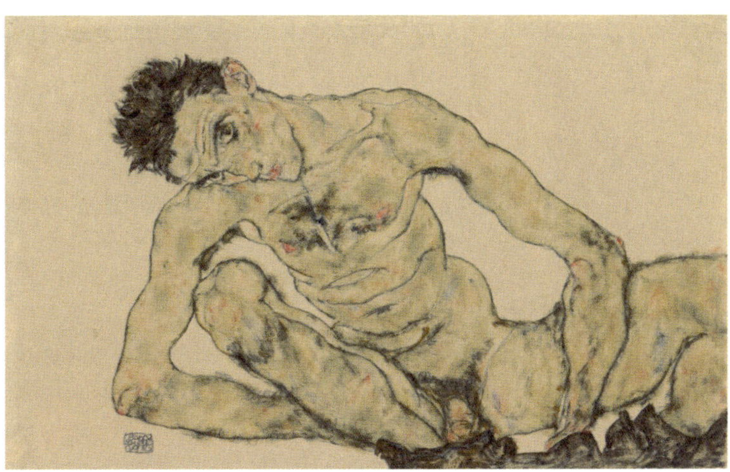

Egon Schiele, *Nude Self-portrait, Squatting*, 1916

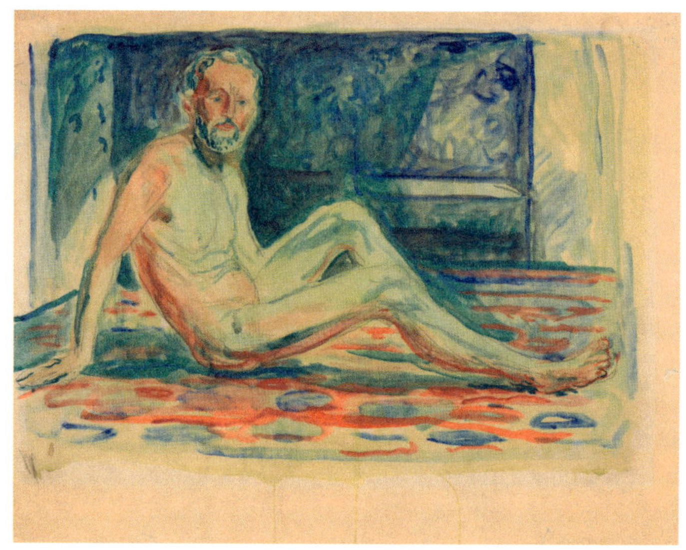

Edvard Munch, *Self-portrait, Sitting on the Floor*, 1921–35

Munch made naked self-portraits throughout his life, as if assessing the effect of age not just on his face but on all of his body.

You might conclude that the majority of Emin's pictures are naked self-portraits. But that is not quite right. She talked in much the same terms in a panel discussion at the Fondation Beyeler in Basel the year before. 'I hope to God that people don't think my personality rests on this bit [gesturing to the area above her neck]. It's all of me, including my soul.' On this occasion she was talking about a different, and even more scandalous, painting than any by Schiele: the work by Gustave Courbet known as *L'Origine du monde* or 'The origin of the world'. This picture, though painted in 1866, was not put on public display until 1995, when it appeared on the wall of the Musée d'Orsay in Paris. Even the year before, when it was illustrated on the cover of a book, the French police asked shops not to display it. It remained controversial into the twenty-first century. In 2011, when a user posted it, Facebook shut down their account (resulting in a seven-year legal case).



*The naked artist*

Before the Musée d'Orsay put it on show, it had been in private collections, and even there discreetly hidden. Its first owner, Khalil Sherif Pasha (1831–79), was an Ottoman-Egyptian statesman, diplomat, and art collector who apparently commissioned it from Courbet. He kept it behind a green curtain. In the late nineteenth century, the writer and collector Edmond de Goncourt was shown it by a dealer, hidden behind 'a small painting of a building in a snowy landscape'. In the mid-1950s, it was bought at auction by the psychoanalyst and theorist Jacques Lacan (1901–81). He – or possibly his wife Sylvia – commissioned a painted cover from her brother-in-law, the Surrealist artist André Masson, to put over this work, which it seemed was still too shocking to display openly,

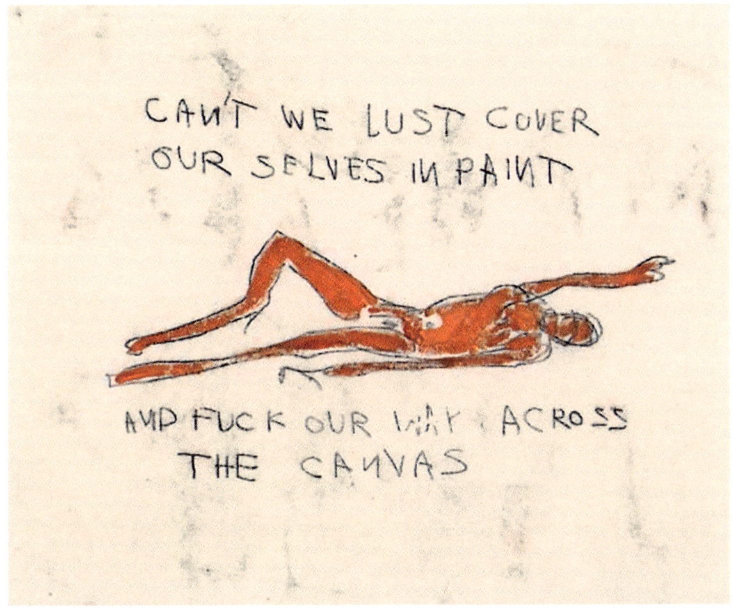


*Untitled*, 1996, from *The Exorcism of the Last Painting I Ever Made*

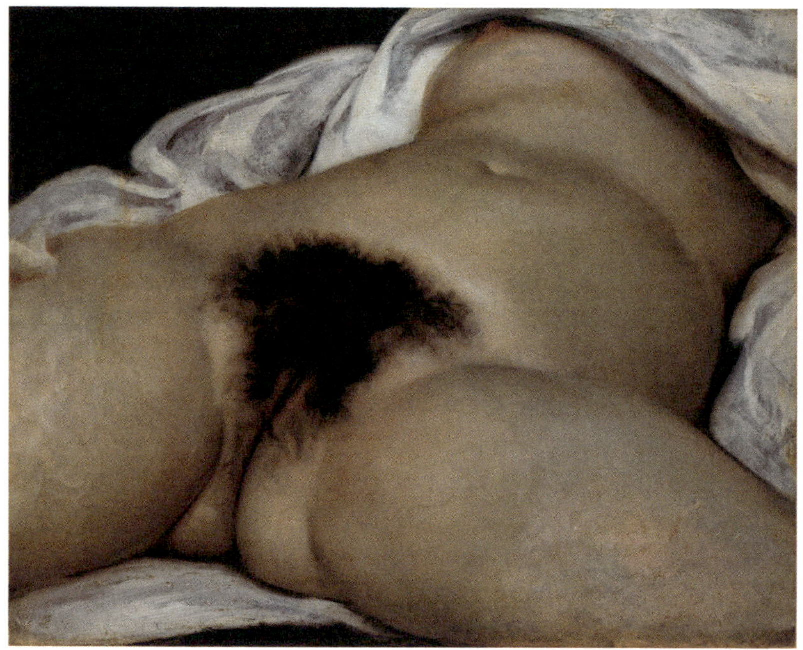

Gustave Courbet, *L'Origine du monde*, 1866

even in Surrealist and psychoanalytical circles. Masson produced a playfully decorative fantasy, in which Courbet's female body was lightly disguised as a wooded landscape.

When Emin was an art student in the early 1980s, Courbet's painting was still more or less 'banned'. At least, 'it really wasn't cool to like this painting', she remembered. 'A lot of feminists would be really, really angry that I liked it.'

> It was almost not allowed to be spoken about, and if
> it was, it would be spoken about in a derogatory way.
> I was just thinking, 'Wow! That's really sexy, that's
> really fantastic.' To me it was an icon of the age.

On another occasion, she concluded, 'For me, it's about female strength, a feminist icon.'



*The naked artist*

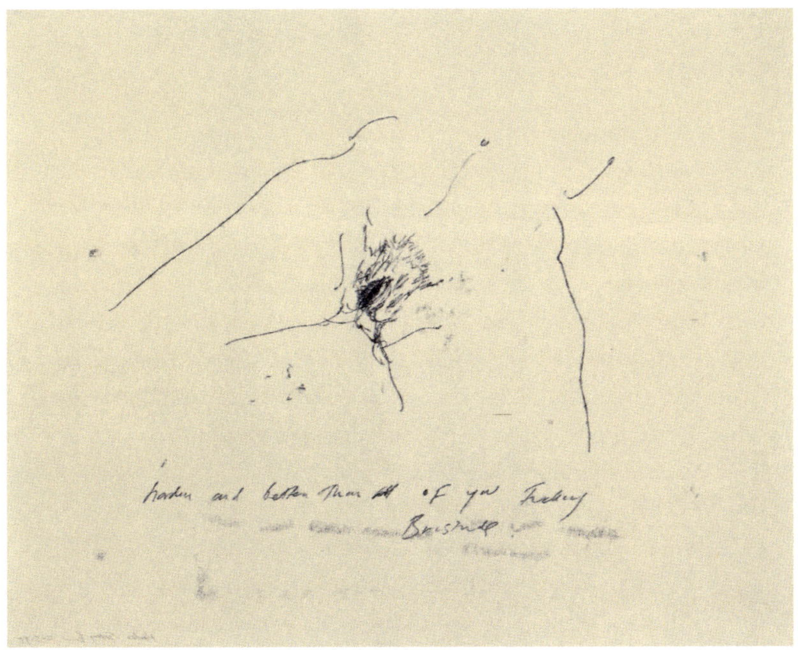

*Harder*, 1995

Look how sexy she is! That pubic hair, you could just
throw your whole body into it. Her personality isn't about
her face; it's about her whole psyche, her whole being, and
it's pulsing through this painting. That wasn't a model.
Courbet was really deeply in love with her. You can see
that. It emanates from the painting. It's so powerful.

For Emin, this is a portrait, but a *body* portrait – like her own
*Harder* (1995), which she has noted was a memory of herself as a
girl but a drawing of a fully grown woman (so a variety of self-
portrait too). She suggested that the really shocking thing about
the Courbet was precisely that it was a depiction of a specific
person: 'a portrait of Whistler's girlfriend'. One theory about the
model's  identity is that she was Joanna Hiffernan (1843–86),
Whistler's model and muse. But many scholars doubt that she

was also the model for *L'Origine*, on the grounds that she was red-haired, which the person in that painting was obviously not. An alternative theory is that the body in question belonged to Constance Quéniaux (1832–1908), a dancer and courtesan who was the lover of the first owner, Khalil Sherif Pasha. In either case, Emin's point holds. This is a picture of a specific person, and love is involved. For Emin, the fact that a work is about sex does not preclude it being concerned with deep emotion and what, for lack of a better word, is called the soul.

The shocking aspect of *L'Origine* is that it ignores a convention that had held, more or less, in Western art (though not, for example, in Japanese) since at least the sixth century BCE. This was, in brief, that everybody pretended that female genitals simply did not exist. The ancient Greeks were much more comfortable with male nudity, which was commonplace in art and reality. Women, respectable ones at any rate, were clad in robes and expected to remain at home. Even naked goddesses generally had their lower limbs covered by robes (like the *Venus de Milo*) or a modest hand (like Praxiteles' *Aphrodite*). If all else failed, their lower bodies were represented as an area of smooth marble with no visible vulva or pubic hair.

During the early Middle Ages, all nudity was a cause of shame. From the Renaissance onwards, unclothed women became a staple subject of art. But with a few exceptions – daring individuals such as Rembrandt and Francisco de Goya (and of course pornography) – the classical convention was maintained. This was true even in an intentionally and explicitly erotic painting such as Ingres's *Le Bain Turc* (Turkish bath) finished in 1862, which was also owned by Khalil Sherif Pasha.

Lucian Freud shared Emin's admiration for this notorious work by Courbet, and he also believed that every part of the human body was distinctively individual. Talking about a nymph in a picture by Titian, he said, 'We could recognise her

  *The naked artist*

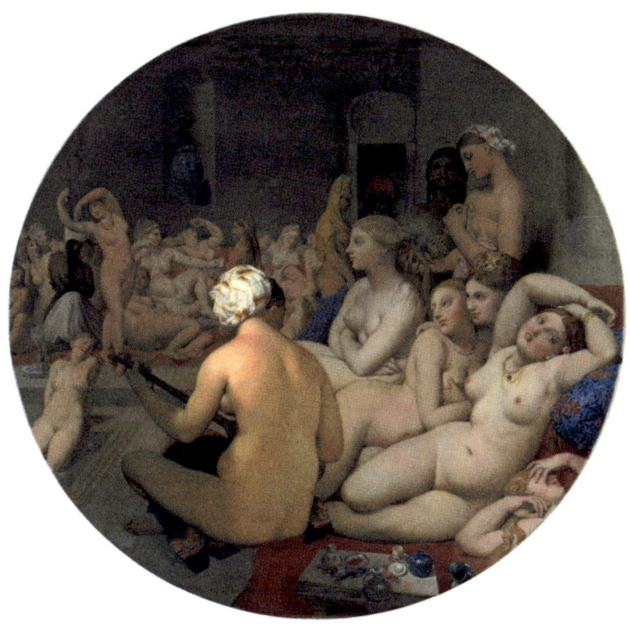

Jean-Auguste-Dominique Ingres, *Le Bain Turc*, 1852–9, modified in 1862

by her toes.' He probably felt the same about each detail of everybody (as Emin does about her soft skin and inward-turning left foot). But his solution was the 'naked portrait', which was the result of careful scrutiny of every part of his subject (treating the head as 'another limb').

As we began by noting, Emin's approach is different. Her nudes are autobiographical but not representational. You might call them psychograms: depictions of how the artist feels, remembers, or imagines herself. In that respect, her pictures are closer to some self-portraits by Frida Kahlo, such as *The Broken Column* (1944). This is a (partly) naked self-portrait, but not a straightforward one. When she painted it, Kahlo had recently had spinal surgery. She represented her backbone as a broken classical pillar, the pain of her numerous injuries and illnesses as nails puncturing her flesh. Stylistically, the picture has a good deal in common with the Surrealism of René Magritte and

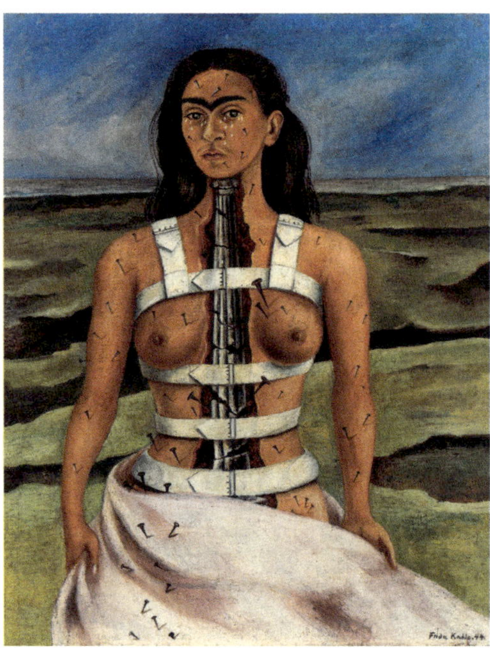

Frida Kahlo, *The Broken Column*, 1944

Salvador Dalí, but you might say it was lived Surrealism: her accidents and sufferings were real.

Emin is an admirer of Kahlo's work, which she first encountered when she was at the Royal College of Art, but with some reservations, as she explained in a short essay.

Some of it makes me feel sick, and makes me think:
I didn't need to know that. But on the other hand,
the fact that she had no proper training, yet obviously
had the talent, is extraordinary. When you look at the
paintings, you see that they are good. She painted what
she saw – and the fact that she actually saw these things
in her imagination is incredible. At the time, there were
many people around her, including the Surrealists, who
were trying to be weird, when she genuinely was.

     *The naked artist*

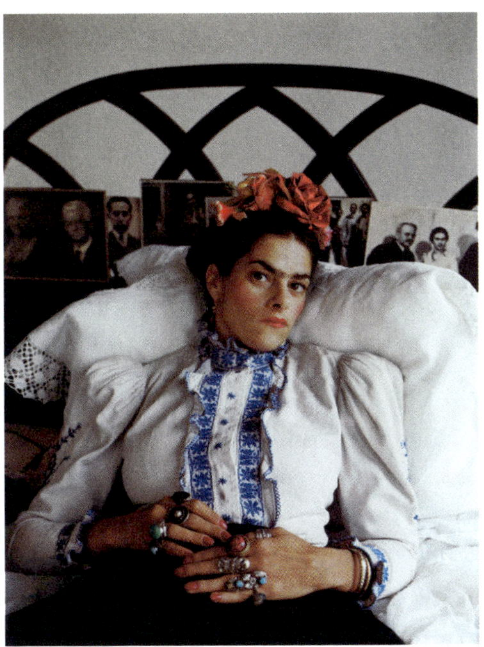

Mary McCartney, *Tracey Emin as Frida Kahlo*, 2000

Emin acknowledges that many people see a resemblance between Kahlo's work and hers, but she believes this 'has less to do with subject matter and more about coincidences – in particular, because I am a woman'. In 2000, she agreed to pose in costume as Kahlo for a photographic portrait by Mary McCartney. The result was a brilliant conceit.

When asked to comment on it more than two decades later, Emin said, 'At the time I really thought I looked like Frida Kahlo, and now I really think I look like me', adding, 'it's a great portrait by Mary.' The first statement is true in several senses. Emin has developed into a completely different kind of painter: loose and free, representational and abstract at the same time, she draws in paint and lets paint cascade like the water of the sea. You could say all of her pictures, naked or not, are self-portraits. And they do not look like Frida Kahlo's at all.

# 22

## *But has it got the thing?*

**MG** Of course, there's good painting and bad painting,
boring painting and thrilling painting. What makes
the difference?

**TE** David Dawson and I talk about the *'thing'*. Painting has
to have the *thing*. If it hasn't got its own entity, the *thing*,
its own being, it has no substance, no sense of being *here*.
David and I have spent years and years and years talking
about painting. About four or five years ago, we realized
what it was that we liked about good painting. What it
was that it had the *thing* in it. And that was about as
much as we could describe it: the *thing*. 'The thing like
the dog in the horror film?' 'Yes, *that* thing!'

Lucian Freud used to talk about something similar. He believed
that every good painting had to have 'a little piece of poison in
it'. He said that one of the reasons he so admired Titian's *Diana
and Actaeon*, which was one of his favourite pictures, was that it
contained just such a morsel of danger. When I asked him what
he meant, he answered: 'In the case of a painting, the poison
cannot be isolated and diagnosed as it could be in food. Instead,
it might take the form of an attitude. A sense of mortality could
be the poison in a picture.' At first glance, *Diana and Actaeon*
looks like a carefree piece of sensuous mythology. But it depicts
a dark myth presided over, as you eventually see, by a skull.
Actaeon gestures in surprise as he comes across a group of

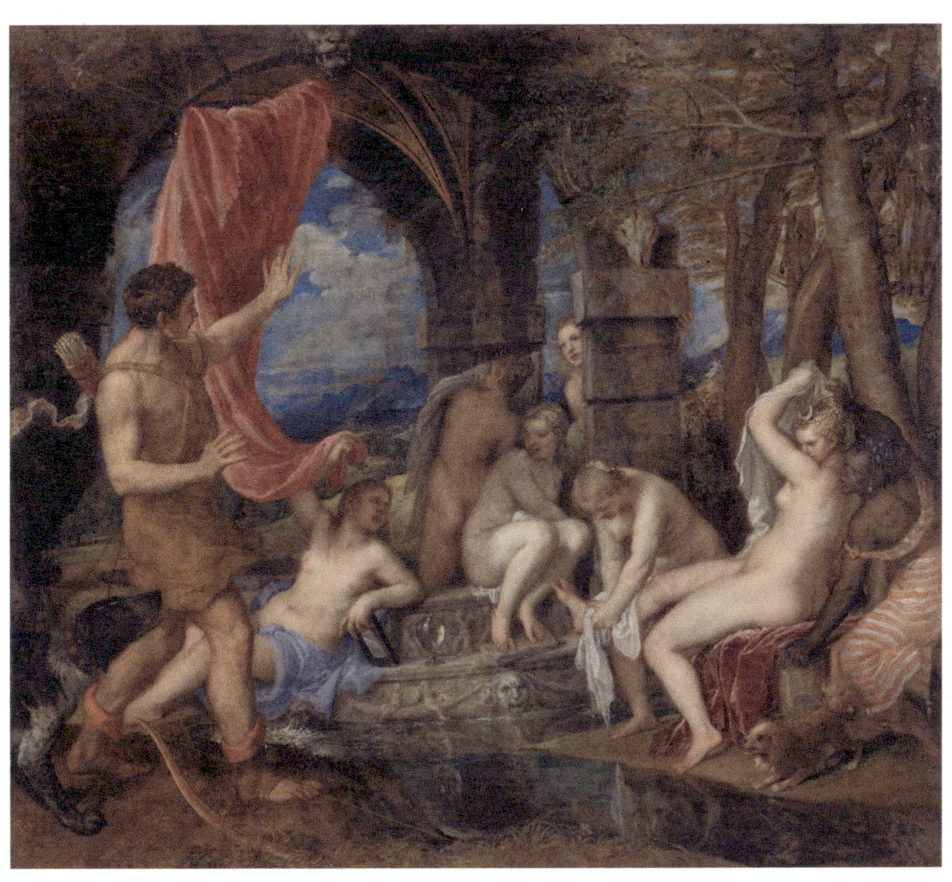

Titian, *Diana and Actaeon*, 1556–9

naked women. But the consequence of this accidental sighting
of the unclothed goddess is death. Diana transforms him into
stag, then he is torn to pieces by his own hunting dogs.

**TE** David worked with Lucian Freud for twenty years. He was
his assistant. The idea of the 'thing' goes back to Lucian's
idea of the little bit of poison, something uncontrollable,
something too much. With a painting that has the thing
in it, the painting has a pulse, the painting is alive, it has
the thing inside it, it's trapped, it's shaking. It has an
emotional vibrance inside and outside the painting. It's
how we react to it when we see it, and it's also the way
the painting reacts when we look at it. It's not one of those
paintings where the eyes move around the room. It has
its own life and its own viscosity, its own stuff. The *thing*.

David looks after Lucian's memory and his estate,
so he can paint in Lucian's old studio. He was doing a
painting of me, and we were trying to paint the *thing*.
That's what we wanted. We were also talking on a spiritual
level. Understanding that it's not just about a *picture*;
it's about this energy from within. It's fascinating, when
someone is doing a portrait of someone, what they are
trying to get from that person. Or a landscape – the
landscape must be *alive*. With my paintings, it's more
the emotional thing that has to be in it. I want you to
look at the picture and feel something emotional.

**MG** The development in your painting seemed to go along
with all other alterations in where and how you worked.

**TE** I changed my life; I had an epiphany. This was before
the cancer. I decided to get rid of my studio in London
and get rid of Fournier Street, get out of the East End.

 *But has it got the thing?*

That was quite a big move after living there for more than twenty years. I realized that I was unhappy. I saw myself from up high, walking towards my studio, a little figure with my head down, really sad, opening the door, going in and then being in some kind of darkness. I didn't like it. To be able to see that so clearly was horrible. Also the drinking, that was a cloud of darkness as well. To change your life on that level, all at the same time, was a massive shake up. To be doing the right thing and in the right place is rare. Maybe if you are a farmer and have always worked on the land, that would be similar.

**MG**  It's a bit like the advice the critic Clement Greenberg once gave to Anthony Caro: 'If you want to change your work, change your habits.'

**TE**  Actually, life's the important thing – living – that's what I learnt with cancer. That's why I didn't mind about dying. My surgeon said, 'You're not scared of dying are you?' I said, 'No. Death looks after itself, I'll look after the living side.' Once I'd got that in my head, everything became really nice. Suddenly. From being a teenage nihilist all my life, I went 'This is nice! 'This is good!' I could see stuff and feel stuff much more than ever before. It was lovely. That's what I hang on to. I don't get very low any more. If I get sad, my sadness now is different. It's to do with being sad about a situation, and I put it right. Whereas before, it would completely engulf everything.

*

David Hockney likes to quote a Chinese saying that painting is an old person's art. One reason for this is that 'the experience of

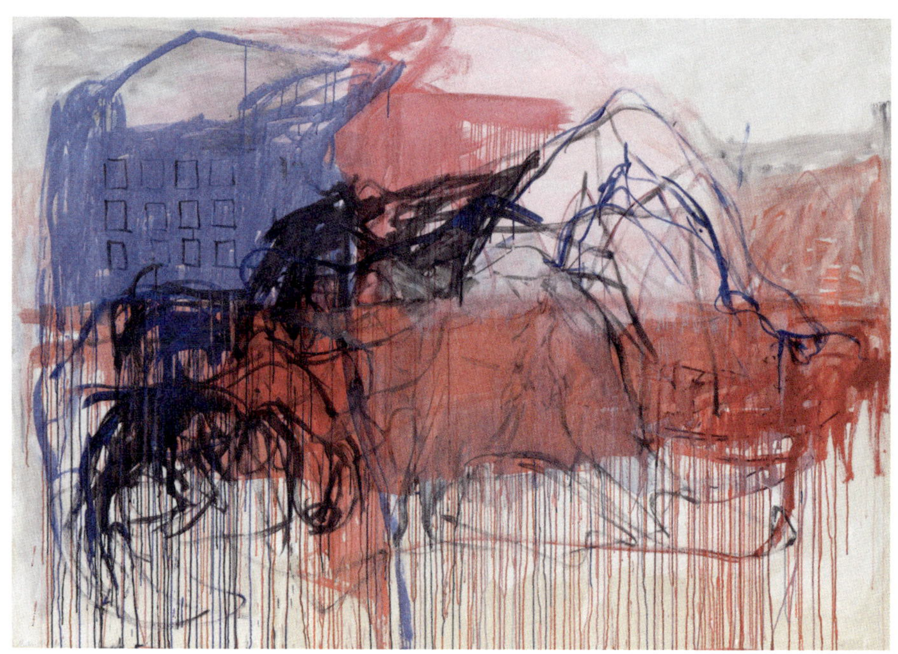

*Another Place to Live*, 2024

life and painting and looking at the world accumulates as you get older'. Of course, there have been young painters who were hugely talented. Masaccio died when he was twenty-seven. But it is also true that painting is an activity that some people can carry on and on throughout long lives, changing and growing.

**TE** If you're young and everything runs away ahead of you, out of control, you lose yourself. You can lose why you're doing it. But if you are sixty-one and wake up and think 'What am I going to do today?' and be really excited about it, it's a fantastic feeling, because there's no cynicism or doubt about why you're doing it. As a painter, or an artist who paints, that's really important: to have that kind of conviction and confidence is really important. Not every painting is going to be good, but it exists, so I have to be responsible for it.



*But has it got the thing?*

**MG** What do you mean by 'responsible'? Are you talking about responsibility for it being good or bad, original or unoriginal?

**TE** I'm not talking about the big blank canvas, taking that on. I'm talking about the conviction – understanding why it should exist and why it should be there. For me, it was after my mum died, when I started painting these pictures of her, dying. How I remembered her in bed. Then I realized how important painting was for me. The ability to pull this from my mind and put it into a canvas and look at it and feel what I was feeling when she was dying was so important. No one else could do that for me. If I had a true conviction, someone else could look at it and maybe understand their own loss. That's a really basic answer.

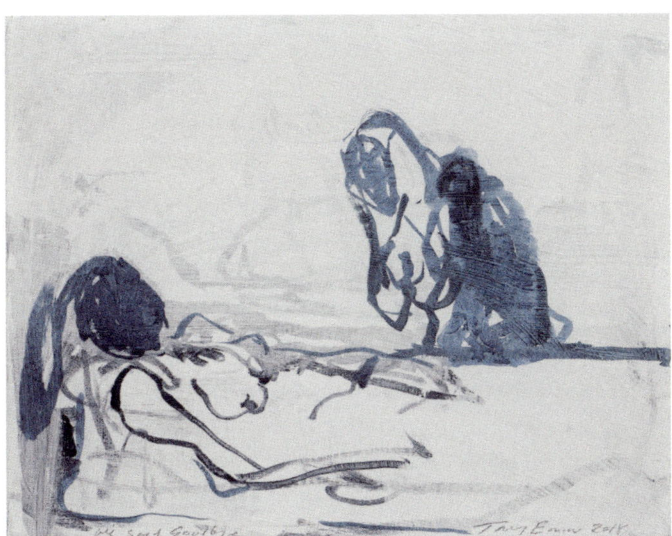

*We said Goodbye*, 2018

The transference of emotion through art is very
important. Because, as I've said, art is nature. It's like
gardening. It's like growing a beautiful garden, having
beautiful flowers, trees, leaves, in spring, autumn, all the
seasons. But art is made by us. It's man-made, woman-made.
Whereas when we plant our garden and it grows, it's nature
doing the work. This is us connecting with *our* nature.

**MG**  There has been art – and painting in particular –
since there have been human beings. In fact, even
the Neanderthals and our other hominid cousins
seem to have made art. It must fulfil a need.

**TE**  I always say this thing about cave people. When they
were painting on the walls of the caves, they weren't out
clubbing each other to death. While we're making art,
we're making a nicer, kinder, better world. It's so obvious.
Because we're nicer, kinder, better people. Pushing our
senses and our nature to our personal limits. It comes
from inside us, grown inside us. It's such a good thing.
What's taken over the world is greed. Forget war, just
greed. When you're making art, it's got nothing to do
with any of those issues. It's got nothing to do with power;
it's got nothing to do with greed; it's got nothing to do
with triumph; it's got nothing to do with everything that
is used against us as humans.

Being an artist right now, making paintings
with my hands from my head is *so* important. I keep
saying to people how important art is. They think
I'm exaggerating or saying this because I'm an artist.
I'm not; I'm saying it for everybody. As I get older, the
intention of art, the reason for making it and the reason
why I do it, is becoming clearer and clearer to me.

  *But has it got the thing?*

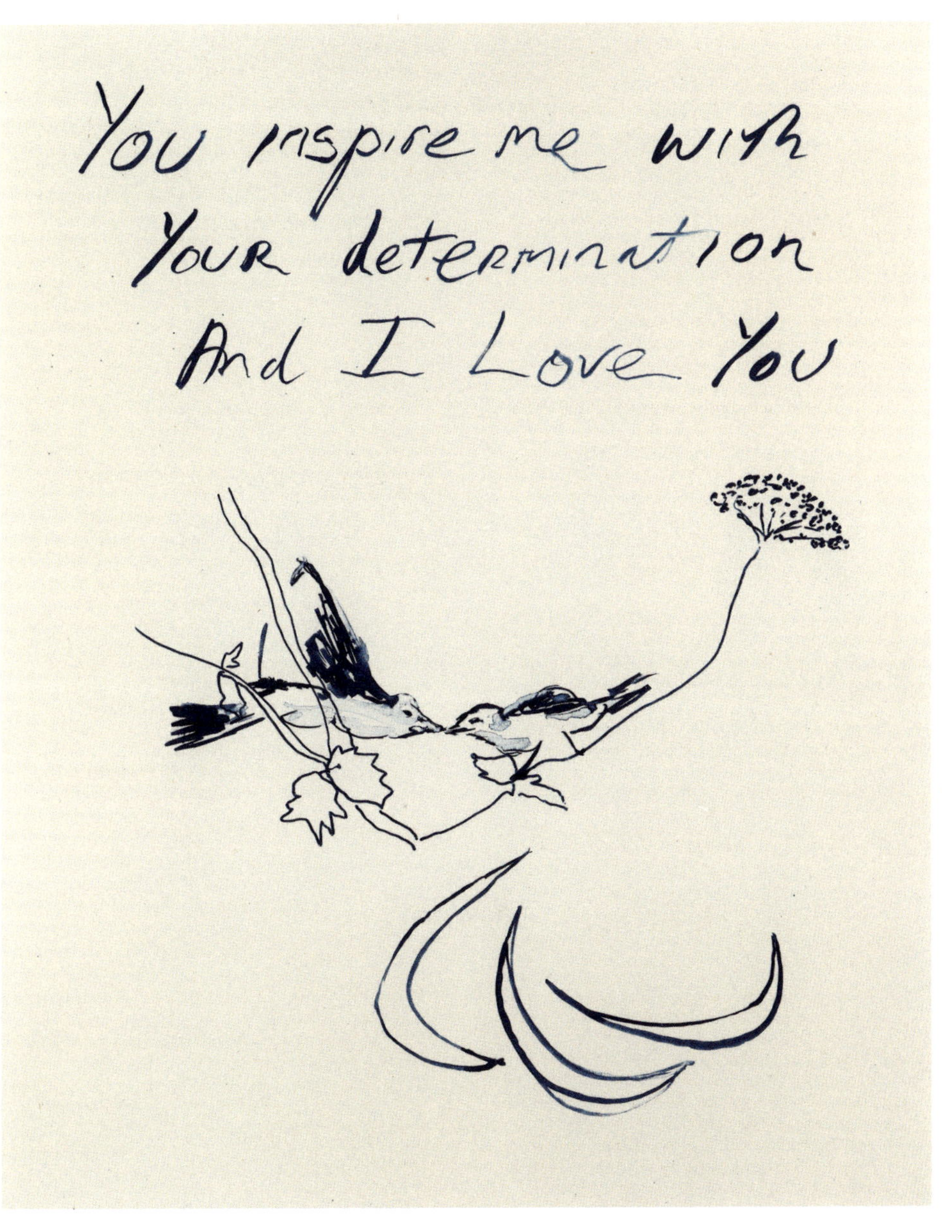



*Birds 2012, 2011*

# Note on the text and acknowledgments

The conversation with Tracey Emin that inspired *My Heart Is This* took place in the summer of 2024, a few weeks after my previous project, *How Painting Happens (and why it matters)* had gone to press. In some ways, what we said that day felt like a continuation of that text. One of the topics we discussed was the extraordinary way her marvellous picture *The Ship* (2019) had come about. Not coincidentally, this was the very work I had discussed in *How Painting Happens* – and the one that first suggested to me that she had blossomed into a truly important and original painter. What I saw and heard that day in Margate cemented that impression.

What Tracey had to say struck me as being as fresh, original, and important as her paintings themselves – which is the reason for this book. As I say in the chapter 'Twilight is the best time', all uninteresting painters are similar in one way – because they are derivative – while all interesting ones are absorbing for the opposite reason: because they are original. The same applies to what brilliant exponents have to tell us about the art of painting. What they say is fresh because they approach the subject from their own novel angle of vision. Remarks by artists with whom I have talked in the past – David Hockney, Paula Rego, Lucian Freud, and Frank Auerbach among them – crop up regularly in this book. What Tracey Emin has to say, I hope readers agree, is as gripping as her pictures.

The essence of *My Heart Is This* – its own heart – consists of her thoughts, words, and works. Most of these are derived from interviews carried out over nine months in 2024–5. No conversation on paper can be quite the same as one between two people in real time and space, partly because so many others need to understand what is said. On occasion, I have expanded my own words so as to supply context that may have been implicit but unspoken in the actual exchanges. Also, in places, words spoken on different occasions about the same subject have been edited together to make a single, continuous statement. In addition to what Tracey said to me in person, I have quoted from her many previous written and spoken utterances, in other interviews, her own books and journalism, and recorded appearances (the quotations from our own encounters are prefaced 'TE').

As always, in writing this text I have contracted some debts – firstly to Tracey Emin herself. To thank her for her generous cooperation would be to understate her contribution. Without her, this volume would not exist. Others have helped along the way. Right from the beginning, Harry Weller has assisted hugely in fielding questions and researching images. As usual, my son Tom Gayford acted as editor of first resort, advising and encouraging the author. Andrew Brown did his usual speedy, super-skilful, and efficient job of editing the text and laying out the pages – and on this occasion also gave wise advice about the ordering of the chapters. The whole process of putting the book together was deftly overseen by Philip Watson at Thames & Hudson. I should like to thank David Dawson for contributing his thoughts and memories, and Honey Luard at White Cube, whose commission to write an essay about Tracey and her latest paintings started the process that eventually led to this book.

# Sources


p. 25 'I like to record the moment': Tracey Emin, 'Ghosts of my past', *Guardian*, 25 May 2009.

p. 25 'It took me years to understand': ibid.

p. 26 '"Nought for Design"': ibid.

p. 40 'Because it's always my face': Hannah Ghorashi, '"I dream of being obscure": Tracey Emin on her new show at Lehmann Maupin', *ARTnews*, 18 May 2016

p. 43 'I really love that painting': Tracey Emin talk at Leopold Museum, Vienna, 28 May 2015, https://www.leopoldmuseum.org/en/exhibitions /66/tracey-emin-egon-schiele

p. 45 'like a bent forefinger': Tracey Emin, *Strangeland*, London, 2005, p. 28

p. 45 'I worked for years': Naomi Rea, 'Turner was a really raunchy Man', *Artnet News*, 13 October 2017

p. 46 'When I did that background': 'In conversation: Tracey Emin with Charles M. Schultz', *Brooklyn Rail*, December 2023

p. 53 Tracey Emin, *Curriculum Vitae Part I*, in Carl Freedman and Honey Luard (eds), *Tracey Emin: Works 1963–2006*, New York, 2006, pp. 146–9

p. 54 'Every time I come here': Tracey Emin, 'Margate should be somewhere I rejoice to come back to. But every time I visit I am filled with dread', *Independent*, 18 April 2008

p. 59 'Since I was little': Tracey Emin, 'I have to battle jellyfish and worse, but nothing beats sea swimming', *Evening Standard*, 14 July 2023

p. 60 'At this point, she noted in her *Curriculum Vitae*': Tracey Emin, *Curriculum Vitae Part I*, op. cit.

p. 66 'When we got there we had on our left': Vincent van Gogh to Theo van Gogh, Letter 79, Ramsgate, Friday

28 April 1876, https://vangoghletters.org/vg/letters/
let079/letter.html

p. 69 'It was a nice feeling. That's what makes you drown':
Stuart Jeffries, 'Tracey Emin on her cancer', *Guardian*,
9 November 2020

p. 69 'My feet went into the sand': quoted in https://
thefridaypoem.com/tracey-emin-and-billy-childish/

p. 71 'always had the idea that birds are angels of this
earth': quoted in https://artuk.org/discover/
artworks/a-moment-without-you-324658

p. 73 'I'm like one of those people who sit in their car':
Tracey Emin, *Independent*, 18 April 2008, op. cit.

p. 75 '[The] cold green waters of the North Sea':
Tracey Emin, 'I have to battle jellyfish and worse,
but nothing beats sea swimming', op. cit.

p. 79 'I had it [insomnia] in my early twenties':
Harriet Lloyd-Smith, 'Tracey Emin lays bare her own
traumas in piercing new show', *Wallpaper*, 27 July 2022

p. 79 'It might seem to have nothing to do': Jonathan
Jones, *Tracey Emin*, London, 2020, p. 62

p. 83 'In 1998 I had a complete breakdown': Tracey Emin,
'Tracey Emin on My Bed', TateShots, 2 April 2015,
https://www.tate.org.uk/art/artworks/emin-my-
bed-l03662/tracey-emin-my-bed

p. 83 'Mattress, linens, pillows, rope, various memorabilia':
Alina Cohen, 'Tracey Emin's "My Bed" Ignored
Society's Expectations of Women', 30 July 2018

p. 84 'He drank whatever he wanted to drink, slept
with whoever he wanted to sleep with': Tracey Emin,
'Tracey Emin on My Bed', op. cit.

p. 84 'When I say "My Bed",': Dalya Alberge, 'Tracey
made her bed but did she lie in it?', *Sunday Times*,
28 December 2014

p. 89 'Every time I reinstall the bed': 'Tracey Emin on her
40-year relationship with Edvard Munch', 22 December
2020, https://www.artfund.org/explore/get-inspired/
features/tracey-emin-on-her-40-year-relationship-with-
edvard-munch

pp. 89–90 'Munch's my favourite artist': Jonathan Jones,
'How Tracey Emin is giving Munch the mother he
never had', *Guardian*, 2 January 2020

p. 93 'I began responding to Munch's work': 'Tracey Emin
on her 40-year relationship with Edvard Munch', op. cit.

p. 94 'Illness, insanity, and death': Sue Prideaux, *Edvard
Munch: Behind the Scream*, London, 2005, p. 37

p. 96 '"As an artist," she wrote': 'Tracey Emin on her
40-year relationship with Edvard Munch', op. cit.

p. 96 'It was Sunday night, and it had to be handed in':
Tracey Emin, *Independent*, 30 September 2005

p. 99 'I realised he was different from the other
Expressionists': 'Tracey Emin on her 40-year
relationship with Edvard Munch', op. cit.

p. 99 'looked together at "a great thick book"': Lynn Barber,
'Truly, madly Tracey', *Sunday Times*, 8 May 2011

p. 101 'It's like the death of the man, the male figure':
recorded commentary in *Emin/Munch: Between
the Clock and the Bed*, BBC television documentary,
directed by John O'Rourke, 9 January 2021

p. 102 'All of Munch's work was directed': ibid.

p. 103 'What I find incredible about Munch is the
way that he painted women': ibid.

p. 103 'Munch had a really deep respect': 'Tracey Emin on
her 40-year relationship with Edvard Munch', op. cit.

p. 104 'As she told Geordie Greig': Geordie Greig,
'Tracey Emin: "What would I have done in the past 40
years if I had been sober?"', *Independent*, 11 May 2024

p. 110 'Dropped out after 1981–82 rail strike': Tracey
Emin, *Curriculum Vitae Part I*, op. cit.

p. 118 'I am interested in the basic human emotions':
quoted in Selden Rodman, *Conversations with Artists*,
New York, 1957, pp. 93–4

p. 121 'I love being alone, I love being in my studio':
author's conversation with the artist, 2025

p. 123 '"his habitual hypnotic stare"': Barbara Novak and
Brian O'Doherty, 'Rothko's dark paintings: Tragedy
and void', in Tam Curry Bryfogle (ed.), *Mark Rothko*,
New Haven and London, 1998, p. 268

p. 127 'I could see that Ken liked Expressionism':
'In conversation: Tracey Emin with Charles M.
Schultz', *Brooklyn Rail*, op. cit.

p. 128 'like amoebae, gradually becoming more and more
specific': quoted in Tate catalogue entry for Ken Kiff,
*Triptych: Shadows, 1983–6*, https://www.tate.org.uk/
art/artworks/kiff-triptych-shadows-t04888

p. 132 'Her personality filled the room': author's
conversation with the artist, 2025

p. 134 'Lynton noted that often': Norbert Lynton,
'Ken Kiff, Obituary', *Guardian*, 16 February 2001

p. 135 'I think I have been labelled': Tate, catalogue entry
for Ken Kiff, *Triptych: Shadows 1983–6*, https://www.
tate.org.uk/art/artworks/kiff-triptych-shadows-t04888

p. 135 'When Kiff talked about art, Lynton wrote':
Norbert Lynton, 'Ken Kiff, Obituary', op. cit.

p. 135 'He was a smallish man with huge eyes':
handwritten memoir posted on Instagram
by the Ken Kiff estate, 18 December 2022,
https://www.instagram.com/p/CmTppuNIQgW/

p. 136 'When Rego and Emin exhibited together':
Gill Hedley, '*Songs of Innocence, Experience, Ambivalence:
Mat Collishaw, Tracey Emin, Paula Rego* at the
Foundling', https://www.gillhedley.co.uk/txt/
Foundling.html

p. 137 'I've felt frustrated': quoted in *Paula Rego:
The Forgotten*, exh. cat., Victoria Miro, London, 2022

p. 144 'cried and cried' and following quotations:
Tracey Emin, *Curriculum Vitae Part I*, op. cit.

p. 145 'I used to make rabbits out of cigarette packets':
Hilton Als et al, 'Remembering Tracey Emin
and Sarah Lucas's 'The Shop', *Frieze*, No. 220
(June 2021), https://www.frieze.com/article/
tracey-emin-and-sarah-lucas-shop

p. 150 'I absolutely hated my body, hated to look at it':
spoken statement, 'Beyond White Cube: Tracey Emin
at Faurschou New York', https://www.youtube.com/
watch?v=1pzSRXVriSg

p. 153 'Painting for me was completely moribund':
Jean Wainwright, 'Interview with Tracey Emin',
in Mandy Merck and Chris Townsend (eds), *The Art
of Tracey Emin*, London 2002, p. 198

p. 154 'What happened when I first got there in
Sweden was that I couldn't paint': 'Beyond White
Cube: Tracey Emin at Faurschou New York', op. cit.

p. 155 '"I'll go through my idea of art history"': ibid.

p. 157 '"I stayed clean", he explained': quoted in MoMA entry for Yves Klein, *Anthropometry: Princess Helena,* 1960, https://www.moma.org/collection/works/80530

p. 158 'You might think Klein': Jean Wainwright, 'Interview with Tracey Emin', op. cit., p. 197

p. 159 'When I was doing the Yves Klein': ibid.

p. 160 'That is one reason why': 'Beyond White Cube: Tracey Emin at Faurschou New York', op. cit.

p. 162 'You know how you have these different phases': Simon Hattenstone, 'The radical, ravishing rebirth of Tracey Emin', *Guardian,* 29 May 2024

p. 165 'She told Lynn Barber': Lynn Barber, 'From party girl to Biennale queen', *Guardian,* 3 June 2007

p. 187 'If it's a full moon and I'm dying to work': Geordie Greig, 'Tracey Emin: "What would I have done in the past 40 years if I had been sober?"', op. cit.

p. 187 'Francis Bacon wrote about how "painting today is"': Francis Bacon, 'Matthew Smith – A painter's tribute', *Matthew Smith: Paintings from 1909 to 1952,* exh. cat., Tate Gallery, London, 1953, p. 12

p. 187 'Bacon, too, spoke of painting as a kind of seance': David Sylvester, *Interviews with Francis Bacon,* London, 1980, p. 140

p. 189 'According to the website of Cancer Research UK': https://www.cancerresearchuk.org

p. 191 'Philip Guston confessed': lecture at the University of Minnesota, March 1978, quoted in Renee McKee (ed.), *Philip Guston,* exh. cat. (London: Whitechapel Gallery, 1982)

p. 191 'Frank Auerbach observed': author's conversation with the artist, 2001

p. 193 'When asked which person from the ancient world': Laura Allsop, '50 questions with Tracey Emin', *AnOther Magazine,* 8 June 2023

p. 194 'There are so many different ways to experience': Waldemar Januszczak, 'Tracey Emin: the unlikely new face of the National Portrait Gallery', https://waldemar.tv/2023/08/tracey-emin-the-unlikely-new-face-of-the-national-portrait-gallery/, 14 August 2023

p. 196 'When she participated in the BBC programme': 'Tracey Emin Who Do You Think You Are?', https://artlyst.com/news/tracey-emin-who-do-you-think-you-are/, 3 October 2011

p. 197 '"At that point", she wrote, "he received an urgent telegram"': Tracey Emin, 'My mother was spat on in the street in Hendon because my father wasn't white', *Evening Standard,* 27 October 2023

p. 197 'Like all great Egyptians, Nubians': Geordie Greig, 'Tracey Emin: "What would I have done in the past 40 years if I had been sober?"', op. cit.

p. 197 'Love of art': ibid.

p. 200 'Everyone focuses on the sexuality of my work': Renée Vara, 'Another dimension: Tracey Emin's interest in mysticism', in Mandy Merck and Chris Townsend (eds), *The Art of Tracey Emin,* op. cit., p. 173

p. 200 'In 2006, Tate invited young artists to ask Emin questions': 'Q&A with Tracey Emin', 13 September 2006, https://www.tate.org.uk/art/artists/tracey-emin-2590/qa-tracey-emin

p. 203 'as Hockney has pointed out, "reality is a slippery concept"': David Hockney and Martin Gayford, *A History of Pictures,* London, 2016, p. 24

p. 205 'Talking in 2020 to Alison Cole about this work': Alison Cole, 'The art world's favourite Easter and Passover images', *Art Newspaper,* 9 April 2020

p. 206 'I shouldn't like to be without suffering': Tracey Emin, *Six Turkish Tales,* Rochester, 1987

p. 208 'He is one of the most inspiring scholar-teachers': 'Keith Critchlow: A life well lived', *Beshara Magazine,* no. 15 (2020), https://besharamagazine.org/metaphysics-spirituality/keith-critchlow-a-life-well-lived/

p. 208 'For those of you out there who don't know what that is': Tracey Emin, *Independent,* 17 November 2006

p. 209 'A lot of my paintings have carpets in them': Gabé Braunstein, 'Don't sell your work, swap your work', *Cultured,* 7 November 2023, https://www.culturedmag.com/article/2023/11/07/tracey-emin-white-cube-exhibition/

p. 209 'When I was a little girl': ibid.

p. 223 'just Louise, a friend of Stuart's': Tracey Emin, 'Tracey Emin on the iconic Louise Bourgeois', *Evening Standard,* 31 January 2022

p. 223 'At the time [in the USA], I was considered': ibid.

p. 224 'The collaboration took me two years to do': ibid.

p. 224 'It's one of the world's largest sculptures': ibid.

p. 228 'It is an art form invented by the Greeks in': Kenneth Clark, *The Nude: A Study in Ideal Form,* London, 1956, p. 15

p. 228 'roots and bulbs, pulled up into the light': ibid, p. 308

p. 229 'I've got a good female nude I can use': Tracey Emin in Carl Freedman and Honey Luard (eds), *Tracey Emin: Works 1963–2006,* op. cit., p. 166.

p. 229 'It's so liberating to be naked': ibid.

p. 230 'The gouaches are self-portraits of me': Tracey Emin talk at the Leopold Museum, op. cit.

p. 230 'I really, really believe that the nature': ibid.

p. 232 'I hope to God that people don't think my personality': 'Art, scandal and the breaking of taboos', talk at the Fondation Beyeler, 9 October 2014

p. 234 'A lot of feminists would be really, really angry that I liked it': ibid.

p. 234 'For me, it's about female strength, a feminist icon': Gareth Harris, 'What are some of Tracey Emin's favourite works?', *Art Newspaper,* 9 October 2014

p. 235 'Look how sexy she is!': ibid.

p. 238 'Some of it makes me feel sick': Tracey Emin, 'Frida on My Mind', *Tate, etc,* No. 4 (Summer 2005), https://www.tate.org.uk/tate-etc/issue-4-summer-2005/frida-on-my-mind

p. 238 'At the time I really thought I looked like Frida Kahlo': Lianne Kolirin, 'When Tracey Emin became Frida Kahlo', *CNN Styles,* 3 March 2023, https://edition.cnn.com/style/article/mary-mccartney-emin-kahlo-photo-snap-scli-intl-gbr

p. 240 'He believed that every good painting': conversation with the author, 2001

p. 244 'the experience of life and painting': Martin Gayford, *A Bigger Message: Conversations with David Hockney,* London, 2011, p. 182

# *List of illustrations*

All works by Tracey Emin © 2026 Tracey Emin.
All photographs are courtesy of Tracey Emin Studio
unless otherwise stated below. Dimensions are given
in centimetres, followed by inches, height before width,
before depth.

# Index